CHINA AND HER NEIGHBOURS

CHINA AND HER NEIGHBOURS

France in Indo-China, Russia and China, India and Thibet

By

RICHARD SIMPSON GUNDRY

GYAN

ISBN : 978-81-212-1590-9(HB)

First Published, 1893

Published, 2018

Published by

Gyan Publishing House
5, Ansari Road
Daryaganj, New Delhi-110002
Phone: 011-47034999, 9811692060
www.gyanbooks.com
E-mail: books@gyanbooks.com

Printed at: G. Print Process, Delhi.

Dedicated

TO

SIR THOMAS F. WADE, G.C.M.G., K.C.B.,

LATE HER MAJESTY'S MINISTER AT PEKING.

INTRODUCTION.

The following essays, which have appeared from time to time in the periodical press, are republished, with such emendations and additions as the development of events seemed to require, in the belief that the retrospect they afford may not be without value at the present crisis in the Far East.

Owing to the time and form of original publication, the chapters may, at first sight, appear somewhat disjointed,—each having been designed to describe a separate episode. But the very fragmentary character of the narrative serves to throw up into stronger relief the continuity of purpose in the various adventures of the Great Powers whose dealings with China and her Tributaries are set forth. It is, indeed, only by bearing in mind this fixed and persistent policy on the part of Russia and France, that the separate episodes of that policy can be properly valued and fitted into their appropriate places in the general scheme.

The series of papers, for example, on French operations in Indo-China, written to elucidate the several events as they took place, will, it is believed, be found to furnish a fairly complete narrative of the whole course of that remarkable enterprise, which can hardly fail to interest the political moralist at the moment when it has culminated in the most cynical aggression of modern times. The dual motive of hostility to England and the glorification of France, which has animated French policy in Asia, has undergone no variation whatever since France had a policy in Asia at all. Monarchies, Republics, and Empires succeed each other, but the spirit remains the same through all these superficial changes. It is candidly avowed, and there need be no delicacy in putting the truth in plain language.

The attempt to gain a footing in Indo-China during the reign of Louis XVI. was avowedly dictated by the hostility to England which is conspicuous in the tone of French journalism at the present day. The facilities which such a position would give for harassing English commerce were frankly put forward, by Mgr. Pigneau de Behaine, as reasons for giving King Gya-long the help which was to be paid for by the cession of Tourane; and the remarkable treaty in which the bargain was recorded exacts privileges that were expressly designed to make Annam an arsenal, dockyard, and recruiting ground for France in Eastern Asia.

And so in the case of Siam. Louis the Fourteenth's remarkable attempt to establish French "influence" in Siam was dictated by jealousy of England and Holland, as much as by a desire to promote French commerce. The two Protestant Powers were believed to derive much of the wealth which enabled them to make head against him, in Europe, from the trade they carried on with Asia; and the French Government of the day rejoiced at the prospect of dealing a blow at that prosperity by installing French garrisons, and setting up a hostile *régime*, at Mergui and Bangkok. The impression that the tale of Siamese embassies to Louis XIV. arose out of a masquerading attempt, by Madame de Maintenon, to amuse a *blasé* and senile king, is hardly yet fairly dispelled. But the first Siamese embassy reached France in 1685, when Louis was at the height of his power and in the prime of life. His garrisons had been turned out of Siam, and the whole project had collapsed, more than twenty years before his death. The detailed account of those embassies and of their political motives which will be found in the following pages may show that the annexations and protective duties of the present day are the modern development of the policy which inspired Colbert and Louis XIV.

A curious feature which may strike us, in connection with each of these attempts, is the share taken by the Church in prompting the political adventure. It is Mgr. Pallu, Bishop of Heliopolis, who inspires the beginnings of French intercourse with Siam, and it is a Jesuit Missionary named Tachard who helps to inflate the conception of military ascendency. It is Mgr. Pigneau de Behaine, Bishop of Adran, who conceives and organizes the whole scheme of French intervention in Annam, and who thus literally and practically laid the foundation of the Indo-Chinese Empire which his countrymen are trying to build up, at the present day. It is the Abbé Huc who suggests to Napoleon III. that the opportunity is a good one for re-asserting French influence at Saigon; and there are mysterious rumours of a (half-caste) Cambodian Christian visiting M. de Montigny, at Singapore, just as he was about starting on a tour of diplomatic visits to the Courts of Eastern Asia, in 1856, to suggest that a French protectorate would be welcomed by [? a section of] the Khmers.

This traditional motive should be borne in mind when surprise is expressed at the apparent divergence between the attitude of the Republican Government towards the Church at home and abroad. Propagandism was connoted with commerce in the projects of Richelieu and Colbert. The Empire was carrying out this policy in striving to exalt the position of France as protector of oriental missions; and the Republic upheld the tradition to the extent, it was understood, of threatening to denounce the Concordat, when it was proposed, some years ago, to break up the system by inducing European governments to undertake, each, the protection of its own missionary subjects. Germany and Italy had acquiesced, and the Vatican had even agreed to appoint a Legate to watch over the interests of the Church, at Peking, when France temporarily upset the scheme by the energy of its opposition.

In the first six chapters of the present volume, an attempt has been made to depict the successive stages in the construction of the French colonial edifice. There is no pretence of describing, in detail, the military operations. Saigon, Cambodia, Tongking, Annam, Siam—each annexation is dealt with, in turn, chiefly as a political episode; and the fact that mention is made, frequently years beforehand, of the next contemplated aggression, may serve to expose the hollowness of the wrongs which were put forward, as excuses for military action, when the convenient moment arrived. The *Intransigeant*, indeed, avowed the other day, with perfect frankness: "We are going to Siam under pretext of avenging an insult to our flag, but really with the idea of making a new conquest." And the admission adequately describes the value of French protestations.

The paper on "France and Saigon" was written for the *North-China Herald* after a visit to the Colony, in 1873, when the idea of gaining a foothold in Tongking was beginning to take shape and the *Saigon Independant* was already advocating a protectorate over the remainder of Annam. De Lagrée's discovery of the Song-Koi had fired the Colonial imagination; Dupuis was engaged in testing its practicability as a channel of commercial intercourse with Yunnan; and de Carné was urging, in the *Revue des Deux Mondes*, that coercion must be employed if the King persisted in obstructing French designs: England was trying to attract the trade to Burmah; and "it is not," he exclaims, "at the moment when, by a stroke of good luck, it depends on ourselves to forestall her, that it behoves us to halt before the susceptibilities of a despot who cannot conceive liberty of commerce without occupation of territory, and who repulses our merchants as if they were the forerunners of our soldiers! When one decides on a war of conquest, it would appear that one accepts beforehand the consequence of success, and the opening of Tongking is a necessary sequel of our establishment in the six provinces of Lower Cochin-China." A protectorate, in short,—or at least complete freedom of trade in the ports of Tongking, guaranteed by the installation of a French Resident at the Annamese capital,—was the only means of securing the desired end and of escaping a deadlock "ou nous acculeraient une timidité sans excuse aussi bien que des scrupules par trop naïfs." One scarcely knows whether most to admire the unconscious tribute paid to Annamese foresight, or the simulated indignation at suspicions whose justice is practically admitted in the concluding phrase. The sentence is, at any rate, worthy of note because it strikes the keynote of French policy in Indo-China. Subsequent proceedings have been precisely characterized by the unscrupulous aggression, disguised under a pretence of moral indignation, which is here commended with such sublime unconsciousness of the incongruity displayed.

The historical sketch which forms the basis of the chapter on "Cambodia" was contributed to the *London and China Express*, at the time M. Thomson was stripping King Norodom of the last shreds of political independence, and premonitory mutterings of derivative claims were beginning to disturb the Court of Bangkok. It had been all very well, ten years previously, for de Carné to expatiate on the political skill and firmness which had defeated Siam and obtained the surrender of Cambodia to the exclusive protectorate of France; but it had been discovered, now, that Cambodia had once been a much larger geographical expression. Garnier had pointed out the necessity of hoisting the flag at Stung-treng and Khong, and had recorded M. de Lagrée's opinion that the province of Tonly Repu ought to be reclaimed: the recognition of Siamese rights over Battambong and Angkor had become a source of acute regret; and Dr. Neïs was beginning to discover that there were tribes, even so far north as the frontier of Tongking, who were held in bondage by Siam.

The essay on "France and Tongking" appeared in the *Contemporary Review*, at the moment when French intervention was taking the form of conquest; and that on "France and Annam" in the *Westminster*, twelve months later, when the action of the French Government had brought China into the field.

"China and Her Tributaries" was written about the same time, for the *National Review*, for the purpose of explaining the nature of China's relations with her neighbours and the continuity of the feudal tie which France was pretending to ridicule in the case of Annam; while "France and Siam" was published two months ago, in the same Review, at the moment when definite expression was being given to the ulterior aspirations that had been foreshadowed, from time to time, in previous essays. A second chapter has been added, to trace the development of the enterprise, and to explain more precisely the English and Chinese interests which seem likely to mar the perfection of the original design. It will be seen that Siam has repudiated vassalage or any kind of tributary relationship to her more powerful neighbour. She cannot, therefore, appeal now, as of right, for the help which China might, or might not, be willing to afford. But the Imperial Cabinet seems disposed to avow a natural anxiety in claims that involve the extension of the French frontier along the southern border of Yunnan. It may not feel much more concerned than England about what happens on the Southern Meikong; but it would hardly be surprising if it shared the distaste of England to annexations of territory that touch China as nearly on the South as they touch British Burmah on the East. French newspapers exhaust themselves in ironical references to former English annexations, by way of retort upon English criticisms of French proceedings in Siam. The annexation of Burmah, especially, is pointed to as a precedent which completely cuts the ground from under our feet. But the fact is overlooked that that annexation was forced upon us by intrigues which were designed to draw Mandalay under the influence of France, and which were alleged to contemplate the annexation to Tongking of the very region which England and China have again stepped in to protect. It is overlooked, also, that our dislike to French encroachments is inspired quite as much by an instinct of commercial self-defence as by any feeling of political jealousy or antagonism. Where England goes, all the world is free to follow: Burmah is as much open to French trade as to English—to Rouen and Lille as to Manchester and Bradford—but where France goes nothing English is admitted, if protective duties can keep it out.

Our interest in Indo-China might easily become acute in presence of a Franco-Russian alliance; and the generally-admitted existence of at least a tacit *entente* may lend interest to the group of essays depicting the relations of China with her northern neighbour. For England's interest in Russian encroachments in the North is scarcely less, or less vivid, than it is in French annexations in the South; and those encroachments are made, in every case, at the cost of the great empire which stretches half across Asia, from Corea to the Pamirs. The chapters on "Kuldja" and "Russia and China," reprinted respectively from the *Times* and the *Fortnightly Review*—though dealing, in the main, with distinct phases of intercourse—will serve to exhibit the political relations between the two giant Powers. The former was written at the moment when the Kuldja difficulty had just been settled by the Treaty of St. Petersburg, in 1881; and the latter while attention was being directed, last year, to Russian proceedings in the Pamirs.

Nor are our interests confined to the neighbourhood of our Indian frontier. It is one of the penalties of our commercial greatness that we are sensitive to any increase in the maritime resources of a possibly hostile Power. We are interested, therefore, in Russian proceedings on the Amoor as well as on the Helmund. Relegated, on the eastern coast of Siberia, to ports which are more or less ice-bound during a portion of the year, Russia would be almost less than human, as well as less than aggressive, if she did not look wistfully across the frontier of Primorsk to the open harbours of Corea. The essays on "Corea" and "Port Hamilton," which are reproduced from the *Westminster Review*, will explain the steps by which the Hermit Kingdom was drawn within the vortex of modern intercourse, and by which its integrity has been safeguarded. The former was written soon after Chinese persuasion and the force of events had induced the little kingdom to open its doors; and the latter shortly after our withdrawal from the group of islands which had been occupied by the British fleet during the disaccord that arose, in 1886, out of Russia's attitude towards Afghanistan, and had nearly burst into flame at Pendjeh. Neither China nor Corea appears to believe too implicitly in the value of the guarantees; but the jealousy with which Russian encroachment would be viewed by others than China, and by others even than Great Britain, may help to render efficacious paper engagements that might prove less reliable with less substantial backing.

In sum, therefore, we find a remarkable similarity

between the political conditions in Asia and Europe. India and China, which ask nothing but to be let alone, are confronted by Russia and France, much as Germany and Austria are confronted in Europe ; and their common interests must tend to ally them in an attitude of mutual defence which would probably command, in an emergency, the sympathy of Japan. For it is evident that, by exercising alternative or simultaneous pressure in the North-west and South-east, the two great Western Powers might create a degree of military tension and political unrest as exhausting as, and even more intolerable than, that existing in Europe. Even neutral Belgium has an Eastern representative in Korea ; and the position of England, in Europe, finds a not inapt parallel in the considerable power of Japan.

The three concluding chapters deal with a topic of less Imperial consequence, but of not less interest, perhaps, to the general reader.

Russian movements in northern Thibet have had, so far, a purely exploratory character; though the facility with which Cossack detachments find their way along the trail of the traveller, and pave the way for emissaries of a less visionary class, may lead us to watch with interest any region towards which Russian attention appears to be directed. Thibet is shielded, at present, in a great degree, by Chinese Turkestan. But frontiers, in these remote regions, are less clearly defined than would appear from school maps ; and there are unsettled districts along the boundary between Kashgaria and Kashmir which account for much Chinese, and some Indian, anxiety about Russian movements across the Pamirs. Our own present interest, however, is confined to re-opening commercial intercourse across the Himalayas. The attempt made by Warren Hastings, in 1774, which was defeated, then, by Chinese antagonism, has been taken up again during this generation, and seems in a fair way of being carried, now, with Chinese goodwill, to a successful issue.

The project inspired the provisions for roads and transit dues which found place in Sir Ashley Eden's treaty with Sikhim, in 1861: it was given diplomatic expression, seventeen years ago, in the Anglo-Chinese Convention of Chefoo, and was taken up with more directness a decade later—though with results that promised ill, at first, for the attainment of the object in view. A mission to Lhassa, which had been organized in India with the consent of China, was abandoned in consequence of the hostile attitude of the Lamas; and the latter, encouraged by this negative success, pushed their antagonism to the point of occupying territory which had long been considered, at Calcutta, as within the British-Indian sphere. They were, of course, driven out; but it has taken several years to re-knit the broken diplomatic threads. Negotiations do not often progress rapidly where China is alone concerned; they were still less likely to do so where Calcutta and Lhassa were involved.

The settlement of the matter seems to have been eventually left to those two capitals; and an agreement was shortly reached in which the project of commercial intercourse was accepted, and the suzerainty of India over Cis-nivean Sikhim formally recognized. A Convention, signed by the Chinese Amban and Lord Lansdowne, at Calcutta, in March, 1890, was promptly ratified at London and Peking, and has been followed by commercial negotiations, at Darjeeling, which are believed to be at length approaching a termination. The papers in which the position was reviewed, at intervals, in the *National* and *Westminster Reviews*, may be useful as collating the several episodes in the story, and conveying some information regarding a little known region of Central Asia.

CONTENTS.

RUSSIA AND CHINA.

CHAPTER VIII.

CHAPTER IX.

CHAPTER X.

CHAPTER XI.

INDIA AND THIBET.

CHAPTER XII.

CHAPTER XIII.

CHAPTER XIV.

CHAPTER XV.

FRANCE IN INDO-CHINA.

CHAPTER I.

FRANCE AND SAIGON.

DURING the reign of Louis XVI. an Annamese Prince appeared at the French Court, under the guidance of Mgr. Pigneau de Behaine, Bishop of Adran, to ask assistance against rebels who had deposed and driven his father to flight. The opportunity was tempting. The titular king could be in no position to haggle about terms: France could exact what political recompense she chose; while the pre-eminence of the Church and the position of its missions could be proportionately strengthened and assured. The Bishop's proposals were accepted, and on November 28th, 1787, a treaty was concluded at Versailles, by which the French King promised the required aid on certain remarkable conditions which were avowedly conceived in a spirit of hostility to England, and with a view to the advantage of having a foothold in Cochin-China in the event of war. Louis was to equip an expeditionary force which would help the deposed monarch to recover his throne; and the latter, in return for this assistance, undertook to furnish, as soon as tranquillity had been restored to his State, all the material necessary for the construction of fourteen ships of the line; and to admit, wherever the French chose to station them, consuls who should be allowed to build ships wherever they chose, and take wood for the purpose from any forest in the kingdom. A corps of French naval officers was to be sent out, in furtherance of this design, who should form a permanent establishment in Cochin-China. The bay and peninsula of Tourane, with two neighbouring islands, were to be ceded to France; the King of Annam was to furnish an army of 60,000 men if the French were attacked in these possessions by any foreign Power, and France was to have the right of levying and drilling 14,000 Annamese soldiers for use in its Indian wars. Circumstances were to prevent the complete execution, or even the ratification, of this remarkable agreement; but the Bishop was able to take back with him to Saigon certain ships, officers, and appliances of war, by whose aid King Gya-long regained his throne; and France never forgot the "interests" and "rights" which she thus acquired. Most of those who had been concerned in the adventure withdrew after it had been carried to a successful conclusion. But Messrs. Chaigneau and Vannier remained more than thirty years in Gya-long's service; and a son of the former, who was born at Hué, has left us a record[1] of events down to the year 1825, in which these last members of the expedition finally retired to France.

[1] Souvenirs de Hué. Par Michel Du'c Chaigneau.

The Kingdom of Annam, as it existed under Gya-long, extended, at that time, over "almost all the littoral of Indo-China, comprising Tongking, Cochin-China, part of Cambodia," and certain islands off the coast, including the well-known Paracels which bear such an evil reputation as a source of danger to navigation in the China Seas. It was bounded, in fact, "on the north by China, on the south by Cambodia, on the east by the China Sea, and on the west by the mountains of Lao, which extend the whole length of the frontier;" and it was divided into eight provinces, of which Sai-Gon was the richest, most extensive, and most fertile. It was in this province of Sai-Gon that Mgr. Pigneau sheltered, in 1774, the then fugitive Annamese King; and laid the foundation, in so doing, of the intimacy that was to eventuate in his European mission and in the present aspirations of his countrymen after Indo-Chinese Empire. It was upon Sai-Gon that the expeditionary force which he was able to organize was directed, and it was here that the military preparations were made which were to establish King Gya-long upon the throne of Annam.

The elder Chaigneau died in 1832, but his son lived to see the province which had been the scene of the Bishop's exploits brought under the dominion of his countrymen, and made the starting point for a fresh career of conquest. The French are, in fact, treading now, on their own account, almost in the footsteps of Gya-long.

It was ecclesiastical influence that was again to

furnish the motive for interference. The outbreak of revolution in France had, as we have seen, prevented the ratification of the so-called treaty which Bishop Pigneau and the advisers of Louis XVI. had seen fit to compose. No attempt had even been made to put its more important provisions in operation ; and the commercial intercourse it contemplated had been fitful and constrained. Ecclesiastical enterprise continued ; but the countenance and support which the missionaries received from a monarch whom they had placed under considerable obligation was withdrawn under his successor. Jealous, no doubt, of the organization and influence they had attained, the advisers of Minh-Man advised a policy of repression, which degenerated into persecution; and the casual visits of French cruisers during the first half of the present century were made chiefly for the purpose of remonstrating against some aggression on missionaries or their converts.

Matters stood thus when the Anglo-French expedition set out against China, in 1857. With the traditional ability and tenacity of his class, which never loses sight of a right once acquired, the Abbé Huc took this opportunity to claim the interest of the Emperor for the cause of the persecuted Church in Annam, and recalled the treaty of Versailles as a useful basis for negociations. The claims of humanity and civilization were a sufficient ground for interfering, to exact reparation for the murder of Catholic priests and guarantees of religious freedom for missionaries and their converts in future; but the provisions of this remarkable treaty might open up further possibilities; the missionaries had pointed out "that commerce would find solid advantages in a fertile country which had numerous and good ports and valuable products certain to find, throughout Europe, important and lucrative markets." It is not clear that any design of annexation existed at the time; perhaps the idea developed with further exploration and the impossibility of bringing the Annamese Government to terms. Had the latter been more compliant, it might have escaped with the fate of China—an obligatory treaty of commerce, and guarantees of religious toleration. The event, however, was to prove that what had been looked forward to as a military promenade was to entail considerable effort. The information which the French had received led them to believe that the Annamese Government was feeble, the people discontented and disaffected, and that active aid might be expected from the Christian converts. The result seems to have completely negatived this expectation. The Government proved well organized, and able to offer prolonged resistance despite constant reverses. The people were more warlike and better armed than the Chinese, and possessed stronger works; though they were of course inferior to European troops.

These were the circumstances in which the Admiral, Rigault de Genouilly, commanding the French squadron then in Chinese waters, was informed that the Emperor "willed to put a stop to the constantly recurring persecutions against Christians in Cochin-China, and to secure them the efficacious protection of France." He was ordered accordingly, after the signature of the treaty of Tientsin, to transfer his forces to Annam to obtain the object indicated. The fleet which had been operating in China was to carry out the Emperor's instructions, with the addition of three ships-of-war and 500 troops which were dispatched to reinforce it from France. The co-operation of Spain was also secured, and the Government of Manilla contributed some 450 native and 550 Spanish troops and the armed despatch boat *El Cano*. Including the latter, the expedition now numbered 13 ships, the *Nemesis*, *Phlegeton*, *Primauguet*, *Avalanche*, *Dragonne*, *Fusée*, *Mitraille*, *Gironde*, *Saone*, *Dordogne*, *Meurthe*, *Durance*, and *El Cano*. With this force Admiral Rigault de Genouilly decided to establish his headquarters in the bay of Tourane, an excellent harbour situated about thirty miles south of the river Hué, on which the capital is situated.

The officers who had aided King Gya-long to regain his throne had superintended the construction, there, of strong fortifications, from which a serious resistance was now anticipated. But in this, as in other respects, the information given proved misleading; for the works defending the bay were taken with slight loss, on September 1st, 1858. Having gained this base of operations, however, Admiral Rigault found himself only at the beginning of his difficulties. The Annamese showed no disposition to treat; heat and illness combined to break down his men; and the forces at his disposal were insufficient to permit an advance on the capital, which experience in China had shown to be the best method of bringing an oriental Government to terms. The only serious movement which appeared open to him was against Saigon—then known to be a fortified post on the river of that name, and to be a depôt of rice for the supply of Hué. The capture of Saigon would, therefore, deprive the Annamese of an important basis of supply and, it was hoped, humiliate it in the eyes of Siam and Cambodia who might be induced to join in attacking their hereditary foe.

On February 9th, 1859, the French squadron destined for this expedition, comprising the corvettes *Phlegeton* and *Primauguet*, the gunboats *Alarme*, *Avalanche* and *Dragonne*, transports *Saone*, *Durance* and *Meurthe*, and the Spanish despatch boat *El Cano*, reached the mouth of the Saigon river; and on the following day the Annamese works defending the harbour of Cap Saint-Jacques were carried. The days from the 11th to the 15th were spent in ascending the river and carrying the various forts and stockades, which offered different degrees of resistance, along the banks.

Saigon was found to be defended by two forts on the south bank of the river and by a citadel on the north. On the 16th the forts were taken, and on the 17th the more serious work of carrying the citadel was accomplished, with slight loss, before noon. This fortress, one of the most important in Cochin-

China, was inhabited only by Government employés and its garrison. According to a description given by a member of the expedition:—"Four gates, which had been solidly barricaded with stones and earth, gave access to it. A large boulevard ran around, and in the middle rose immense buildings destined to warehouse the tribute rice from the provinces of the south. A few dwelling-houses of the high officials alone broke, by their quaint architecture and the brilliant colours with which they were covered, the monotony of the great buildings. The stable of the war elephants also occupied a considerable space." Saigon was, in fact, a fortress and depôt of the first importance, and we may judge from the Admiral's despatch how serious a loss it must have been to the Annamese Government. "Two hundred guns [he writes] of iron or bronze have fallen into our hands, and we have also taken a corvette and seven or eight war junks still on the stocks. The citadel contained a complete arsenal. Counting what we found in the forts, we may estimate the hand arms at 20,000 gingals, guns, pistols, lances, pikes, and sabres. We found, everywhere, enormous quantities of powder. The citadel alone contained eighty-five tons in cases and barrels, without counting an enormous quantity of cartridges. The projectiles were in proportion; the magazines also contained saltpetre and sulphur, lead and military equipments of every kind, enough rice to feed 6000 or 8000 men for a year, and a military chest containing *cash* to the value of 130,000 francs. In property taken or destroyed, comprising the value of the citadel, which I purpose razing from top to bottom, it may be estimated that the Annamese Government will sustain here a loss of 20,000,000 francs."

The disaster did, in fact, bring King Tu-du'c to the point of opening negociations; but he was not yet sufficiently humiliated to acquiesce in the cession of Saigon, the recognition of French "rights" at Tourane, and the opening of his principal ports to commerce, which Admiral Rigault prescribed as bases of agreement. Hostilities were accordingly resumed. But before the French had had time to push their advantage, the renewed outbreak of war in China led to the recall of all the available forces from Cochin-China, to join in the second expedition to Tientsin. Tourane was definitely abandoned; and a sufficient garrison, only, was left in Saigon to hold its own until circumstances should permit the resumption of active operations.

The Annamese availed themselves of the opportunity to hem in their adversaries. Saigon is situated on the point of a peninsula formed by two branches of the river; and when the conclusion of the Chinese war enabled Admiral Charnier to go to the assistance of his countrymen, the Annamese had constructed a treble line of earthworks, studded with cannon, from bank to bank, about a mile in the rear of the French position. Operations were promptly begun, with the object of dislodging them from this position. The French carried the first line at the point of the bayonet, to find themselves checked by a point blank volley from the second; and when their artillery had so far silenced the Annamese batteries as to enable the stormers to carry this also by assault, they found themselves in presence of a third work, from which a still hotter reception was experienced, and which caused still heavier loss as the excited soldiery refused to retire for the operation of their artillery, but pressed forward with the bayonet. This was the chief engagement of the war; and though plucky resistance was afterwards experienced at every available point, the whole of lower Cochin-China was gradually overrun and subjugated, and finally constituted a French dominion, of which Saigon is now the capital.

It was not, however, till two years after the close of Admiral Charnier's campaign that the Colony attained its full dimensions. The old vice-royalty of Sai-Gon, it may be remembered, contained six provinces; but only three were at first annexed. The treaty of Saigon, concluded on June 6th, 1862—after providing, of course, for the toleration of Christianity and protection of converts—ceded to France the three provinces of Bien Hoa, Gia Dinh, and Dinh Tuong, with the island of Pulo Condore. French merchants and French war-ships were to have full rights of navigating the great river of Cambodia (le grand fleuve de Cambodge) and all its branches. Annam undertook to make no cession of territory to a foreign power without the assent of France. The ports of Tourane, Balat and Kwang-o were to be opened to French and Spanish commerce. In cases of future diplomatic intercourse, French or Spanish envoys were to be received by the king at Hué. Annam undertook to pay an indemnity of 4,000,000. And then follow two curious articles, affecting the three remaining provinces of the old satrapy, which were soon to furnish an excuse for incorporating these, also, in the new dominion. By Art. X. the inhabitants of these three provinces (Vinh-luong, An-gian and Ha-tien) were to be allowed to traffic freely in the three French provinces; while Article XI. ran as follows :—

> The Citadel of Vinh-luong shall be occupied for the present by French troops without, however, interfering in any way with the Annamese officials. It will be surrendered to the King of Annam as soon as he has stopped (aura fait cesser) the rebellion which exists at present by his orders in the provinces of Gia-dinh and Dinh Tuong . . . .

What might have been expected of course followed. These three provinces became a form of annoyance for the French; and Admiral Grandière incorporated them, in 1867, in French territory.

The town of Saigon is situated on a deep but rather narrow river of the same name, sixty miles from Cap St. Jacques. It is said to have been once the capital of Cochin-China, under the earlier Nguyen sovereigns, while Tongking was still the dominant state and before King Gya-long had succeeded in welding the whole littoral under his supremacy by Bishop Pigneau's aid; but the Court was subsequently moved to Hué, out of reach of the pirates who found convenient haunts in the numerous creeks that intersect the low land between it and the sea. The country on either side of the river, for the first thirty miles, is swamp covered with dense jungle inhabited by monkeys and tigers. But marks of habitation become more frequent as you ascend, until the neighbourhood of Saigon is richly and completely cultivated. The creeks which intersect this plain afford admirable means of carriage, and make the town a natural *entrepôt* for the commerce, as well as a convenient political centre, of the colony. A writer, who was present at the first capture of the city, says "all the country surrounding the citadel was occupied by the town of Saigon, composed chiefly of wooden houses covered with straw; though there rose here and there, in the midst of these, a few built of brick and roofed with tiles. These houses, nearly all constructed with a good deal of art, had each a well cultivated garden, and were surrounded by great trees whose shade protected them against the burning rays of the tropical sun. At the furthest extremity of Saigon was the Chinese district, which was the commercial quarter of the town, and recalled by its appearance the cities on the coast of China." But hardly one stone of the citadel is now left standing on another. The Annamese town has also nearly disappeared, the houses having no doubt been destroyed for military reasons during the siege; and a great portion of the site is now covered by the broad streets and more ambitious buildings of the French conquerors. The irrepressible Chinaman, only, holds his own. Choleyn, as the Chinese district is called, is still the commercial quarter of Saigon, and a great proportion of the trade of the colony passes through Chinese hands. The Annamese, who are fewer than one would expect, live chiefly along the south branch of the river, and in detached villages on the outskirts.

It is almost needless to say that, in laying out the foreign quarter, the French have displayed the characteristic taste of their nation. The streets are broad and well lined with trees, after the fashion of Boulevards; and a fine esplanade forms an agreeable lounge on a summer evening. A large building at the eastern end, which first strikes the eye in coming up the river, belongs to the Hongkong baker from whose shop came the poisoned bread in 1859; but he pleads, I believe, innocence of that crime, throwing the blame on one of his subordinates as having been seduced by the Canton officials. Most of the business premises are, naturally, either on the river or nearly adjacent. Further inland, the houses are much scattered, and stand back in compounds shrouded with rich tropical foliage. An extensive Botanical Garden has been laid out in the environs, and a Zoological collection made in it, after the Parisian model. The Gardens are distant about half an hour's drive from the landing place, and the road to them gives a very fair view of the town and suburbs. A missionary edifice in their neighbourhood, La Maison de Sainte Enfance, carefully closed as usual against intrusion by the curious, attracts attention from the peculiar semi-oriental style of its architecture. A handsome palace built for the Governor, after the model of the Tuilleries, is worth a visit; and one drives, of course, to the Chinese quarter, if one wishes to take away a complete impression of the town; but the houses here, like the "gharry" in which you travel, are identical with those at Singapore.

A favourite drive is to the tomb of Bishop Pigneau de Behaine; partly because of the half-romantic interest attaching to the spot, partly because the drive is interesting in itself, and gives as good an idea of the surrounding country as the drive to the Botanical Gardens does of the town. The same writer whom I have already quoted, speaks enthusiastically of "the great plains cultivated with sugar-cane and rice, the centenarian trees rising majestically aloft and spreading wide their leafy branches, the plantains and lemon trees with their green foliage lighting up the vast fields"—which adorn the environs. But though these features are undoubtedly present, his brilliant word-painting conveys rather too gorgeous an impression of the reality. The Plain of Tombs, in which the famous "Tombeau de l'Evêque d'Adran is situated," lies four or five miles to the back of Saigon, and is dotted, as its name implies, with graves—of which many are said to date from the time when Saigon was a royal city. The road runs through a plain, rich in tropical vegetation, and sparsely studded with homesteads of the Annamese peasants. We pass through one large village which, in the multiplicity of pigs, fowls and children, the huts open to the road, and general characteristics, recalls, again, the outskirts of Singapore; for in personal appearance, as well as in characteristic habits, the Annamese greatly resemble the Chinese, to whom they are of course a cognate race. Even the dress differs in fashion rather than in character; that of the officials almost exactly resembling the old Chinese style under the last (Ming) dynasty.

I have said that Bishop Pigneau's tomb is, for various reasons, one of the lions. But—in my experience at least—linguistic and other difficulties rendered getting to it nearly as hard a task as reaching one of the ruined cities of the interior. The search occupied from 11 a.m. to 6.30 p.m.; involving two separate excursions and the complete exhaustion of two ponies. Indeed we only discovered it at last by wandering about the country with a photograph which we had bought in Saigon, and which a peasant more intelligent than the rest at last recognized. He succeeded in directing the driver to the neighbourhood; and after much further wandering, we were at last guided into the heart of a clump of trees and found ourselves in front of the long-sought mausoleum. It proved to be essentially Chinese in character—exactly like a small Chinese temple—with screen in front and walled all round. A large expanse of roof with the familiarly curved gables, supported on wooden pillars;

in the centre a raised bed of whitened brick, bearing no inscription; and at the back an altar and tablet, also in Chinese style and bearing Chinese characters. Here was the last resting-place of the man who may be regarded as the pioneer of his countrymen in Cochin-China.

We have seen that the colony now comprises six provinces. The population is estimated at about 2,000,000. Its natural resources are said to be great, and it may, with good government, become a valuable possession. Admiral de la Grandière made the fatal blunder, at first, of repelling the Hong Kong merchants who showed an inclination to open branch establishments at Saigon: the colony was French, and all advantages were to be for the French! But the error of this policy was soon recognized when it was found that few Frenchmen came forward; and commerce has been carried on by English, German, and Chinese merchants. Rice is the principal export, the suitability of the plains for its cultivation enabling the production of a far greater quantity than is needed for the food of the comparatively few inhabitants; but the land is fertile and well suitable for the production of other tropical products.

[The Report of Mr. Tremlett, the British Consul at Saigon, states the export of rice during 1892 at 540,000 tons, valued at 2,200,000*l.* The other principal exports were fish, coprah, cotton, pepper, silk, &c., aggregating some 450,000*l.* No statistics of imports were available.]

CHAPTER II.

FRANCE AND CAMBODIA.

WITHIN twelve months after the signature of the Treaty of Saigon, it was found that French interests required the extension of a protectorate over Cambodia. Buffeted between Cochin-China and Siam, that unfortunate State had ended by becoming tributary to both; and it appeared inconsistent with the dignity and duty of France to abandon an inherent right which she had of course acquired with her new possession.

The origin and history of the Khmers have been the subject of keen discussion ever since Mouhot's researches disclosed to the world the splendid architectural remains which every succeeding visitor appears to view with equal admiration. It seems, however, to be now generally admitted that tradition and the evidence of style point to an Indian source; how much soever the race may have been debased by Malay and Mongolian admixture. The ruins of Angkor clearly represent what was once the centre of a rich, powerful and civilized State. At what date that civilization was founded, and how long it endured are among the most interesting and difficult problems offered by the Indo-Chinese peninsula.

It is clear, at any rate, that it must have lasted during several centuries, and then, from causes which can only be surmised, was rapidly extinguished. A considerable State implies considerable resources; and the country is, in fact, fertile, metalliferous, and admirably watered. All prosperity has, however, long since disappeared under conditions of chronic warfare. For the last hundred years, at any rate, Cambodia has been a battle-ground for Annam and Siam; and its political structure has been knocked to pieces, and its old civilization effaced, by their continued blows. The three provinces of Vinh-luong, An-gian and Ha-tien, last annexed by the French to Saigon, are said to have once belonged to Cambodia, but to have been reft away by the Annamese. It is certain that its power extended, once, much farther up the valley of the Meikong, for a Dutch embassy which ascended that river in 1641 mentions that its sovereigns were being driven back by the repeated attacks of the Laos: and one of the first acts of the reigning dynasty in Siam was to annex the provinces of Battambong and Angkor, on the east of the Great Central Lake which is a distinguishing feature of the country.

The whole peninsula seems to have been at that time in a turmoil. Annam had rebelled against Gya-long, who was trying to recover his throne by French aid: a change of dynasty had occurred simultaneously in Siam; and Cambodia seems to have been buffeted helplessly in the general disturbance.

The Siamese legend is that the Cochin-Chinese and Cham Malays who occupy the southern seaboard had combined to drive out the reigning Khmer princes, and that the intervention of Siam was with the object of restoring the latter to power. The help was, at any rate, effective; and, as usual in such cases, the country fell completely under Siamese influence. The Annamese were too much occupied with their own troubles to interfere; and when, in 1795, the Siamese replaced a Cambodian prince in power, they retained Battambong and Angkor, and affirmed a protectorate—which, in Asia, means suzerainty and tribute—over the remainder of the kingdom.

It seems evident, from even the imperfect materials available, that a normal and fertile cause of Cambodian decadence has been family dissension and intrigue. Fraternal jealousies have led to quarrels at home and intervention from without. If one prince leant on Siam, the other fled to Annam; and each court was willing to support a claim in which its own pride and influence were involved. Cambodia thus became a chronic battle-ground between opposing factions, instead of offering a solid front to the aggressor. The intrigues of Annam evidently recommenced with the recovery of its internal tranquility; and differences arose among the Cambodian princes as to the advisability of leaning towards a State that was developing preponderant power. Dissensions of this kind invariably meant disturbances at home, and appeals for help by the disputants to one or other of the neighbouring powers. The upshot in the present case seems to have been first war, and then an agreement that the king should be reinstated and should pay tribute to both his neighbours.

The years 1830-40 were evidently another epoch of general turmoil in this unfortunate region. This is the period during which French maps show Annamese authority as extending over Cambodia and the valley of the Meikong. It was, in fact, a period when the Laos of Wienchang rebelled against Siam, and when the Annamese evidently succeeded in excluding Siamese influence, temporarily, from the Khmer kingdom. As Siamese records express it, "The Cochin-Chinese came and directed the affairs of the country by laws and modes entirely Cochin-Chinese, at which the Cambodians were indignant, and unanimously rose and slaughtered them in every province. They then placed themselves, anew, under Siamese protection, and entreated that a Siamese army should be sent to aid them." The result, as a matter of fact, clearly was that the Siamese regained the upper hand, quelling the revolt of the Laos, and recovering their predominant position in Cambodia. Hostilities lasted, however, several years; and were only terminated in 1845 by the surrender of the Annamese claim to supremacy, and a return to the former system of tribute payment to both Hué and Bangkok. The prince who was confirmed on the throne of Cambodia, as a consequence of these events, was Nuck Phra Ong Duang, the father of the present king. He died in 1860, at the moment when France was breaking down the Annamese power at Saigon; and his son, Nuck Phra Ong Rajawaddy, whom the French call Norodom, began to reign in his stead.

The chronic dissensions, however, at once revived and facilitated the extinction of the last vestige of Cambodian independence. King Norodom had hardly ascended the throne before his brother, Ong Wartha (or Si Votha, as the French call him), excited a revolt which the Siamese temporarily suppressed, but which we shall find again in active operation during the earlier stages of French rule.

It is generally difficult to get at the first origin of anything. The attempt usually discloses some anterior motive, which has probably arisen out of some other collateral consideration. It is difficult, for instance, to say in the case of France whether policy or religion—the priest or the statesman—first started the nation, in any given case, on the quest of glory and territorial dominion. We are indebted to M. Moura[1] for the information that, so long ago as 1854, there appeared in Singapore a Christian mandarin of Portuguese descent, who represented to the French Consul that he had been sent by the King of Cambodia to contract a French alliance. What motive can have impelled him to this step, seeing that France had at the time no "interests" east of Pondichery, is a question which French missionaries might perhaps be able to answer. The news had

[1] Le Royaume de Cambodge. Paris, 1883.

possibly got abroad that M. de Montigny was about to visit certain Eastern countries, with a view to open up relations and intercourse. As a matter of fact he did visit Bangkok the following year, and negociate a treaty between France and Siam—of which French merchants, however, neglected to avail themselves to any appreciable extent. But he appears to have been imprudent enough to mention a purpose of going on to Cambodia, in pursuance of this mysterious invitation; whereupon the King of Siam sent a messenger to forbid his vassal indulging in any such divagation; and M. de Montigny, after waiting a while at Kamput, in expectation of a communication from Udong which never came, had to go on to China, *re infectâ*. Moura further asserts, on we know not what authority, that the intention of the king had been to place Cambodia under the Protectorate of France, and to cede to the latter the provinces of Saigon which the Annamese had reft from his ancestors' possession! Is it possible that we have, here, the germ of the idea that was to expand into Saigon-Cambodian dominion? The story sounds improbable in so far as concerns King Ong Duang, who appears to have been a genuine friend of Siam; but it is not impossible that the mission may have had a less responsible origin. The cession would, at any rate, have been a cheap one, as the provinces in question had long since passed out of the Cambodian grasp.

However this may be, the French Protectorate was imminent. And the plea for its assertion was ready to hand in the tributary relations already existing between Cambodia and Annam. The first move towards its establishment was made in 1863, when Admiral de la Grandière visited the then capital, Udong; and, under cover of the prestige arising from recent French conquests, seems to have found little difficulty in persuading the King to accept a treaty of which the first article ran:—"The Emperor of the French will assist and protect Cambodia." It is true, Norodom is said to have protested, at Bangkok, that he had signed under a sense of powerlessness to refuse; but though Siam showed great jealousy of the encroachment on ground where she had long been predominant, she could not venture on open resistance. The question, however, soon came to a head. There had, as yet, been no opportunity for the ceremony of coronation, amid the troubles attending Norodom's succession; and the King of Siam wished him to come to Bangkok for the purpose. The French objected to this implicit recognition of a suzerainty which it was their policy to discredit and evict: but an understanding was eventually come to that the coronation should be performed at Udong, by Siamese and French representatives having equal powers; and an opening was thus effected for further negociations which eventuated in the well-known treaty of 1867, by which Siam formally recognized the French Protectorate, and relinquished all claim to tribute or other mark of vassalage for herself—on two precise conditions. France undertook never to take possession of Cambodia for the purpose of incorporating it in Cochin-China; and agreed that the provinces of Battambang and Angkor, which had, as we have seen, been Siamese since 1795, should remain in Siamese possession. It was agreed, further, that the boundary between Cambodia and the provinces in question should be surveyed and defined by a joint French and Siamese Commission, and this was done in 1868. Since 1867, Siamese influence may be said to have disappeared from the councils of Cambodia.

We have, however, somewhat anticipated the course of events, in order to complete the elimination of Siam from the scene. Fresh internal troubles had in the meantime arisen, under the leadership of one Pucombo, who appears to have established a great personal ascendency over the people; and the rebellion initiated by this leader, on the East, was supplemented by another insurrection under one Assoa, in the South. The French accused the Annamese mandarins of the border provinces of sustaining both, or at least of allowing them to use Annamese territory as a base. The latter eventually vindicated themselves, in one direction, by giving up Assoa; but Pucombo overran the country almost to the gates of the capital; and the French had an opportunity of exercising their protective duties by sending an expedition (under Colonel Reboul), which broke up the insurrectionary force and compelled its leader to seek safety in flight. His death, twelve months later, ended a rebellion which had at one time spread over the whole kingdom except the metropolitan province. During its course the capital was removed to its present site, Phnom-peng; and at its close (in 1867) Admiral de la Grandière annexed the Annamese provinces of Vinhluong, Angian, and Hatien, whose Governors he accused of having favoured the insurrection. By June, 1867, order had been so far restored that two hundred men and two gunboats, stationed at Phnom-peng, were considered a sufficient garrison.

A note of antagonism to Siam was struck when, in 1868, the King addressed, or was caused to address, to the French Government, a protest against the establishment of Siamese Customs at the northern end of the Great Lake. He, at the same time, asserted his rights over the little provinces of Molu-prey and Tonli-repu—the occupation of which by Siam was alleged to be recent and irregular; and of these, as well as Battambong and Angcor, we may some day hear again, though nothing seems to have come of the protest for the moment. French authority was, in the meantime, being steadily consolidated, by extending and defining the power of the Resident and in other ways. In June, 1874, right of free transit was granted to produce coming from Battambong and Angkor to Cochin China: the same prerogative had been granted, a few years previously, to Laotian produce having the same destination; and these measures, together with the neutralization of the lake, which had been agreed on between the French and Siamese Governments with the object of removing all obstacles to trade and fisheries, proved of some advantage in promoting the flow of commerce to Cochin China.

So far, however, the hand of France had been felt but lightly. The time was approaching when her interference would become more active. In the course of May, 1876, the Prince Si Votha—whom we have seen showing active dissatisfaction at his brother's nomination to the throne—furtively quitted Bangkok, where he had been practically interned, and made for the region bordering on the river Meikong. He appears to have gone first to Tonly-repu, where he set to work to raise partisans and prepare for an invasion of Cambodia. In this region, and in the neighbouring Cambodian territory —where there was, according to M. Moura, much agitation and discontent owing to the bad administration of the provincial mandarins—his agents were able to raise numerous recruits. They had, we are told, "orders to be considerate to the people, to enrol only volunteers, and to pay in full for whatever was damaged or consumed. And this novel method of proceeding in time of trouble filled the people with astonishment and admiration, and gained them over more than aught else to the cause of the pretender." The Siamese Government despatched a special commission to Siem-rap, the capital of Angkor, to maintain neutrality on Siamese territory; and wrote to the French expressing anxiety at Votha's escape, and saying they had sent mandarins in pursuit with orders for his arrest, and forbidden the supply to him of arms or provisions in all districts under Siamese rule. The French seem to have contented themselves, at first, with sending two gunboats into the Meikong, to reassure the population and prevent their fleeing from the threatened trouble. Votha's proceedings were not, at any rate, greatly hampered; for he was strong enough, in June, to invade the province of Kampong Sorai and besiege the citadel, though he was defeated and driven into the border province of Molu-prey. The repulse, however, was only temporary, as he managed to enlist under his banner the remnant of Pucombo's following, who had been living in the half-settled provinces east of the Meikong, and was soon in a position to resume his incursions. Offers of a pension at Saigon, or a welcome and forgiveness at Bangkok, failed to tempt him; and by February, 1877, he had made such headway that the French judged it necessary to organize an expedition, by which he was finally defeated and driven into the forests of Stiengs; and so, for the second time, King Norodom was secured on his throne.

It will be remarked, however, that his protectors were somewhat tardy in coming to the rescue. The rebel prince was able to invade Kampong Sorai in June, 1876; but it was not till February, 1877, that the French undertook to suppress him. Admiral Duperré appears to have seized the opportunity to dictate certain reforms in the constitution, which were probably much needed, but which the King and his entourage showed no disposition to accept.

The Governor, however, had means of pressure by withholding help; and on January 15th, 1877, his Majesty acquiesced in a scheme, of which the following were the principal features. Certain exalted titles which involved huge retinues and a useless drain upon the State resources were abolished, and a fixed income was allotted to the Royal personages who held them in lieu of the provinces which they had previously held as appanages. A portion of the revenue was set aside for public works, instead of the whole passing under the King's control. The country had been split into a ridiculous number of provinces, and these were to be reduced, with a corresponding decrease in the number of functionaries. Officials were forbidden to trade. Villages were to have the right of electing their own head men. Taxation was re-organized. Labourers were to be allowed to redeem, for a small sum, the ninety days of labour they owed to the State. The duration of leases was to be extended (the State being constitutional owner of the land). Slavery without redemption to be abolished; increased facilities to be given for redemption, with severe penalties against the capture of slaves in the bordering (savage) districts; and the French Resident was to have the right of *entrée* into the King's Council. Having secured the promulgation by edict of these and other reforms, the Admiral, as we have seen, organized an expedition which promptly defeated and put the rebels to flight.

But though the King had been persuaded to

accept the scheme, it by no means followed that it would be put in immediate operation. The history of the next few years seems, in fact, to have been one of effort towards this end, resulting in the tightening of pressure and the gradually increasing introduction of the French element into the administration. To meet the cost of this increasingly active intervention, a new convention was dictated, in November, 1881, whereby the produce of certain taxes, amounting to about $100,000, was especially reserved for the expenses of the protectorate. The judicial powers of the Saigon tribunals were extended, so far as Europeans were concerned, all over Cambodia; and Franco-Annamese immigrants were withdrawn from Cambodian, and placed under French or Mixed, jurisdiction, according as they alone or Cambodians also were concerned. Other changes were effected in the following year, and other restrictions imposed, which it is unnecessary to trace in detail as everything is comprised, over-ridden, and swamped in the exhaustive list of concessions exacted by M. Thomson in the final treaty (!) of June 17th, 1884.

The story of the negotiations which preceded the signature of this document was told at the time, in the *Saigonnais*, with an unconscious satire amusing to those who read between the lines of the semi-official record. The ostensible object of M. Thomson's visit was to obtain the King's consent to the inclusion of Cambodia in the Customs Union, lately imposed from Paris upon the new Indo-Chinese Empire. And Article XVI. of the Treaty of 1863—

by which "the Emperor of the French [undertook] to honestly assist the King so as to enable him to collect duties from traders and enable them to proceed to sea"—was relied on as giving right and power to insist on acquiescence. It is difficult to say what may have been the precise object in view when this clause was penned, but we may assume that it hardly contemplated the imposition of a Customs tariff devised at Paris, and its collection by French officers. The King, at any rate, whatever he may have thought of the advantage of inclusion in the proposed Union, seems to have shown a strong objection to handing over the collection of his revenues to French officials. He urged, apparently, that his prestige would be destroyed if he agreed to entrust foreigners with the administration of his Customs, and insisted ("without," remarks the *Saigonnais*, "perceiving the personal rudeness of the demand"!) that the Governor should telegraph to Paris for fresh instructions. His struggles were, however, of course useless, and resulted only in plunging him deeper in the mire. As he declined to recognize the logic of the deduction from the Treaty of 1863, M. Thomson decided to have a treaty about which there should be no future possibility of mistake. Without recapitulating the measures taken in pursuance of this view, it will be sufficient to note that as the King kept him at arm's length M. Thomson, having caused the Palace to be surrounded, informed him that there was no longer any question of the Customs convention, but of a new arrangement "which, confirming the Treaty of 1863, would enable France to fulfil thenceforth, in the Kingdom of Cambodia, the functions incumbent on her and would prevent a repetition of the insults to which the Government of the Republic had been exposed." What passed subsequently, the *Saigonnais* knows not. "It is reported that the Governor used the words 'submission or abdication.'" In any case, a quarter of an hour had hardly elapsed before "the King of Cambodia, overcome by the energy and withal calmness of the Governor," signed the treaty.

The purport of this remarkable document is sufficiently implied in the first article, which sets forth that "The King accepts all the administrative, judicial, financial, and commercial reforms which the French Republic may think well to introduce, in the future, to facilitate the accomplishment of its protectorate." A shadow of power is reserved to him by Art. II., for the purpose probably of keeping within the lines of the Franco-Siamese Treaty of 1867, which promises that France will not incorporate Cambodia in Cochin-China; but that power is gradually whittled away, in eight more articles, till little but a shadow and a pension of $300,000 remain. It is an indication of the sweeping nature of the changes, that individual proprietorship was henceforth to be substituted for the State ownership of the land. The King roused himself, subsequently, to address a protest to the President against a treaty "imposed upon him by force, and at the bayonet's point;" and there was some disposition at first, in Paris, to evince sympathy with him and to blame M. Thomson for his harshness. But it appeared that the latter had really acted under directions from home; and nothing more was heard of this last phase in the history of Cambodia as an independent kingdom.

A Proclamation which was issued to the Cambodian people, on the day after the King's signature had been obtained, affirmed once more the beneficence of French rule and the brilliancy of the future which awaited Cambodia under its new constitution.

REPUBLIQUE FRANCAISE.

"By a Convention signed at Phnom-penh on June 17th, 1884, H.M. Norodom King of Cambodia, and M. Charles Thomson Governor of Cochin-China acting in the name of the Government of the French Republic, agreed to realize the reforms recognized as necessary in the interests of the Cambodian people. The new arrangement confirms and completes the fundamental treaty of August 11th, 1863, between France and Cambodia, and respects the ancient laws and customs of the kingdom as far as they are compatible with the eternal principles of right and human progress, which alone make nations great, happy, and free. In consequence of this accord and the goodwill which exists between the two Governments, measures will be taken in the immediate future by which slavery in Cambodia will disappear, in order that all Cambodians may enjoy their liberty. The land, which has up to the present belonged to the Crown, will be ceded to communes and individuals in full ownership. Churches and temples will retain the lands they actually occupy. French officials will be sent to the provinces, to direct matters in concert with the Cambodian authorities, so that justice may be rendered equally to all, and that the taxes be applied to works of public utility—the construction of bridges, roads, canals, telegraphic lines, serving to facilitate communication in all parts of the kingdom. A municipality will be charged to administer the town of Phnom-penh. Commerce and industry will become more prosperous, order and tranquility guaranteed, individual property constituted; and the welfare of all Cambodians will increase daily. Such, briefly, will be the chief results of the new Convention by which H.M. Norodom I. has just cemented the bonds of friendship which have so long united France and Cambodia. The Government of the French Republic, Protector of Cambodia, will always have for its end to ensure, by wise dispositions, the liberty and welfare of the Cambodian people. H.M. the King of Cambodia and the Governor of Cochin-China reckon on the zeal and devotion of the Cambodian officials to impart to the population the intentions of the two Governments, and to aid them in the accomplishment of the work of peace, justice, and civilization.

(Signed) The Governor of Cochin-China,

CHARLES THOMSON.

Done at Phnom-penh, June 18th, 1884.

Five months after the signature of the new treaty, M. Thomson took the opportunity of personally installing the first members of the new Municipal Council; pronouncing an oration which is reported at length in the *Journal Officiel* of Saigon, and which was read, doubtless, with a glow of patriotic satisfaction by every Frenchman whose sense of humour did not overcome his national appreciation of dramatic effect. "To liberate and regenerate Cambodia, to raise the moral and intellectual level of its inhabitants, to initiate them in the principles which are the basis of modern society, while respecting their religious and national creeds, to develop the natural riches of the country, while caring for all wants and respecting all rights: such is the great and noble mission which France, faithful to her historical traditions, has undertaken; such is the work which will be accomplished, avec le concours de toutes les intelligences et de toutes les bonnes volontés." The English language is hardly adapted to an explicit rendering of these final expressions, so they may well be left in their native vagueness and beauty.

To ask that the picture should be immediately realized would be to prove oneself void of poetic imagination. But it may be hoped, for the sake of the Cambodians themselves, that they will make the best of the inevitable, and accept the destiny which France and civilization have decreed. Assuming, as we do, that their independence is irretrievably lost, it were well that they accepted quietly the new régime. For, though we are far from thinking French rule an unmixed blessing to native races, it offers a guarantee of order which alone will be welcome to a people whose recent history had been one of chronic civil war and invasion. However harsh the course adopted, much may be forgiven the French if, by restoring order and respecting native rights, they render possible the fulfilment of one tithe of the brilliant programme which M. Thomson enounced.

CHAPTER III.

FRANCE AND TONGKING.

THE consolidation of French dominion in the south was followed, shortly, by the discovery of interests in Tongking. "On June 5th, 1866, the harbour of Saigon offered the common enough spectacle of two little gunboats making their final preparations for a start."[1] The travellers on board "were commissioned to ascend the great river, whose fertile delta they and those around them had so often traversed, and no limit of distance or time was assigned to the enterprise. The thoughts of the colony had long been turned with curiosity and impatience towards this interior about which such great uncertainty prevailed. The period of conquest was past. . . . It was to the organization and exploration of the country that the attention of the local Government now required to be directed. Here was a vast field still open to the ambitions of the expeditionary troop, and one promising results more fertile, and discoveries more glorious, than the sterile pursuit of pirates who

[1] "Voyage d'Exploration en Indo-Chine." Par Francis Garnier.

could never be caught, or unequal combats against an enemy who was always beaten." The Government had, in fact, decided on the exploration of the valley of the Meikong; and the journey was to lead to the annexation of Tongking.

The history of Tongking as a separate State may be said to date from the early part of the fifteenth century. Till then it had been at times a vassal, at times a virtual province of China. So early, indeed, as the ninth century it seems to have made an effort to throw off the yoke, and succeeded in asserting a partial independence; but it was not till about 1428 that it extorted a final recognition of its autonomy.[1] A general named Le then succeeded in expelling the Chinese troops and founding a dynasty which endured, through various vicissitudes, for more than three hundred years. The forms, customs, and prejudices of Chinese civilization still prevailed, and the supremacy of the Chinese Emperor was still admitted: the Kings of Tongking received investiture at the hands of his delegates, on their accession, and sent tribute periodically to the Celestial capital. But the conditions were changed: they were vassals, henceforward, instead of subjects. The Le dynasty received its first shock, and was well-nigh overthrown, about a hundred years after the death of its founder. It was, however, re-established by a general named Nguyen, who forthwith assumed the title of Regent; the monarchs falling into the position of *rois fainéants*, from which they never recovered. The death of this

[1] "Lettres Edifiantes, etc.: Tableau Historique du Tonquin."

minister was the signal for a division of power which caused untold misery to the country and its inhabitants. He was followed in his dignity of Regent by a son-in-law named Trinh, while his son Nguyen Hwang was appointed governor of a dependency corresponding approximately with the region known to us as Annam, which had been conquered and detached from the adjoining kingdom of Chiampa. What ensued may be guessed beforehand. Chafing at the control of his brother-in-law, Nguyen Hwang threw off the yoke and, while admitting the nominal suzerainty of Tongking, proclaimed himself otherwise independent. Efforts to reduce the southern kingdom to submission gave rise to constant hostilities, but the Nguyens maintained their independence and gradually extended their rule over the remainder of Chiampa, a district nearly represented by the present French colony of Saigon.

Matters were in this position when, towards the close of the eighteenth century, a formidable revolution occurred, which overwhelmed Le, Trinh and Nguyen in a common ruin. Court intrigues had led to the usual appeals for external aid. The Tongkingese had been invited to enter Annam, and had taken the normal course of setting up as masters where they had been asked to intervene as friends. A successful insurrection against them had been followed by a counter-invasion of Tongking, which was subjected, in turn, by the victorious Annamese. The last "Le" king fled to China, where he died; while the last "Nguyen" fled to

Siam, where he was persuaded by the Bishop of Adran to solicit, from France, the help that was to enable him to recover his throne and to weld the whole Eastern littoral into the kingdom over which we find him reigning under the style of Gya-long.

But to be governed by a Nguyen meant, in the eyes of the Tongkingese, to be subject to Annam; and they seem never to have acquiesced willingly in the change. They wished, at the time, that the Le dynasty should be restored in the person of a brother of their last sovereign; and "Le" pretensions have ever since been a thorn in the side of Annam. Powerless though it must have been to stave off its eventual fate, the Annamese Government might probably have held out longer against France, in 1860, but that it found itself attacked on two sides. The partisans of the former dynasty had taken the opportunity to break out in rebellion in Tongking, under a reputed scion of the ancient house.[1] Numbers of Tongkingese appear to have joined the movement; and within less than eight months the insurgent leader had overrun a great portion of the country. An army sent against him was utterly defeated; and the Court of Hué was driven to make peace with France and Spain, to save itself from overthrow. Relieved thus from pressure in the South, it was able to put forth its whole strength against the in-

[1] Le Phung, said to be a Christian pupil of one of the local Catholic Seminaries. He was wrecked, taken and executed, two years later, in an abortive attempt on the Annamese capital.

surgents; and eventually succeeded in crushing the movement.

It was natural that the rebel leaders should make overtures to the foreigners who were operating against the common enemy; and, if the French had then cared to annex Tongking, here was no doubt an easy opportunity. In addition to the prestige of his birth, the pretender was supposed, as a Christian, to have the sympathy of the Christian population whom it was the avowed object of the expedition to protect; and it was believed that a simple demonstration would encourage a general rising in his favour. The Spanish commandant was inclined to espouse his cause, but Admiral Bonard refused to acquiesce:[1] the reputation of Saigon was then in the ascendant, and it was there the French flag was to be planted: the Red River was not yet known, nor could the importance its discovery was to give Tongking be possibly foreseen. The step which was to turn French attention to the north, was the despatch of the expedition whose departure Garnier has described for us in the opening lines of the present chapter. One of the problems of the day was to open up commercial intercourse with the western provinces of China; and it was hoped that this river, which descends from the mountains of Thibet, traverses the whole length of the Indo-Chinese peninsula, and discharges itself through French territory into the China Sea might prove a practicable route. The result was disappointing so

[1] "Histoire de l'Intervention Française au Tongking," par F. Romanet du Caillaud.

far as the Meikong was concerned, as its channel proved to be broken by impassable rapids: but the travellers made an unexpected hit. The Mahommedan rebellion was then at its height in Yunnan, and the objection of the Chinese officials to their passage through rebel territory compelled them to quit the Meikong soon after passing the frontier, and pursue an easterly route. The result was that they reached, at Yuen-kiang, the banks of a river coming out of Yunnan and tending towards the Gulf of Tongking, which promised a solution of the problem. Credit cannot be claimed for the discovery as a new one in a geographical sense, for the river is laid down in the old Jesuit maps; but it was certainly reserved for M. de Lagrée and his companions to call attention to its existence and to its capabilities as a commercial route. It is this river, known as the Hung Kiang, or Red River, in Chinese territory, and Song koi, in Tongking, which has excited all the subsequent interest of the French in Tongking. To hold Tongking was not only to possess a fertile province, but to control a highway of communication with Yunnan; and France became as anxious to obtain that hold as China and Annam were loth that it should pass into her possession.

The first to explore the new route was a Frenchman named Dupuis. Yunnan was still in the worst throes of the rebellion which had so long defied the efforts of the Imperial Government for its suppression, and Dupuis resolved to visit the Imperialist headquarters, establish relations with the mandarins, and endeavour to utilize the Red River for the import of arms and munitions of war. Yunnan is famous for metallic wealth, and he calculated on taking payment in ores which he would carry away by the same route to a foreign market. Having found the officials at Yunnan-foo ready to accept his overtures, his next step was to ascertain that the river was really practicable for his purpose; and he succeeded in making his way down its course sufficiently far to satisfy himself on that point. The navigation became practicable at the town of Manghao, which is well within the Chinese frontier. There were rapids of doubtful practicability for steamers between that and Laokai, some seventy miles lower down, but none which could not be surmounted by native boats. There are, however, other than physical difficulties to be considered, when it is a question of transit through Asiatic kingdoms. Nature may provide highways; but the obstructiveness of the governing powers, or the existence of local disturbance, are obstacles nearly as difficult to overcome as natural barriers. Although the frontiers of China and Tongking were supposed to be contiguous, there existed, between the limits of the strictly settled districts, a strip of territory inhabited by aboriginal tribes more or less submissive, but partially independent of either. The area of this doubtful borderland and the degree of authority exerted over it by the neighbouring governments depend, no doubt, to some extent upon the measure of tranquility in the adjacent provinces. If these are in insurrection, or the hands of the authorities are otherwise weakened, the borderland escapes from control, and becomes a field of refuge for the scum that is cast off in the turmoil of Oriental warfare. This was the case when Dupuis made his exploratory journey. The Taeping and Mahommedan rebellions had disorganized the adjoining provinces of China: the French war and insurrections in Tongking had seriously weakened the Government of Annam. Before the Mussulman insurrection, Manghao had been under the authority of a border chief, tributary to China, whose principal residence was at Laokai. Certain Cantonese appear to have profited by that outbreak to displace him at these two stations, but none the less maintained order and successfully promoted trade. They were still in possession of Manghao at the time of Dupuis' visit, but had been ousted from Laokai by a body of Taeping refugees from the Chinese province of Kwangse; and these, under the name of Black Flags, on account of their distinguishing colours, become the Kroumirs of the tale.

His explorations ended, Dupuis returned by the same route to complete his arrangements with his Chinese clients. By them he was commissioned to procure large quantities of arms and munitions of war; letters of credence were given him to the Annamese officials; and extensive commercial operations, having for their basis the metallic products of Yunnan, were, it is said, promised countenance and support as soon as peace was restored. So far, all seemed promising enough. Unfortunately, however, a very small error is sufficient to upset an elaborate calculation, and the error in this case seems to have been a misconception of the probable attitude of the Annamese Government. It was too much taken for granted that the letters of the Yunnan Mandarins would smooth away obstacles, and that the fact of the arms being destined for China, a friendly and suzerain State, would ensure them against hindrance. The illusion was natural, perhaps, but it was complete; and the result proved, for the hundredth time, how unsafe it is to rely on Orientals acting in accordance with Western logic. In the meantime, however, happily ignorant of the obstacles he was to encounter, Dupuis made his way back to Hankow, and from thence to France, for the purpose of executing his commission. His endeavours to interest the French Government in his project appear to have been fairly successful, though he was refused official support. One request only was granted. Dupuis wished to repair in person, on his return, to the Annamese capital in order to obtain recognition of his character as a Chinese emissary. He was persuaded that it would assist him in this object if he were allowed to make the visit in a French ship; and he was promised that measure of support. But the Government would do nothing further; he must act, in other respects, at his own risk.

Thus assured at least of the sympathy of his Government, Dupuis purchased and shipped the supplies of which he was in quest, and set out on his return to make the necessary preparations for their transport. Hong Kong offered the greatest facilities for the purpose, and it was there he organized his expedition. As the extent of these preparations is an important feature in the case, we may note that they involved the purchase of two discarded English gun-boats and a small steam sloop, besides the hire of a 400-ton junk—the whole manned by a crew of twenty-five Europeans and 150 Asiatics armed with breech-loaders. The Annamese mandarins may well have been startled when such a flotilla came to seek passage through the heart of Tongking. Having all in readiness, he went next to Saigon, to ask for the man-of-war which he had been promised should convey him to Hué. The despatch vessel *Bourayne* had, in effect, been designated for this service; but her commander, M. Senez, who had just returned from an exploring expedition along the shores of Tongking, strongly dissuaded him from the project. His opinion was that, so far from seeking authorization from the Court of Hué, the best chance of success lay in anticipating any action the latter might possibly take. The expedition would, he considered, become unrealizable directly the Annamese Government was informed of it, and more unrealizable still if the Government of Saigon recommended it.[1] It is important to note that this advice tended materially to alter the scope of the enterprise, and to reduce it from a pioneer expedition which was to prepare the way for the formal opening of the Red River, to a sort of dash past a blockade which, even if successful,

[1] "L'Intervention Française au Tonkin," p. 57. I have been greatly indebted to M. Romanet du Caillaud's compendious work for the facts of this narrative.

would be more likely to leave the Annamese authorities irritated at the intrusion than disposed to favour a second attempt. From the point of view of an adventurer wishing to make a single lucrative voyage, the more high-handed proceeding probably held out the best chance of success. From the point of view of the French Government, desirous of opening up Tongking and the Red River to foreign trade, there were two courses open. The more legitimate was to let Dupuis incur the opposition of the Court of Hué, and make that opposition a starting-point for diplomatic insistence. The other was to let him *far da se*, with the certainty that, if he failed, a complication would be created in which France could intervene, and which would give her an opportunity of dictating terms. The French Government would probably have preferred the former course. It was interested in the experiment, but was too much under the influence of recent disaster to approve any procedure that might entail complications. The Saigon authorities, more absorbed in their own affairs, and already looking on Tongking as a vital object of colonial policy,[1] were probably less

[1] "Notre établissement dans ce riche pays limitrophe de la Chine et débouché naturel de ses riches provinces sud-occidentales est, selon moi, une question de vie ou de mort pour l'avenir de notre domination dans l'Extrême Orient. Nous devons y prendre pied soit comme alliés du roi Tu Duc, pour y retablir son autorité et l'y faire respecter, soit par une occupation militaire qui ne serait que trop justifiée le jour ou la cour de Hué nous aurait donné la preuve de sa mauvaise foi et de sa repugnance à conclure avec nous un arrangement définitif."—*Despatch of Admiral Dupré to the Minister of Marine and the Colonies*, d. May 19th, 1873.

unwilling to see the waters troubled. Be this as it may, the advice of M. Senez was followed. The visit to Hué was abandoned; Dupuis was to present himself unannounced off the mouth of the Red River, and endeavour to ascend it in his double capacity of merchant and Chinese emissary, offering to pay all legitimate dues and charges that would be exacted from a Chinese or Annamese trader. He returned accordingly to Hongkong for his flotilla; and the *Bourayne*, which was about, by a happy coincidence, to start on a second voyage of exploration, preceded him into Tongkingese waters.

M. Senez' instructions were to visit the Bay of Cua Câm, through which the Red River flows into the Gulf, and to ascend the river itself as far as Hanoi, the capital city of Tongking. These objects were carried out. On November 1st, 1872, he entered the estuary; and on the 6th, having left his ship at anchor, arrived in a launch before the walls of Hanoi. Almost simultaneously Dupuis arrived off the port of Cat-Ba. M. Senez' reception at the Tongkingese capital was not cordial, nor was it without a considerable display of firmness that he was able to exact the attention he considered his due. He succeeded, however, in the end; and, after visiting the provincial cities of Bac-Ninh and Haï-Dzuong, made his way to Kwang-yen, where the Annamese Viceroy was at that moment residing. It was in the neighbourhood of this city that Dupuis' flotilla was anchored; and when M. Senez and the Annamese Commissioner exchanged visits, his project naturally came up for discussion. What passed at the interview might have been safely predicted. The Viceroy listened to M. Senez' argument, and seemed impressed by his enumeration of the advantages that would result from the opening of Tongking to commerce: "but," he asked, "would they appreciate all those advantages at Hué?" He objected, moreover, to the authority with which Dupuis had been furnished by the Chinese Commander-in-Chief, as seriously informal: a viceroy, only, was in a position to address the Annamese Government; and again, not the Viceroy of Yunnan, but the Viceroy of Canton was the official with whom communication was always held. Nothing, in short, could now be done but refer the question to Hué for decision; and as M. Senez assured him that the French Government took an interest in the enterprise, he would exert his personal influence in Dupuis' favour. Eighteen days was named as the time required for the receipt of an answer, and it was agreed that Dupuis should anchor below the forts in the interval.

Having thus done all that lay in his power to promote the enterprise, M. Senez left on November 20th on his return to Saigon; but with his departure the spirit of obstruction regained the ascendant. The natives were forbidden to have dealings with Dupuis or his people. He was given to understand that the answer from Hué might very likely be three months, instead of eighteen days, in arriving; and the advisability was suggested of his returning to Hongkong, and there awaiting the decision. To have acquiesced in these intimations would, of course, have been to abandon the enterprise. He replied that he would wait the eighteen days; and then, answer or no answer, would proceed on his voyage. The expiry of the term found the officials as far as ever from sanctioning his advance. He acted, accordingly, as he had declared, and made his way to Hanoi, which he reached exactly a month after the departure of the *Bourayne* for Saigon. It is needless to dwell on the turmoil which a step so unprecedented caused in the minds of the Annamese officials. The gates of the citadel were closed, and the guard was placed under arms. Dupuis appears to have succeeded in calming their fears, but not in allaying their opposition. He must still wait for the reply from Hué! And they hid away every native boat out of sight, in the meantime, that he might not be able to tranship his cargo for the river voyage. Dupuis, however, again got tired of waiting for the answer that never came. Having obtained a hint where he would find some of the hidden boats, he went the length of helping himself to three; and, transhipping to these as much of his cargo as they would carry, succeeded in making his way with them to the Yunnan frontier. No actual resistance was offered; the officials contenting themselves with putting difficulties in the way of getting food or labour along the route. Even the Black Flags did not oppose his passage; though, as on the occasion of his first visit, there was a lack of cordiality in their reception! The authorities in Yunnan appear to have been pleased with his success.

The Viceroy gave him fresh letters of recommendation to the chief Annamese officials, and moved the Viceroy of Canton to write also in his favour.

He had started from Hanoi on January 18th. He got back there on April 30th—to find his new letters as little efficacious as the first. The former Viceroy had left, and his successor displayed uncompromising hostility. Orders were issued forbidding the inhabitants to have any dealings with Dupuis or his companions, to sell them any kind of provisions, or to hire them boats for transport. The further precaution was taken of barring the northern reaches of the river, to prevent any renewed attempt to ascend; and, this done, the Commissioner threatened to burn his ships if he did not quit Tongking. Dupuis, who had taken the precaution of bringing 120 Chinese soldiers as boatmen from Yunnan, enlisted 150 more who offered their services—a proceeding which raised his forces to 500 men—and awaited the attack. It is hardly necessary to add that the Annamese hereupon delayed execution of their threat. They appealed, instead, to the Governor of Saigon, to rid them of his contumacious subject.[1] And this brings us to the first act of French inter-

[1] It is right to add that the Annamese Government had already addressed Admiral Dupré on the subject, and had elicited the following sensible advice :—"Mon avis est," the Admiral wrote, "que le parti le plus sage à prendre serait de laisser M. Dupuis continuer son voyage, s'il consent à payer les droits établis, à ne pas susciter de troubles, à ne debarquer ni armes ni munitions sur toute votre territoire."

vention—an episode which resembles a chapter of Dumas, rather than a tale of modern history.

We have seen that the Government of Saigon, eager to strengthen its position and extend its influence in the Far East, was inclined to a more adventurous policy than its superiors. The question of Tongking was, in fact, not the only one pressing for solution. Although the King of Annam had been compelled to cede, in the treaty of 1862, the three provinces which formed the nucleus of the colony, he had not recognized the subsequent annexations which had doubled its area. A new treaty was wanted, to settle this and other questions, but the king showed no inclination to sign one, and the Saigon authorities were getting irritated at the delay. On his return from his voyage of exploration through the estuary of the Red River, M. Senez advised the use of Tongking as a lever to extort the concession; and, whatever we may think of the morality of the scheme, he must be allowed credit for discernment. Tongking was the most vulnerable and most valuable part of the Annamese monarchy, and disturbance in Tongking always meant a compliant disposition at the Court of Hué. A military occupation would be preferable; but, as such a project would have small chance of approval under existing circumstances, he suggested the encouragement of insurrection as an alternative: a "Le" Pretender to be placed at the head of the movement, and some mercantile house in Saigon to furnish arms under the secret guarantee of the colonial Government. The last insurrection had only succumbed, he considered, for want of arms: if these were provided the Tongkingese had an excellent chance of recovering their independence, and would be glad to place themselves under the protectorate of France. M. Senez appears to have found in Admiral Dupré a willing listener, and we shall see hereafter that the seed did not fall on barren ground.

In the meantime, Dupuis' proceedings were being made the subject of urgent complaint by the Annamese Government; and Admiral Dupré appears to have so far admitted the justice of the remonstrance as to point out that the existing treaties forbad French subjects to reside in the interior, and that he had therefore better withdraw. Dupuis refused. He was, he said, an emissary from the Government of Yunnan, to begin with; but he was entitled to do what he desired, even as a Frenchman: the treaty gave Frenchmen all the privileges of the most favoured nation and, consequently, the same rights as were possessed by the Chinese who traded and travelled with full liberty throughout the kingdom of Annam. He sent, moreover, an agent, in the person of M. Millot, who seems to have given the Admiral a favourable impression of his proceedings; the upshot being that His Excellency not only promised to endeavour, semi-officially, to obtain for Dupuis an indemity of $250,000 for the hindrance he had encountered, but actually gave an official guarantee for a loan of $30,000 from a local bank, to meet his immediate requirements.

The political condition of Tongking was naturally discussed, and M. Millot was able to report one fact of especial interest. The partisans of the "Le" dynasty were again agitating, and had even made overtures to Dupuis for help, which the latter, however, had refused, on the ground that politics were not within his province. It is easy to conceive that, to a mind impressed by M. Senez' suggestions, the opportunity offered by such a complication must have been very seductive.[1] Admiral Dupré appears to have regarded it as too favourable to be neglected. The Court of Hué had begged him to send an officer with a small escort to settle the Dupuis difficulty: he would do so; and selected for the purpose Francis Garnier, the senior surviving member of the expedition which had first brought the Red River into notoriety. He telegraphed to France a statement of his intentions and his reasons, accepted all the responsibility, and asked to be let alone to do his best.

The instructions Garnier received appear to have left him wide discretion, both in regard to Dupuis and his own proceedings. He himself, in a letter to his family, says he had full liberty to act as he

[1] "Sans doute alors l'amiral, quand il eut fait faire à M. Dupuis une avance de trente mille piastres, pensa-t-il avoir trouvé cette maison de commerce, dont parlait le projet de M. Senez, qui sous la guarantie financière occulte de la France pourrait fournir des armes aux insurgés. Une grande partie du matériel de guerre de M. Dupuis . . . était encore à Hanoi: et d'un jour à l'autre on pouvait armer les insurgés."—*L'Intervention Française au Tongking*, pp. 79, 81.

thought best.[1] In an official letter to his Government, Admiral Dupré speaks of having told him to establish himself securely at the spot which he might consider most convenient for carrying out his mission. A despatch to the Court of Hué, written at the moment of Garnier's departure, tersely recapitulates outstanding grievances,[2] and insists on the opening of Hanoi and the Red River to trade. "Here I am," Garnier wrote from Hanoi, "en train de fonder soit un protectorat français soit une nouvelle colonie, selon le dégré d'obstruction que montrera la cour de Hué." Indeed, the admiral frankly expresses this threat, two months later, when even the capture of Hanoi had failed to induce compliance with his demands. "Si vous ne vous hâtez de faire le traité," he writes to the Annamese Government in December, "notre séjour au Tongking se prolongera; nous serons forçés d'en compléter l'occupation pour administrer directement le pays, ou de chercher dans la famille royale ancienne celui de ses membres qui a le plus de droit pour régner sur le pays, à l'établir, et le soutenir de nos armes." He was, in fact, resolved to establish French influence, either by treaty or annexation, and Garnier was to take the steps he thought most conducive to that end.

[1] "Comme instructions carte blanche! l'amiral se rapporte à moi."

[2] "Démarches des Annamites auprès du gouvernement étranger de Hongkong, mauvais traitemens infligés aux Chrétiens, mépris des passeports delivrés aux missionaires."—*Admiral Dupré to the Government of Annam*, October 11th, 1873.

The strength of his escort appears somewhat inconsistent with the magnitude of the design. It comprised thirty soldiers under Lieutenant de Trentinian, besides the crew, fifty-six in number, of the despatch boat *D'Estrées*, in which he sailed. Two more gunboats, however, were shortly sent after him, raising his total force to 212 men, of whom twenty-four were Asiatics, and eleven guns. Garnier reached Hanoi on November 5th, 1873. The chief Annamese authority in Tongking was Nguyen Tri-phuong, the general who had opposed the French in the campaign of Saigon. He had the reputation of being intensely hostile to foreigners, and it soon became evident that there was little chance of an amicable understanding. Garnier said he had come to negotiate a treaty of commerce which should open the Red River to navigation. Nguyen declared he had no power to entertain that question, and requested him simply to judge and punish Dupuis in accordance with the request which had been addressed to the Governor of Saigon to that effect. Garnier posted a proclamation that, as the Annamese Government had sent to Saigon for assistance, he had come to see how things were going on; and that the French intended to drive away pirates, foster commerce, and so bring wealth to the country. Nguyen immediately posted another, forbidding native or Chinese merchants to have any intercourse with the French Commandant, who had been sent to drive out Dupuis and had no right to meddle in the affairs of the country. The position, in fact, became so strained that, only three days after his arrival, Garnier had resolved to attack the citadel, and was only dissuaded by Bishop Puginier, who apprehended that such a step would lead to reprisals on the Converts, to the abandonment of their posts by the Annamese officials, and the consequent access of serious disorders in the province.

The delay, however, was only temporary, as Garnier conceived an alternative measure which it was im-impossible the Governor could tolerate. Failing to persuade the latter to open Tongking of his own motion, and dissuaded by the Bishop from a resort to force, he resolved to place himself alongside the Annamese authorities, and himself give the necessary orders! He accordingly issued a proclamation declaring the Red River and various ports open to trade under French protection, and fixing a customs' tariff. Of course the Mandarins had the placards torn down as soon as they were put up. Garnier then presented an ultimatum demanding the disarmament of the citadel, the issue of orders to all the governors of provinces to obey the instructions of the French envoy, and permission for Dupuis to enter freely into Yunnan. The ultimatum was ignored; and on the following day the citadel was attacked and carried.

Hanoi was taken on November 20th, and Garnier at once put forth a proclamation disclaiming any idea of annexation, and throwing the responsibility of what had happened on the local Mandarins. He had been sent there by the Governor of Saigon to open up commercial intercourse, but the Mandarins were obstinate and regardless of the interests of the people; he was obliged therefore to depose them, and was about to invite the co-operation of the respectable and intelligent classes in filling their places and maintaining order. He requested, at the same time, all the minor officials to remain at their posts, and caused fresh seals of office to be prepared, which asserted the protectorate of France over Tongking. This was practically to assume, at any rate for the time being, the government of the province; and for the time being, also, M. Puginier's prediction was fulfilled. The greater part of the officials ran away, others tried to organize resistance, and bands of brigands scoured the country; anarchy reigned supreme.[1] It may seem strange that, having gone so far, he did not play the card which M. Senez had indicated, and encourage a revolt in favour of some "Le" pretender. He did, in fact, take into his service, in the capacity of adjutant-general, the chief of the "Le" party, who assured him he could dispose of four or five thousand followers. But M. Puginier appears to have dissuaded him from going further, doubting the possibility of finding a "Le" who would fulfil the required conditions of capacity and descent; and Garnier seems to have abandoned the idea. At any rate, the insurgent card was not played, and respect for the king was blandly affirmed, while the royal fortresses were captured and the royal officers superseded and imprisoned.

[1] "L'anarchie etait à son comble."—*L'Intervention Française, &c.*, p. 123.

It would carry us far beyond our proposed limits to describe in detail the incidents of the ensuing month. With feverish energy, but with resolution and success, Garnier set to work to organize the territory he had practically conquered, and to extend his authority over the neighbouring districts. With an audacity born no doubt of first success as well as of conscious superiority, handfuls of men were sent off to destroy forts and coerce recalcitrant officials. M. Balny d'Avricourt, with the gunboat *Espingole* and seventeen marines, received the submission of the governor of Hungyen, took the fortified town of Phu-ly,—if that can be called "taking" where the defenders fly without firing a shot,—and on December 5th carried by assault the provincial city of Haidzuong. On the same day, by a course of procedure which may be described as unscrupulous and violent or clever and dashing, according to the view taken of Garnier's whole procedure, M. de Hautefeuille obtained possession of Ninh-Binh. The successful officer was, in each case, installed as governor of the province he had conquered; and the capture of Nam-dinh by Garnier himself, who placed Dr. Harman in charge, completed the subjection of the delta of the Red River. The Annamese authority had collapsed like a house of cards.

Events had passed so rapidly that there had been no time, as yet, for the intervention either of the Saigon Government or of the Court of Hué. Delegates from both quarters were about to arrive, and the occupation of Tongking was to terminate as quickly as it had been effected. Among symptoms that some at least of the royal officers were beginning to recover breath, was the formation of an army in the province of Sontay, having in its vanguard the famous Black Flags of the Upper Red River, which began to advance menacingly in the direction of Hanoi. Garnier had made arrangements for attacking this army with all the force at his disposal when, on December 19th, there came an ambassador from Hué, whose instructions gave promise of an understanding in the sense desired by the Saigon Government. He refrained accordingly from carrying out his design; issued a proclamation announcing the suspension of hostilities; and, relying on the ambassador's promise that this should be forwarded to the Annamese camp, relaxed the vigilance which seemed now unnecessary. He was actually engaged in discussing the terms of a treaty with the royal envoy, when the alarm was given that the Annamese army was advancing and that the Black Flags were actually firing on the ramparts. The attack was repelled; but, in attempting to follow up his success, Garnier found that he had to deal with opponents less contemptible than the Annamese. Firing occasionally, as they retreated, the Chinese eventually halted behind an earthwork and faced their pursuers. Garnier attacked them with a handful of men, at the point of the bayonet, but it was his last act of daring. He stumbled and fell while running forward in advance; and in an instant the Black

Flags were upon him, and stabbed him with their spears, while his followers fell back to escape a similar fate. Rallying, at a short distance, the latter succeeded in again compelling the Chinese to retire, by the superiority of their fire, and recovered the bodies of their leader and of another soldier who had fallen; but both had been decapitated, and their heads carried off in triumph. Nor was this all. M. Balny d'Avricourt, having also repelled the assailants on the side of the citadel which had been entrusted to his care, sallied out, in ignorance of what had happened, to support his chief; and again the contempt of the enemy which the French had learnt during the first days of their success, was to prove fatal. He found the Black Flags in position behind an entrenched village, which he, like Garnier, thought to carry with a rush. They did not, however, even wait for his attack. After a volley which killed one of their assailants, they sallied forth to meet the remainder. M. Balny was surrounded and killed; and his handful of followers were obliged to beat a rapid retreat. These successive disasters at length taught discretion. M. Bain de la Coquerie, upon whom the command now devolved, confined himself to strengthening his position in the citadel, and awaited the reinforcements which he had already heard were on their way. Three hours had not elapsed, in fact, after the events described, when a letter was brought from the Commander of the *Décrès*, announcing his arrival with 100 marines and a supply of food and munitions of war, which removed all apprehension for the safety of the garrison.

Thoroughly alarmed by Garnier's proceedings, the Annamese Government had, in the meantime, followed up its written remonstrances by sending ambassadors to endeavour to arrange matters with the Government of Saigon. These had been met, as the local authorities in Tongking had been met, by a declaration that the Dupuis affair was a matter of detail; the first and essential thing was the conclusion of the required treaty. Negotiations had thereupon been entered into, and terms practically arranged, when the envoys declared their powers insufficient to bring matters to a conclusion. Nguyen-Van-tuong returned accordingly to Hué, accompanied by M. Philastre, for further instructions; and, having obtained the king's assent subject to the settlement of affairs in Tongking, went on to the scene of action to bring about the desired arrangements. The two emissaries arrived in the Bay of Cua-Cam on December 24th; Garnier had been killed on the 21st; the conduct of affairs fell, therefore, entirely into their hands.

We fail to discover what were M. Philastre's precise instructions, but it is not hard to divine the motives which influenced his proceedings. The French Government had sent out orders forbidding a military occupation of Tongking: he had a promise that the treaty should be signed directly affairs in that province were settled; and he appears to have been in haste to terminate a situation which his own judgment condemned.

M. Philastre and Nguyen Van-tuong arrived, as we have seen, in the bay of Cua-Cam on December 24th. They reached Haidzuong on the 29th. Three days later, the French garrison of that town was withdrawn, and the citadel restored to the Annamese. They reached Hanoi on January 3rd, and orders were issued for the evacuation of Ninh-binh and Nam-dinh with equal promptitude. A convention[1] for the surrender of Hanoi quickly followed; and provision was made, in this, for the movements of Dupuis. He and his expedition were to withdraw to Haiphong, whither the French troops were also to retire and to remain pending the formal conclusion of the treaty. If Dupuis wished to pursue his journey into Yunnan, he was to be at liberty to do so, but with a limited escort and sufficient armament only for his personal defence in the districts which were beyond Annamese control; nor was he to return till the Red River had been formally opened to foreign commerce. A French resident was to be stationed at Hanoi; Garnier's tomb there was to be respected; and a plenary amnesty was promised to all who had been compromised during the French occupation.

The evacuation took place on February 12th, and M. Philastre returned to Saigon in company with the Annamese delegate. Garnier's labour, however, had

[1] "Convention du 6 Fevrier, relative à l'évacuation de la citadelle de Hanoi."

not been lost. His action, to quote the words of a letter written to him by Admiral Dupré's aide-de-camp, had simplified everything. M. Senez' advice to use Tongking as a lever had been followed and had been successful: the treaty was assured. The worst sufferers were the unfortunate Tongkingese who had accepted Garnier's overtures, or had been otherwise compromised or suspected during the French occupation. M. Philastre had exacted, it is true, a promise of plenary amnesty for the past and a guarantee against persecution for the future; but the promise, as might have been foreseen, proved hardly worth the paper it was written on. Massacres and persecutions of Christians ensued immediately on the withdrawal of the French troops; and the temporary officials whom Garnier had appointed were driven to seek safety in flight. A number petitioned to be taken to Saigon. Some were massacred with their families. Mr. Rheinart, indeed, who had been appointed in the new capacity of French Resident at Hanoi, found his position so intolerable, in consequence of these events and the unfriendly attitude of the Viceroy, that he withdrew to Haiphong and subsequently resigned altogether a post he found to be untenable.

We have seen that the terms of a treaty had been nearly arranged before M. Philastre's visit to Tongking. That visit had been paid on the assurance that, when matters had been settled there, the treaty should follow. It remained, now, to exact fulfilment of that promise; and after some further demur the document was signed. Two days later, the chief ambassador, Le Tuan, died—it was suspected by his own hand, in dread of the reception that might await him on his return to Hué. By this treaty[1] the annexation of the three provinces taken by Admiral De la Grandière, in 1867, was formally recognized. Chinese suzerainty was tacitly set aside by a clause recognizing the entire independence of Annam in respect of every foreign Power; and the supremacy of France was implicitly substituted, by the king's undertaking to conform his foreign policy to that of the Republic. He was promised, in return, any help he might require to maintain internal order in the kingdom, to defend it against foreign attack, or to put down piracy on the coasts. He was to have an immediate present of five gunboats, with a quantity of munitions of war; and France was to place at his disposal drill instructors, engineers, experts to organize a Customs Service, and professors to found a College. What remained unpaid of the indemnity exacted, in 1862, for expenses incurred in the conquest of Saigon, was remitted: full tolerance was promised to teachers and professors of the Christian religion: three ports in Tongking and the whole course of the Red River were to be open to foreign trade. French Consular agents were to be appointed at the several open ports, and given authority over foreign residents of whatever nationality. French subjects or other foreigners desiring to settle

[1] "Traité conclu à Saigon le 15 Mars, 1874, entre la France et le Royaume d'Annam."

at any of the aforesaid ports must register themselves with the French Resident: Frenchmen or other foreigners desiring to travel in the interior must procure a passport to be granted by a French authority: disputes between Frenchmen and other foreigners, or between foreigners and foreigners, were to be judged by French tribunals; and disputes between foreigners and Annamese, by a French and Annamese magistrate sitting together; while crimes committed by Frenchmen or other foreigners on Annamese territory were to be judged at Saigon. This treaty was followed six months later by a second, designed to regulate commercial intercourse; and in this France explicitly renewed "the promise made to the Annamese Government in Art. 2 of the Treaty of March 15th, to make every effort to destroy both land and sea pirates, especially in the vicinity of the towns and ports opened to foreign commerce." Some difficulty was experienced in obtaining the assent of the Annamese to this supplementary treaty; but the event again proved the wisdom of M. Senez' remark, that the lever to move the Court of Hué was to be found in Tongking. A fresh insurrection, which followed the French evacuation, reduced the Government to submission; but placed the French in the disagreeable position of having to fight those who were most friendly to their presence: for, however distasteful some of the conditions imposed may have been, the king promptly showed his appreciation of others by claiming the help promised to maintain order in the State. The help was given; the "Le" flotilla was captured or destroyed, and the insurgents were driven back into the mountains of Cat-ba. It is superfluous to add that the disinclination of the Annamese Court to give effect to the treaty revived with the disappearance of the danger, and that it was with difficulty Admiral Dupré exacted the exchange of ratifications. Eventually, however, the formality was accomplished. Consuls were appointed, and Customs officers sent to Haiphong and Hanoi in pursuance of its terms; and on September 15th, 1875, Tongking was declared open to foreign commerce.

The treaty of 1874 was to settle all pending questions, and to place the relations between Saigon and Hué on a clear and definite footing; it was to assert French influence in Annamese politics, and to maintain French supremacy in Tongking. As a matter of fact it failed in two cardinal points. By establishing the machinery of a Protectorate in one clause, while it affirmed Annamese independence in another, it placed French authority in an equivocal position towards other Western Powers: and it failed to secure the capital object of opening up a peaceful channel of commercial intercourse with Yunnan.

No Power could allow its subjects residing in a country recognized as independent, to be subjected to the jurisdiction of French agents or carried off into French territory to be judged; and more than one European Government refused to recognize it on those grounds. A new treaty was therefore required, explicitly asserting a Protectorate, if that position was

F

to be maintained, and the Governor of Saigon was instructed to seize the first opportunity of re-opening the question.[1] But that was not all. Seven years after the Red River had been declared open to the frontiers of Yunnan, its waters were still closed to foreign commerce; and the state of the country generally was worse than before. Whether those remarkable Black Flags, who appeared at one time as invaders, at another as allies, and seem really to have been paid mercenaries of the Annamese Government—whether the obstruction were really of their creating, or whether a general state of lawlessness were the cause, there could be no doubt that the country was unsafe for foreign travel. Nor is it surprising this should be the case. The disorganization caused by the operations of Garnier and the repeated insurrections, in Tongking, would tax a stronger Government than that of Annam to repair. We have seen that insurrection followed immediately on the withdrawal of the French in 1874. Again, in 1878, a force collected in China by a general named "Le," who had previously held a commission in the Chinese army, overran four provinces, penetrated to Bac Ninh within twenty miles of the capital, and was only suppressed by the help of a Chinese contingent. A French subject named Francelli was murdered near Hanoi in 1880; other Frenchmen were attacked in the following year, and the waterways generally were notoriously unsafe.

[1] Despatch from the Minister of Marine and the Colonies to the Governor of Saigon, d. January 10th, 1879.

Obviously, however, the French could not be expected to let the clauses affecting the Red River lie dormant. If the Annamese Government had not been able, in seven years, to restore order, they might fairly urge that the time had come for them to undertake the task. By the treaty of 1874 they had promised to do all in their power to put down piracy and disorder, and they were willing to fulfil the pledge. Nor was this all. The French had persistently declined to admit the presence of Chinese interests or authority in Annam, and had gone so far as to stultify their own position by inserting in the treaty of 1874 a clause expressly designed to combat any such assumption. Yet the fact was obtrusively evident that Chinese influence was a substantial element in the situation. In the words of a Saigon correspondent of the *République Française* :—

> "Les Chinois, réguliers ou irréguliers, impériaux ou drapeaux noirs, prenant de plus en plus pied sur le territoire tonkinois, y gênant de plus en plus le commerce et y parlant décidément en maitres, on a prié Hué d'agir et de se débarrasser de ces hôtes gênants, de ces intrus, les seuls qui tirent profit de nos traités de 1874. La cour de Hué, qui d'ailleurs est de connivence avec tous ces Fils du Ciel, cela n'est douteux pour personne, répondit qu'elle était trop faible et à elle seule impuissante."

It was resolved, accordingly, to send a fresh expedition; and in March, 1882, Captain Rivière set out from Saigon with two sloops-of-war, eight gunboats, and 620 marines, for the ostensible purpose of strengthening the garrison of Hanoi, and of taking order with the irregularities that were neutralizing

F 2

the treaty stipulations with regard to the Red River. If the Black Flags got in his way, they must be brushed aside; but he was to avoid hostilities as far as possible, and especially to avoid conflict with Chinese Imperial troops. M. de Vilers' instructions, in short, were unexceptionable. Yet Rivière seems to have acted as though he had been directed to precipitate a crisis.

The expedition was despatched in accordance with the terms of the treaty by which France engaged to help maintain order; but the Annamese officials seem to have viewed the matter in a strangely different light. If France was bound to afford help when asked, Annam was not bound to ask it, nor to accept it unasked: so far, therefore, from welcoming the French troops, they closed the gates of the citadel, while the Commander-in-chief of the province drew his forces together as though to resist their action. Considering that these preparations amounted to actual menace, Rivière seems to have resolved on decisive action. He not only informed the Viceroy that his attitude was calculated to provoke hostilities, but required the acceptance of a new convention which exacted, among other trifles, the withdrawal of all Chinese troops from Tongking. The Viceroy replied, of course, that he had no power to entertain any such question; and as he maintained this inability, in face of a threat to use force, Hanoi was bombarded and carried by assault. The Viceroy and Commandant committed suicide; the Governor was held a prisoner in his palace, and the French Commander-in-chief took possession of the Custom-houses where the duties were ordered to be collected for the benefit of the French treasury. A situation had been once again created which would give France an excuse for employing her strength to impose what terms she chose on the Court of Hué.

So far as between France and Annam. There was, however, a third Power, which the French had shown a disposition to ignore, but which seemed disinclined to let itself be so quietly effaced. We have seen that China claimed Annam as a vassal and tributary State; and there could be no doubt that the claim rested on centuries of recognition and on the possession of a very real influence in the country. The kings of Annam had been always invested, on their accession, by delegates of the Emperor of China; the ceremony taking place in the very city of Hanoi which had now, again, passed into French occupation. Once in four years an embassy bearing tribute was sent to Peking; and we have seen, more than once, an appeal made by Annam and granted by China, for help in cases of emergency. The contest was, then, really between French and Chinese influence in the country, and events were tending to define that position. Nor was the tie of suzerainty and vassalage the only one which would lead China to espouse the cause of her tributary. Just as France would consider an aggressive movement by Germany on Belgium a menace to her own safety, or as England would oppose Russian encroachment in Afghanistan, so was China interested in the threatened supersession of

Annamese authority on her southern frontier. The substitution of a powerful and militant for a weak and submissive neighbour might, indeed, disturb a less conservative nation; and when, to this consideration, was added the avowed object of obtaining control over the course of a river which rises in Chinese territory and constitutes a channel of communication with the sea, it would be strange if Chinese statesmen acquiesced calmly in the change. It would have been wiser, no doubt, if they had taken up a decided attitude sooner; but they are slow to move, and notoriously indifferent to danger while it is remote from their doors. When the treaty of 1874 was communicated to China, in common with other Powers, Prince Kung took occasion, certainly, to remark[1] that Annam was tributary to China, that what Chinese troops were there had been sent at the request of a tributary power, and that the stipulations for commerce with Yunnan appeared to overlook the fact that Yunnan was not open to foreign trade. But it was not till the preparations of the French, in 1880-1, gave evidence of renewed activity, that the Imperial authorities showed themselves alive to the urgency of the question. Current rumours as to French projects led the Marquis Tseng to remark, then, at the French Foreign Office, that China had not ceased to regard Annam as a vassal State nor, either in her character as suzerain or neighbour, could she view with indifference anything which might alter the international relations of the country; but his overtures

[1] Prince Kung to Count de Rochechouart, June 15th, 1875.

were treated with so much brusqueness that it would seem the Government had decided to override a position they found it impossible to contest. Annam, wrote M. Barthelemy St. Hilaire—and China was invited to take note of the fact,—was free from any bond (affranchi de tout lien quelconque) to any other Power than France; and the French Government could not, therefore, enter into any explanations with a foreign Government about circumstances of which it must be the sole judge. It had so long been the fashion to regard China as an inert mass, devoid of energy or impulse, that it was no doubt thought in the last degree unlikely she would be moved to active interference on behalf of her tributary. The patience with which she persisted in trying to find a diplomatic solution probably encouraged this impression. Yet the manner in which she wakened up when threatened by Russia in Central Asia might have shown that she could assert her dignity, on occasion, and might even prove a troublesome neighbour to the French in Tongking.

CHAPTER IV.

FRANCE AND ANNAM.

At a moment when French proceedings in the Far East are attracting general attention, when intervention in Tongking has led to annexation, and the idea of a protectorate over Annam has expanded into a dream of Indo-Chinese Empire, it may not be uninteresting to review the earlier stages of the adventure, and to read afresh the story of ecclesiastical intrigue and military adventure involved in the career of the missionary bishop who laid the foundation of French interests in the country. The facts are instructive, as evincing the continuity of national policy despite governmental changes, and have, besides, a dash of romantic interest which may help to relieve the painfully commonplace details of annexation and exaction that have characterized more recent proceedings. The date is the close of the last century: the curtain rises upon a scene of rebellion and anarchy such as Oriental histories too frequently disclose.

About 1765–70, the reigning king of Annam nominated as his successor the son of a concubine, in supersession of his legitimate heir. At his death, a minister whom he had interested in the design carried it into execution, but made himself so obnoxious that an influential party invited the intervention of the King of Tongking. The latter marched south at the head of a formidable army and exacted the surrender of the culprit. Not satisfied, however, with having achieved this object, the Tongkingese set about overrunning the country on their own account; whereupon one Nhac incited the people to resistance, and succeeded in driving out the invaders. He placed, then, a prince of the blood royal temporarily on the throne; but soon quarrelled with and put him to death, and declared himself king. The (illegitimate) prince whose usurpation and weakness had caused the trouble had, in the meantime, been captured and killed also; and Nguyen-anh remained sole legitimate pretender to the throne. His efforts to make head against Nhac met with some success at first, in the southern provinces; but the success was ephemeral, and he had to seek safety in flight.

A somewhat similar drama had in the meantime being played in Tongking, where a king who died in 1782 had also nominated as his successor the son of a concubine. The leading mandarins combined to set him aside in favour of the legitimate heir, with the usual result of creating two factions; and a state of anarchy ensued which led to an appeal for help to Annam. Nhac, who was now supreme in the south, willingly obeyed the summons; overran the country and of course, in his turn, refused to quit; thus reversing the scale and subjecting Tongking to Annam.

It will be readily understood that the Catholic missionaries, who had gained a firm footing in Annam, found their position jeopardized in the prevailing anarchy. Among these was M. Pigneau de Behaine, Bishop of Adran, who seems to have been in high credit with the (legitimate) royal family, and is said even to have saved the life of Nguyen-anh, by concealing him in his house when hard pressed by the rebels, in Saigon. His is the central figure in the following story, which we open by quoting a letter written by him, from Pondichéry, to the College of Foreign Missions at Paris :—

In the month of March, 1782, obliged to abandon Cochin-China, I withdrew to Cambodia with the College. The famine was very severe, and if I had not taken the precaution to send provisions, we could not have subsisted there. Hardly had we arrived when the rebel chief despatched troops thither. I went and hid myself with my scholars and the rest of our people in the most frightful deserts, where I remained two months. Then, the king of Cochin-China having re-entered his States, I returned near him with my people; but it was only, alas! to prepare for a fresh flight. This time we had no other refuge to seek but the islands of the Gulf of Siam. I made all necessary preparations, and at the first news of the approach of the rebels we set out. Never, since my arrival from India, had I enjoyed such tranquility as I found in the island where we stayed. We occupied ourselves there solely with our salvation and that of our people, who were perfectly resigned to endure the trials which Divine Providence seemed to have in store. In effect, we soon heard that the king was at not more than half a day's distance, and that the rebels were pursuing him. The king gave battle, which he lost, together with nearly all the naval force which remained to him.[1]

[1] Lettre de Mgr. d'Adran à MM. du Séminaire des Missions Etrangères, March 20th, 1785.—It may be well to explain that, by "Cochin-China," the bishop means more particularly the southern portion of the Annamese kingdom.

Seeing all hope of return to Cochin-China cut off by this fresh disaster, the bishop fled with his neophytes to the capital of Siam, where he found means to bestow them in safety; and seems to have been trying to make his way to Pondichéry when he came again in contact with the fugitive prince. Having missed the monsoon, he (the bishop) had, with his followers, been spending some months at the island of Pulo-way; and at this point we will again take up his narrative:—

After having repaired our little barque, we quitted our solitude with the greatest regret, and sailed for Pulo-punjan, with the intention of traversing from that point the Gulf of Siam. Here we met, for the second time, the king of Cochin-China, who told me how he had been carried off to Siam, and dwelt on the duplicity of the Siamese, who, under pretext of replacing him on the throne, had only made use of his name to pillage the people. It was there that he confided to me his son, aged six, whom I have brought hither.

After describing his voyage, and lauding the devotion of his Cochin-Chinese attendants, the bishop continues:—

Another matter in which I want your help, is to procure the education of the young prince with whom I am charged. I should like, whichever way things may turn, to have him brought up in the Christian religion, and to compensate him for the temporal crown he has lost by the hope of another much more precious and more durable. It is only you who can render me this service. . . . If, eventually, the king should turn to the English or the Dutch, who will not fail to re-establish him in his States, you perceive how useful it will be to have done at least what one could for his child. He is only six years old, and already knows his prayers. He is full of intelligence and of ardour for all that concerns religion. A thing which seems inconceivable to many people is that he should have attached himself to me without regretting his father, mother, grandmother, nurses, and more than five hundred men who all burst into tears when he left them. The Christians attributed it to the special grace of God, and drew from it conjectures very favourable to our religion. The gentiles, who were less well-informed, said I had bewitched him. The two mandarins, his governors, and six soldiers, who constitute his guard, are already well instructed, and will be baptized at Pentecost.

The meeting here described took place in 1784; and Mgr. d'Adran is said to have led the fugitive to hope for help from France. However this may be, the answer to the letter we have quoted seems to have been an order to come in person with his pupil to Europe. He obeyed, of course, and we find them, in 1787, at the Court of Versailles, appealing to Louis XVI. for help to place Nguyen-anh on the throne he had never yet been able to occupy. The thought may suggest itself, that the negotiations which ensued were slightly one-sided: on the one hand a child of eight with his (French) guardian; on the other, the royal ministers, in a position to exact what terms they chose for their assistance. Such as they were, however, they seem to have marched merrily. The good bishop evidently lost no time, after his arrival, in pressing his views; and it must be confessed that the following memorandum, in which he embodied them, contains a great deal of worldly wisdom for one who had been so long isolated from the world and devoted to religious pursuits. It is interesting, as showing the spirit of hostility to England in which the negotiations were conducted, and especially interesting at the present moment, when French ambition is again striving to create a rival empire in the East.[1]

"The political scale in India appears so heavily inclined to the side of England that it must seem very difficult to redress the balance. Perhaps an establishment in Cochin-China would be the most certain and efficacious method that could be employed. In effect, if you glance at the productions of Cochin-China and the situation of its ports, it is easy to conceive the great advantage that would arise from establishing ourselves there, both in peace and war.

1. We may assume that the most certain means of combating the English in Asia is to ruin or weaken their commerce. In time of peace we should much diminish the profit they derive from their trade with China, by carrying it on at less cost and with greater facility than they.

2. In time of war it would be easy to interdict this commerce to any hostile nation; for by cruising about the exit from the Straits, or more surely still at the Bocca Tigris which is at the entry of the Canton river, we should be sure of hindering all coming out or going in, whenever we chose.

3. We should find, in Cochin-China, easy and inexpensive means of repairing and careening ships, and even of building new ones.

4. We should find everything needed for revictualling our squadron, and supplying other colonies with necessaries.

---

[1] *Vide* "La Cochin-Chine et le Tonquin," Par Eugène Veuillot. Paris 1859. M. Veuillot is frankness itself on this score: "La France n'accepte qu'avec peine et provisoirement la suprématie maritime de l'Angleterre. Cependant nous venons, dans les mers de l'Indo-Chine, au sixième rang—après le Portugal (Introduction, p. iii.). . . . . Nous ne sortirons de cette position humiliante que le jour on le pavillon français flottera dans l'Asie orientale sur une terre Française. . . . . L'empire d'Anam nous est ouvert, et c'est là que nous devons nous établir. [The Indian mutiny was in progress at the time, and M. Veuillot goes on to say, p. xiv.], La France n'a point a craindre un malheur semblable à celui de l'Angleterre, et ne veut point le mériter. Le motif determinant de son enterprise est puisée dans les profondeurs du sentiment général, il est généreux et chrétien!"

5. We might, in case of need, find there help in men, troops, seamen, &c.

6. We should be able easily to check the English in the projects they seem to entertain, of spreading themselves towards the East (*s'étendre à la côte de l'Est*).

The force of the bishop's arguments appears to have quickly approved itself to Louis XVI. and his advisers; for we find his projects exactly embodied in a convention signed at Versailles, on November 28th, 1787, by the Comte de Vergennes and the Comte de Montmorin on behalf of the French king, and by the little prince Canh-dzué on behalf of his father. This document is sufficiently curious to deserve full translation, both as an evidence of the political schemes of the day, and because it is frequently appealed to by the French as a basis of their rights in Cochin-China. If it is difficult, for outsiders, to regard a treaty composed under such conditions as serious, it is evident that the French negotiators were very clearly alive to the advantages which might be extracted from it:—

1. There shall be an offensive and defensive alliance between the two kings of France and Cochin-China; they shall be bound to lend each other, mutually, succour and assistance against the enemies of one or the other of the contracting parties.

2. In consequence, there shall be equipped and placed under the orders of the king of Cochin-China, a squadron of twenty French ships of war, of such a standard as the requirements of his service may exact.

3. Five European regiments, and two regiments of colonial native troops, shall be embarked without delay for Cochin-China.

4. His Majesty Louis XVI. undertakes to furnish, within a few months, the sum of one million dollars, of which 500,000

shall be in specie, and the rest in saltpetre, cannons, muskets, and other military armament.

5. From the moment the French troops enter on Cochin-Chinese territory, they and their generals will receive the orders of the king of Cochin-China.

On the other hand:—

1. The king of Cochin-China undertakes to furnish, as soon as tranquility shall be restored in his States, and on the simple requisition of the French ambassador, everything necessary in the shape of equipment, rigging, and provisions, to put on the sea without any delay fourteen ships of the line; and for the perfect execution of this article there shall be sent from Europe a corps of naval officers and warrant officers who shall form a permanent establishment in Cochin-China.

2. H.M. Louis XVI. shall have resident consuls on all parts of the coast of Cochin-China, wherever he shall judge fit. These consuls shall be authorized to construct, or cause to be constructed, vessels, frigates, and other ships, without interference, on any pretext, from the Government of Cochin-China.

3. The ambassador of H.M. Louis XVI. at the Court of Cochin-China shall have the right to cut wood for the construction of vessels, frigates, and other ships, in all the forests wherever he may find any suitable.

4. The king of Cochin-China and his Council shall cede in perpetuity to His Most Christian Majesty, his heirs and successors, the port and territory of Hansan (bay and peninsula of Tourane), and the adjacent islands of Fai-fo on the south and Hai-wen on the north.

5. The King of Cochin-China engages to furnish the necessary men and materials for the construction of forts, bridges, roads, wells, etc., which shall be considered necessary for the safety and defence of the concessions made to his faithful ally the King of France.

[Article 6 merely regulates the conditions of government in the ceded districts.]

7. In case His Most Christian Majesty determine to make war in any part of India, it shall be permitted to the commander-in-chief of the French troops to make a levy of 14,000 men, whom he shall drill in the same manner as in France, and who shall be instructed according to French discipline.

8. In case any Powers should attack the French on Cochin-Chinese territory, the King of Cochin-China shall furnish at leas: 60,000 soldiers, whom he will equip and maintain at his cost, etc.

This remarkable treaty, in which the infant son of a fugitive prince is made to grant such immense concessions, has two grave defects. It was never ratified, and never executed. The revolution which broke out in France two years later effaced, for the moment, all thought of such distant projects; though sufficient help was actually afforded the Cochin-Chinese prince, to give a semblance of justification to the claim that it found practical acceptance. And this brings us to the second phase of Mgr. d'Adran's curious adventure.

When the bishop—who had been named plenipotentiary, and charged with the execution of the treaty he had brought about—arrived at Pondichéry, he found the governor inclined to look askance at the projects he was desired to forward. M. de Conway had been ordered to provide, as vanguard of the expeditionary force, four frigates, 1600 men, and some field artillery. He seems, however, to have hesitated and delayed till the French residents at Pondichéry themselves took up the project, and equipped two ships, besides providing arms and ammunition. Certain volunteers accompanied this expedition, and the governor consented, some months later, to place a frigate and several officers at the bishop's disposal.

Mgr. Pigneau reached Saigon in 1789. Nguyen-anh had been able in the meantime to regain a footing in that province, but the French contingent

—however inadequate to carry out the terms of the treaty—was sufficient to give useful help. The French officers set promptly to work to organize an effective force; helping to cast cannon, build ships, and drill troops with whom the king was able to take the offensive and reduce the whole littoral to submission. Frequent reference is made to the presence of French officers, in the course of the long campaign; and the fortifications of Hué and Hanoi, the capitals respectively of Annam and Tongking, bear evidence of European design. Curious collateral evidence of the reality of the political position came under the notice of Lord Macartney, during his memorable expedition to China, at this very epoch. The opening up of commercial relations with Cochin-China was, in fact, one of the avowed objects of the mission, in pursuance of which he called at Tourane, in 1792, during his outward voyage. He deferred presentation of his letters, judging it more politic to wait till he had accomplished his primary mission to Peking. He took occasion, however, to deliver his presents, with which the king was much pleased, permitting the English to travel into the country and examine it as much as they desired. Lord Macartney[1] found the district, "with a considerable part of the kingdom of Cochin-China," still in possession of the usurper, whose antagonist (i.e. Nguyen-anh), "the descendant of the former sovereigns of the country, was in possession of some of the southern

[1] V. "Macartney's Embassy to China." By Sir George Staunton, Bart. Vol. i. p. 328.

districts of the kingdom, and was in daily hope of such succour from Europe as might enable him to recover all the possessions of his ancestors. . . . Some individuals from France" had already joined him, and given hope of further assistance; of which the party in power at Tourane were fully cognisant, as they at first feared that the English fleet represented the threatened expedition. And a letter to Lord Dundas, then President of the East India Board, gives a curious confirmatory hint of the projects and political motives that were inspiring the French adventure. "They supposed," writes Lord Macartney, "that the quantity of gold extracted from the Cochin-Chinese mountains, and the vast quantity of sugar manufactured in its plains and sold at a price lower than in any other part of the world, would render a settlement in the neighbourhood profitable. But, above all, they conceived that, by stationing frigates there on the approach of war, they might easily intercept our ships bound for or returning from Canton."

It is beyond our purpose to follow the incidents of the civil war, with which we are concerned only so far as it involves the action of Mgr. d'Adran and its consequences. Nguyen-anh's gradual recovery of authority over Saigon and Annam, his conquest of Tongking, his ascent of the throne under the style of Gya-long, and his recognition (in 1804) by China are matters of historical notoriety. The bishop did not live to see the complete triumph of his *protégé*, but he reached the threshold, as it were, of the final scene; and the occasional glimpses we catch of his career show him in a position of high regard and influence at the Annamese Court. It was natural that the services he had rendered should gain for him this place in the king's esteem, and equally natural that it should excite the jealousy and envy of the native mandarins. A letter (May 30th, 1795) written by him from Saigon will serve to illustrate both his position and the assaults to which it was obnoxious:—

Nineteen notables (*grands du royaume*) joined in representing to the king that prudence forbad my being left any longer charged with the education of the young prince; that, being a foreigner and of a different religion, it was impossible but that I should imbue him with my principles. They besought his Majesty accordingly to place him in the hands of *literati* (mandarins lettrés), who would give him an education similar to that of his ancestors. The king, indignant, threw the memorial on the ground, recalled all the services which I had rendered to the State, to himself, to his son and his family, and added: "It is astounding that, after having done so little in recogniton of so many benefits, you should dare to urge me to the most monstrous ingratitude."

The bishop seems, however, to have deemed it wise to bow to the storm; and affirms that he not only dissuaded the king from punishing the intriguers, but persuaded him that it would be wiser to let him partially efface himself, than to excite the enmity of his Court. Some fear of his Majesty's conversion, if we may trust Mgr. d'Adran's narrative, seems to have been at the bottom of the movement. One of the principal mandarins had shown a strong proclivity towards the new doctrine, and people argued: If so able and erudite a man could not hold out against the reasoning of the foreign bishop, how would it be with the king and the prince?

The influence of the prelate, however, and the intrigues of the mandarins were soon to be terminated by the action of a greater power. Mgr. d'Adran died, four years later, while travelling with his pupil; and, making all allowance for the enthusiasm of his colleagues, we cannot but infer from the description of his obsequies that it was felt, even at Court, that a great figure had passed away.

> The light of Cochin-China [writes M. Lelabousse] is extinguished; the pillar of the kingdom is overthrown; desolation is everywhere; mourning is general. Mgr. d'Adran fell ill early in August, in the province of Qui-nhon, whither he had gone with his royal pupil, who never moved without his wise mentor. The king sent his physicians, and employed all possible means to save the life of one who had so often saved his. He even came in person with his son to visit him, and shed many tears on perceiving the uselessness of his endeavours.[1]

The bishop died on October 9th, 1799, in his fifty-eighth year, and was buried on December 16th, at a spot of his own selection, in the environs of Saigon, which may still be discovered by the curious visitor. It was, at the period in question, "a pleasant country garden, which he had himself been in the habit of cultivating, some three miles from the town;" but the garden has disappeared, and the tomb is now smothered amid the brushwood which has overgrown the locality.

[1] Lettres Edifiantes.

Thither (we are told) the prelate had been in the habit of retiring from time to time, with his royal pupil, for relaxation from the worry of the Court and the fatigue of study; thither he went with the missionaries, to refresh them by a little repose from their toil; and there he found a remedy for his own troubles, declaring that he forgot them directly he arrived.

And there, with almost royal pomp, the king caused his remains to be interred. We pass over the description of the religious ceremonies with which the Roman Church so well knows how to exalt the memory of the dead, while appealing to the imagination of the living. The reader will easily conceive the crowd of converts, the blaze of tapers, the display of images, ornaments, and tapestry: it is more to our present purpose to describe the Annamese share in the procession:—

All the king's guards, comprising more than 12,000 men, without counting those of the prince his son, were under arms and drawn up in two lines, the field guns in front; 120 elephants with their escort and their officers marched on either side. Drums, trumpets, military music, both Cochin-Chinese and Cambodian, fusees, fireworks—nothing was lacking. More than two hundred lanterns of different shapes, besides a prodigious number of torches and tapers, illuminated the mournful procession. At least 40,000 people, both Christians and pagans, followed the funeral. The king was there with all the mandarins of the different corps; and, strange to say, even his mother, his sister, the queen, his concubines, his children, all the ladies of the Court considered that, for a man so above the common, everyday customs should be set aside; all came, and went the whole way to the tomb.

It would require a literal translation of M. Lelabousse's letter to enumerate all the marks of esteem and regret which the king showered on the memory of the deceased prelate. The identical flags which his Majesty was in the habit of having carried alongside him in battle were carried alongside the coffin on its way to the grave. A handsome tomb (in native style) was erected to his memory; and, in pursuance of native custom, the king issued an edict eulogizing his services and his abilities and expressing sorrow at his loss.

The young prince with whose fortunes he had been so intimately associated survived him only two years, and it is easy to conceive that his death was a severe blow for the Missions. Still, the goodwill which Mgr. d'Adran's services had gained seems to have endured after his death; for though we find occasional complaints of the king's lukewarmness—resulting probably from the fact that he had to consider the prejudices of his people, while the missionaries would have liked him to exalt Christianity by edict—we find, also, instances in which he supports them and their cause. An attempt made by Louis XVIII. to revive the dormant treaty of Versailles seems to have alarmed the Court during the closing years of Gya-long's reign, and to this introduction of the political spectre the persecution which broke out under his successor may perhaps be traced.

M. Michel Chaigneau,[1] who was born and bred at Hué, tells us how his father was stirred by the appearance, in 1817, of two French ships in the bay. For twenty years the adventurers had been apparently forgotten: Revolution, Republic, and Empire had

[1] Souvenirs de Hué. Par Michel Du'c Chaigneau.

come and gone since they had sailed from France: a Bourbon was again on the throne; and the Duc de Richelieu had written, asking M. Chaigneau's opinion as to the best means of developing commerce. The incident seems to have awakened a desire to revisit France, and Chaigneau set sail, with the King's consent, in 1819. But the parting was final: Gya-long died in 1820, and with his death may be said to terminate the first chapter of French intervention in Annam.

With his death, also, passed away the glamour of the influence which the French, and especially the Missions, had enjoyed as a consequence of Mgr. Pigneau's personal and political prestige. M. Chaigneau returned the following year, with the rank of consul, and with a number of presents from Louis XVIII. to the reigning king. It would have been better, perhaps, if he had brought nothing more. But he was the bearer also of instructions to conclude a treaty. Gya-long had, as we have seen, died in the interval; his successor appears to have received the French king's letter and presents with fitting courtesy; but he declined absolutely to entertain the question of a treaty. It was, he said, useless: his people could not go to France, and the French were already at liberty to come and trade at Tourane like other people. It was a political mistake to press the matter, in presence of these dispositions. Minh-Mang refused altogether to receive a fresh letter brought soon after by Captain Bougainville, who was accredited as envoy to the Annamese

Court; and MM. Chaigneau and Vannier judged it wise to withdraw, in 1824, from a country where they felt themselves objects of distrust.

It was not, however, till five years later that the growing dislike of the new king to the foreigners and their converts broke out into open violence. The native Christians were the first to suffer; but in 1833 the persecution extended to the missionaries also; and from that year to 1840 thirteen French and Spanish priests were executed or died in prison. For a moment then the king seems to have been alarmed at what he had done. His father had recommended him to diplomatize—to discourage Christianity, but not to persecute; to keep the missionaries at a distance, but not to kill them, as that might lead to French intervention which was to be avoided at all cost. In 1839, accordingly, he sent a mission to France, which Louis Philippe declined to receive; but the report which the members brought back seems to have convinced him that he had nothing to apprehend. His death, about the time of their return, was followed by renewed persecution under his successor. An opportune visit of a French corvette in 1843 secured the release of five priests who were in imminent danger: a similar visit, next year, procured the surrender of another who was under sentence of death; and Admiral Lapierre, who visited Tourane in 1847, found occasion to destroy the Annamese fleet by which he believed himself menaced. The persecution continued under Tu-duc, who came to the throne a year later; a visit by M. de Montigny, in 1857, only aggravating the evil. These casual visitations, indeed, seem only to have increased the irritation of the Annamese sovereigns against the class to whose presence they attributed the annoyance. M. de Montigny had been commissioned to negotiate a treaty, having for its leading features—free exercise of the Catholic religion; freedom of commerce; the residence of a consul at the capital, and the cession of Tourane or of a neighbouring island for the establishment of a French factory; but he found himself unable to open serious negotiations. It was soon after his return, *re infectâ*, that the Emperor Napoleon resolved on the expedition under Admiral Rigault de Genouilly, at the close of the China war, which resulted in the acquisition of Saigon and has entailed the annexation of the whole kingdom.

The circumstances which induced French intervention in Tongking,[1] and which have led on, step by step, to the annexation of that province and to the declaration of a protectorate over Annam have been described in a previous chapter. The immediate impulse seems to have come from Saigon; but it will be seen, from the foregoing pages, that it was an impulse in consonance with a policy devised during the last century and that has always had warm supporters in France.

The Annamese might, possibly, have staved off

[1] "Voyage d'Exploration en Indo-Chine, 1866-8," par Francis Garnier.

their fate by favouring, instead of obstructing, the commercial projects which had fascinated French imagination. But the official and semi-official correspondence which is freely quoted by M. du Caillaud tends to justify the impression that, although Garnier's mission was ostensibly diplomatic, there was a perfect willingness at Saigon to create a "situation" which should lead to more vigorous intervention, and to the acquisition of a permanent foothold on the banks of the river which had become an object of interest. The course of action adopted was, at any rate, eminently calculated to provoke the hostilities which ensued; for no nation which retained a shred of power or self-respect could tolerate the assumption of superior authority which provoked the mandarins to resistance.

France was, however, still gasping, after her death-struggle with Germany, and unprepared as yet for the colonial enterprises into which she has subsequently plunged. The fortresses Garnier had occupied were given up, and the expeditionary troops withdrawn after the Saigon Government had exacted, as the price of evacuation, a treaty which secured, on paper, most of the privileges which it professed itself anxious to acquire. Ports were opened, and consuls and customs officers appointed, in 1875, in accordance with the provisions of this document; but no sustained effort appears to have been made to enforce the provisions, regarding the navigation of the Songkoi, which had been the avowed motive of the expedition. Complaints were frequent, however, of piracy, Black Flags and other obstacles, for which the Annamese Government was held responsible; and eventually, in 1882, Commander Rivière was despatched, with a force as inadequate as Garnier's, to insist on, and effect, the suppression of these evils. History repeated itself. Received with a coolness verging on repulsion, by the officials he came ostensibly to reinforce, Rivière, like Garnier, took umbrage, and took Hanoi, without apparently reflecting that he was thereby justifying the suspicions he deprecated. Again the remarkable spectacle was seen of a handful of Frenchmen invading the delta; and again the Annamese appealed to the Black Flags for help. Again these redoubtable auxiliaries advanced; and again the French, repeating the mistake of rating them at the same value as the Annamese levies, incurred a severe repulse. Rivière was killed, under almost the same circumstances as his predecessor; and his death sealed the fate of Tongking.

France had recovered, by this time, from the exhaustion of her great war, and was ready to approve the cry that Rivière must be avenged and French prestige restored. Saigon urged its favourite idea of political expansion: financiers dwelt on the reports of metallic wealth, of which there had always been a tradition, and which Dupuis' adventure[1] had fostered: credits were voted, and troops sent freely forward. The colonial "idea" burst, in fact, into full bloom. What was to have been merely an avenging

[1] Dupuis' own narrative of his journey will be found in the *Bulletin de la Société de Géographie*, July and August, 1877.

expedition grew into a war of conquest. All pretence of merely avenging Rivière's death disappeared. Not only was the annexation of Tongking demanded; but Annam itself was attacked, on the plea that it was wickedly obstructing execution of the treaty of 1874—fostering resistance, in other words, to the French invasion. Its capital, Hué, was taken; a treaty dictated, by which the king recognized the protectorate of France over all his dominions; and the seal of office, which he and his predecessors had held for centuries as vassals of China, was destroyed.

The defects of the treaty of 1874 had now been technically cured, but the French were farther than ever from that peaceful and lucrative traffic with Yunnan which had been alleged as the high motive of their policy. China, alarmed at the prospect of a conterminous frontier with a militant and restless power, intervened on behalf of her vassal. Despite the warnings of its Representative at Peking, the French Government had chosen to disregard her protests with a persistence which suggested a very willingness to provoke war; and the presence of Imperial troops in the Annamese ranks showed that she accepted the challenge. It seemed for a moment that a solution had been reached, under the auspices of M. Bourrée, by which China was to retain control over the northern region, abandoning the territory south of the Songkoi to France; but this settlement was condemned as inadequate at Paris, and excessive at Peking, and the struggle went on.

The intervention of the Chinese had been, so far, indirect. Imperial soldiers had been encountered; but Sontay and Bac-ninh had been avowed as the first stations of Imperial interest: to attack Sontay would be to attack China, and its garrison had been strengthened accordingly. To leave the Chinese in Sontay, however, would be to stultify the rejection of the Bourrée convention; so the French pushed forward to the attack and, after several months of preliminary fighting, succeeded in occupying the disputed posts.

The Marquis Tseng had, in the meantime, withdrawn from Paris; but the Grand Secretary, Li Hung-chang, who had shown a wise disinclination to commit his country to war *à outrance*, consented to re-open negociations which resulted in the signature, at Tientsin, on May 11th, 1884, of a treaty eminently favourable to France, by which China undertook to withdraw from Tongking, to recognize the French treaties with Annam, and to open her adjacent frontier to commerce; France agreeing, on her side, to hold the frontier inviolate, and to respect the fiction of a Chinese suzerainty.

The series of mishaps—to use no stronger word—by which, first its representatives in the East, and subsequently the French Cabinet itself contrived to upset this arrangement, form one of the most curious episodes in the diplomatic history of this remarkable campaign. Captain Fournier's presentation of a memorandum to the Chinese plenipotentiary, naming the dates on which he required the several fortresses to be handed over, commenced the difficulty. The Chinese affirm that they protested against the dates named as impracticable, and that Captain Fournier thereupon ran his pen through the contested clauses; while the latter affirms that he did nothing of the kind, and that Li Hung-chang had specifically accepted the dates and stipulations called in question. The correspondence, in which these antagonistic statements were affirmed and denied before the world, must surely be unique in the annals of diplomacy.

Captain Fournier's view of the case is contained in the following letter to M. Ferry :—

I affirm, upon my honour, that I neither altered nor cancelled, either by erasures or in any other way, any of the dates and stipulations of the note of May 17th, handed to Li Hung-chang. I affirm that Li Hung-chang expressly told me that the evacuation of the Chinese garrisons would be effected by him within the time fixed in that note. I affirm that it was with his entire assent that I addressed to the President of the Council (M. Ferry) and to General Millot the telegrams inserted in the Yellow-book. I may add that I gave all possible publicity to the agreement concluded in this last interview. I reported it immediately to Admiral Lespès, who had to see the Viceroy on the very next day and converse with him on the same subject. I handed in the telegram sent by me to General Millot in French, at the Chinese telegraph office in Tientsin, where all the officials are the functionaries of the Viceroy's Yamên. An hour afterwards Li Hung-chang had this telegram in his hand, which he could read, and which, like all political telegrams, was transmitted to the Tsung-li Yamên. Such a step taken by the French negotiator; the Viceroy's silence, after

all the opportunities thus given him of protesting against the telegram which he had in his hands, and which so distinctly committed him—a telegram which was then published in the Chinese newspapers, and the stipulations and dates of which were publicly read on May 20th before the Chamber of Deputies by the President of the Council—can they leave the slightest doubt as to the perfect certainty on my part, that no misunderstanding could exist between the Viceroy and myself on the questions treated in the note of May 17th?

Whereupon Li Hung-chang's Secretaries addressed the following affirmation to the *North-China Herald*:

Tientsin, *November 24th*, 1884.

SIR,—Being informed that Captain Fournier, in a letter that has been made public, denies having made the erasures in the Fournier Memorandum presented to Li Chung-t'ang on the 17th May last, we beg to state that we were present at the interview Captain Fournier had with His Excellency on that day, and we positively declare that we saw with our own eyes Captain Fournier with his own hand make the said erasures and put his initials thereto.—We remain, yours obediently,

MA KIEN-TSCHONG.
LO FONG-LOH.

"Devant ces suzerainetés là," wrote a witty Frenchman, speaking of Chinese pretensions in Annam, "on salue et on passe." Before contradictions such as these, one might exclaim, we can only hold our peace dumfounded. It is clear, at any rate, that the Chinese Minister did not sign the document which Captain Fournier left on his table—mangled or intact as the case may be; and more careful diplomacy would surely have exacted this precaution before taking action upon it. Colonel Dugenne was, however, sent forward, on the date named, to occupy the city of Langson, not only with a force lamentably insufficient, but with means of interpreting so inadequate that he was unable to translate a letter in which the Chinese commander responded to his summons. The whole embroglio, in fact, from this point becomes simply inconceivable. Colonel Dugenne's instructions were to halt and communicate with his superiors, if the Chinese showed signs of opposition. He was met, as we have seen, by a letter which, when eventually translated (at Shanghai !), was found to acknowledge the Tientsin treaty, but to plead that the writer had not yet received instructions to withdraw, to deprecate precipitancy, and to suggest reference to Peking. We can, perhaps, not blame him for ignoring a communication he could not read, though we may stand aghast at the negligence which left him in that predicament. But he was clearly able to communicate in some degree, for he understood that the Chinese commander subsequently asked ten days in which to complete the evacuation; and yet, in the face of that demand and of his own instructions, he responded by requiring the latter to quit at once, intimating that he would recommence his forward movement in an hour. He did so, was fired on, and forced to retreat with loss.

These circumstances, which we find admitted in evidence taken before a Committee of the Chamber, and corroborated by Colonel Dugenne's recall, scarcely justified the assumption on which M. Ferry precipitately acted—that there had been wilful treachery on the part of the Chinese, for which a heavy indemnity should be paid or heavy reprisals inflicted. It is likely that no one regretted, subsequently, more deeply than the French Premier, the precipitancy which led to the overthrow of a useful treaty and the commencement of a useless war. It has been suggested, indeed, that there was a willingness to keep up the quarrel, in order to exact an indemnity, if not to carry out a suggestion made by Rivière, that the three southern provinces of China should be added to Tongking; but we acquit M. Ferry of any such extravagant design. If it had, at any rate, ever seemed to him practicable, he was soon to realize more clearly the degree of resistance to be expected.

M. Challemel-Lacour had spoken of China as a *quantité negligeable*, and the French Government declined even to recognize, as "war," the operations which it was about to undertake. It was simply going to punish, and exact an indemnity for, one of those acts of treachery from which it seems to be the destiny of the French so frequently to suffer. Fighting was, however, resumed not only in Tongking but on the China coast. Taking advantage of a condition of things which was not "war," Admiral Courbet made his way peacefully past the forts that guard the entrance to the Min; and then demanded the surrender of a much inferior Chinese squadron that lay in the harbour of Foochow. A hopeless resistance simply entailed useless slaughter; and Paris had news that the first act of retribution had been accomplished. The blockade of Formosa had less glorious results; General Liu Minchüan succeeded, in fact, in repulsing an attack on Kelung: but the blockade was maintained, and might have been kept up till now without affecting the result of the struggle, if French naval superiority had not enabled the Admiral to exert pressure in the north. The Chinese soldiers improved their reputation, too, amid the Highlands of Tongking: it was only after much fighting that General Négrier was able to occupy, on February 13th, 1885, the citadel of Langson which would have been surrendered in the previous June, if Colonel Dugenne had had patience to wait a fortnight. That disaster, however, combined with the uneasiness which Admiral Courbet's cruisers were creating in the neighbourhood of the Yangtze, impelled the Chinese to make peace. It is possible that they might have been less pliant if they had been less hasty, for Langson was recovered, and General Négrier wounded and compelled to retreat, on March 28th; but the Protocol of Paris had been signed in the interval, and China adhered to the agreement.

The first article of this Convention was in itself an admission that France had gained nothing by the campaign to which M. Ferry had committed her; for it simply provided for the ratification of the Fournier Convention.

"China consents to ratify the Convention of Tientsin of May 11th, 1884, and France declares that she has no other end in view than the full and complete execution of that treaty."

Hostilities were to cease at once: the blockade of Formosa was to be raised: Chinese troops were to withdraw within the frontier of Yunnan; and the Annamese kingdom was tacitly surrendered into the hands of France by the recognition of the treaty which had been dictated at Hué.

The Protocol of Paris was the virtual outcome of Bishop Pigneau's predication. In acquiring the foothold he had indicated, the Republic was really requiring Annam to fulfil the bargain which had been entered into by her fugitive prince, a century previously at Versailles. No one familiar with the far-reaching policy of the Roman Church will fail to apprehend that the Bishop's design was twofold, and that the more intimate purpose was probably not that put most frankly forward. The extension of French influence and French dominion in the East meant the extension of her protectorate over Catholic missions, and increased opportunity for the extension of those missions themselves. What more likely to produce these results than a scheme of military adventure and eventual dominion, eminently consonant with French character and aspirations? Political exigencies delayed its execution. The downfall of the monarchy and the Napoleonic wars abruptly broke the threads; but, even with the accession of Louis XVIII. we see a tentative effort to reknit them; and the Abbé Huc is at hand to awaken the attention of Napoleon III., when the close of the Anglo-French war with China left a powerful expedition available, in 1858, for driving home the wedge which Louis XVI. had pointed. The treaties of Saigon of 1862 and 1874, the treaty of Hué of 1883, and the treaties with Cambodia in 1863 and 1884, are the political offspring of the treaty of Versailles in 1787. After the lapse of a century, the dream of the Bishop seems approaching realization. The flag of France has been planted along the whole eastern seaboard of Indo-China, and the foundation of the empire which was to compensate for the loss of India has been laid.

When the Governor of Saigon seized a pretext to extort from King Norodom, in 1884, a treaty practically handing over Cambodia to French rule, the *Saigonnais* took occasion to predict that the whole trans-Gangetic peninsula was destined to come under the protectorate of France. The expression was sweeping, considering that large districts of the peninsula were already owned by England; but it was well understood that Siam was proximately indicated. Materials for quarrel, when the moment might arrive—in the south, in the shape of two provinces that once belonged to Cambodia, but which have passed under the rule of Siam; while Dr. Néis was making scientific researches among the Laos tribes in the north—and making treaties with them, it is said, as well, to bring them within the fold of the great protectorate. The very thought of further aggression was of course repudiated at Paris; but so were, once, the ideas of annexing Tunis and Tongking; and the Court of Bangkok can hardly be blamed for feeling alarm at the attitude of its new neighbour.

II.

As we set out on our historical excursion in company with Mgr. Pigneau de Behaine, it may be worth while glancing back at some contemporary and even earlier writings, for a notion what Tongking was like before dynastic wars and outside interference had wrecked its prosperity. For Tongking was not always the *terra incognita* it had become early in the present century. Portuguese, Dutch, and English merchants had factories there during the seventeenth century; and even after these were abandoned, a desultory commerce appears to have been kept up till towards the close of the eighteenth. It was in 1637 the Dutch first landed in the country, and they found the Portuguese already established. The English seem to have arrived nearly about the same period; and a flourishing foreign settlement is said to have existed, at one period, at Hung-yen, which was then the centre of foreign commerce. We will let Captain Alexander Hamilton,[1] "who spent his time from 1688 to 1723 trading and travelling by sea and land," tell the story of their withdrawal:—

Tonquin is the next place I must steer to, of course, where the English and Dutch both had their factories; but the English Company's affairs being a little out of order, they withdrew theirs in 1698; and the Dutch, finding but little advantage by their trade in Tonquin, withdrew theirs about six years after. However, the English had a private trade pretty good till the year

[1] "A Description of the East Indies." By Captain Alexander Hamilton. Pinkerton's Collection, vol. viii. p. 483.

1719, that (*sic*) an English ship from Bengal ruined it by an act of violence. The ship, being laden and ready to sail, fell down the river to Catcheo, the capital city of Tongking; and in defiance of the known laws of the country, the supercargo got a Tonquin girl on board, in order to carry her with him; but her friends, missing her, informed the civil magistrate, who sent to demand her; but the supercargo would not resign his mistress; whereupon acts of hostility ensued, and some were killed on both sides, and Captain Wallace, who commanded the ship, had the fortune to be one of the slain. However, the English bravely carried off their prize; but I never heard anything more of the Tonquin trade since.

The depredators, however, or some others of their countrymen, must have subsequently made their peace, for we learn from Père Richard,[1] who wrote in Paris, in 1778, that English ships still traded to Tongking; though they were debarred from ascending the river on account of another act of impropriety. Up to 1730, or thereabouts, they had been allowed to come up to the capital; but a certain ship was found smuggling some copper, and fought its way out to escape seizure. Trade was thereupon suspended till 1742, when the English again made their peace, though they were excluded from the river.

As to the articles of which the Tongking trade consisted, we are inclined to again rely on Captain Hamilton, who was evidently a man of much experience:—

The country is prodigiously fruitful in all things necessary for the conveniency and support of life. They have abundance of raw silk, and manufacture part of it in wrought silks, but none fine. Their baaz is the best, which they generally dye black. It

---

[1] *Vide* Pinkerton, vol. ix.

wears very long, because it is soft and well spun, and the oftener it is washed, the colour looks brighter, if blacker may be so called. They make bowls, cups, and tables of rattans, and cover them very neatly with lack of various colours, and gild them. They have also some porcelain, but very coarse and ill-painted. And those are the commodities for exportation from Tonquin.

Earlier, however, than either of these writers, we have an exhaustive paper by one S. Baron,[1] who appears to have been born in Tongking, but to have been of English nationality. He bears somewhat similar testimony as to the articles of export, among which silk was evidently the most important; but adds a remark discouraging to those who lay stress on the metallic wealth of the country:—

Neither have they any gold but what comes from China. Their silver is brought in by English, Dutch, and Chinese trading to Japan. They have iron and lead mines, which afford them just enough of those minerals to serve their occasions.

He is contradicted, however, on this point by Richard, who declares that gold is found in the sands of the rivers and the clefts of the rocks, adding that there are, besides, (gold) mines which are worked by the Chinese, while the natives themselves work mines of copper, iron, and lead.

Baron, who wrote about 1685, seems to have been unsuccessful in his trade, and a little put out with Tongking: a prince by whom he had got himself adopted, went mad on the death of his grandfather, "which was," he says, "the overthrow of my busi-

[1] "A Description of the Kingdom of Tonqueen." By S. Baron, a native thereof. Churchill's Collection, vol. vi.

ness, by incapacitating him to protect me in my greatest trouble and necessity." His description of the country, government, institutions, etc., is, however, exhaustive; and the following paragraph has especial interest:—

> Though the Chova (Regent) values foreign trade so little, yet he receives from it, embarrassed as it is, considerable annual income into his coffers, as taxes, head-money, impositions, customs, etc. But though these amount to vast sums, yet very little remains in the treasury, by reason of the great army he maintains, together with several other unnecessary expenses. In fine, it is pity so many conveniences and opportunities to make the kingdom flourishing should be neglected; for if we consider how this kingdom borders on two of the richest provinces of China, it will appear that, with small difficulty, most commodities of that vast empire might be drawn hither; and great store of Indian and European commodities, especially woollen manufactures might be vended there. Nay, would they permit strangers the freedom of this inland trade, it would be vastly advantageous to the kingdom; but the Chova (jealous that Europeans should discover too much of his frontiers, by which certainly he can receive no injury) has, and will probably in all times to come, impede this important affair.

Richard's remarks on the same subject bear a suspicious resemblance to Baron's, whose paper he evidently had before him when writing his own. He, too, opines that a considerable trade would be possible if greater facilities were allowed. "But the administration has not yet opened its eyes to these sources of public prosperity; they keep in a false dread of revolutions and invasions from foreign forces which they fear the pretence of commerce might favour":—a remark which has a curious significance at a moment when this "pretence of commerce" has led to the very real invasion of the French.

Rumours of mineral wealth always possess a strange fascination. Père Regis once wrote of a hill of pure silver in Korea; and a tale that Korean kings were once buried in golden coffins led, not many years ago, to a filibustering expedition to rifle the graves. Korea proved, however, to be a very ordinary country indeed when foreigners gained access to it; and it seems probable that the French will have a like experience in Tongking. Mineral wealth figured largely in the pictures of rich resources and abundant trade which they were told would become theirs when Annamese obstruction had been put down. A commission appointed to investigate the question under the presidency of the Inspector-General of Mines reached, however, a more qualified conclusion. The presence of gold and silver is indicated in Thai-nguyen, gold and tin in Cao-binh, and copper in Tuyen-kwan and Hung-hoa. Official exploration was, however, advised, to gather more precise information; the chief sources, at present, being Annamese documents and common report. Only "with regard to the coal measures on the coast of Tongking and the adjacent islands," was it admitted that information and investigation were sufficiently advanced for work to be commenced at once.[1] Nor did the very thorough inquiries under-

[1] A Company has been formed in Hong-Kong to work these mines, mainly with British capital, under the title "Société Française des Charbonnages du Tongking," with a capital of 4,000,000 frs.

taken by Mr. Colquhoun, on the spot, lead him to much more halcyon conclusions. The "wealth," it will be remembered, lay in two directions: it awaited development in Tongking itself, and it was to be drawn down the valley of the Songkoi from Yunnan. Here are Mr. Colquhoun's[1] conclusions on both heads:—

> The principal source of Yunnan wealth is mineral; but China must effectively open the Songkoi, and allow the mines to be worked, before any great afflux can come from this source. Most of the mines are far removed from the Songkoi, and the river is not navigable to a degree which can create any great carrying trade. For that purpose, according to the French themselves, a railway is needed. Finally, what is urged in regard to the mines of Tonquin—namely, the fact that mines far removed from the scene of industries do not pay—must be borne in mind . . .
>
> The (Hongay) coal might perhaps compete with the Australia, China, and Japan coal, sold at Hong-Kong; analysis has shown its quality to be excellent. Iron, lead, zinc, tin, and gold, exist in different parts—mainly in the Songkoi basin—but whether it will pay to exploit them, I cannot offer any opinion.

In regard to the agricultural resources of the country, he speaks with greater confidence. The principal staple is rice, of which there are two crops annually; other products being the castor-oil plant, mulberry, cotton, sugar-cane, plantain, and sweet potato; silk is largely produced, but the quality is poor; the tobacco is condemned as insipid; in-

Further considerable sums have been sunk. Large quantities of coal appear to be in view, but it has not yet been made available in marketable quantities, although shareholders are assured that they are on the verge of success.

[1] "The Truth about Tongking" (Correspondence of the *Times*). By Arch. R. Colquhoun, London, 1884.

ferior indigo and false gambier are also produced. Little tea is grown; but in Laos, bordering on Yunnan, a fine quality known in China as Puerh tea is produced, and the French hope to divert the export to Tongking—an expectation in which, however, Mr. Colquhoun appears to doubt their success, unless they make a rail along the whole course of the Songkoi—the very river whose alleged value as a waterway was the alleged motive of the campaign.

More significant, however, than even the doubts thrown on the truth of the prospectus by which France was persuaded to plunge into the Indo-Chinese adventure, was the small share she had succeeded in acquiring, of the trade that had actually been done since she acquired a footing in the country by the treaties of 1874. Taking the year 1880 as a fair instance—before commerce had been disturbed by the recent invasion,—Mr. Colquhoun pointed out that 97½ per cent. of the imports into Tongking came from Hong-Kong, and only ½ per cent. from Saigon; while 79 per cent. of the exports also went to the British colony, and only 16 per cent. to Saigon. And resort would, he predicted, be had to protection, in the endeavour to reverse all this, directly the French deemed themselves in a position to act. The prediction was promptly verified. Early in 1884, the Saigon Government was requested to submit to the Colonial Council a Customs tariff whose operation, it was intended, should embrace Annam and Tongking. Saigon had been free, so far, from Customs dues.

A restrictive policy was tried when the colony was first organized, but it was found so absolutely prohibitive of progress that more liberal principles were adopted, and the field thrown open to foreign enterprise which had built up what trade the port enjoyed. With the exception of an export duty on rice, the Colonial Budget depended on internal and direct taxation, such as on land, licenses, and excise; and the colonists were able to plead that, under this system, the finances had flourished, and a surplus of $400,000 had been accumulated against accident or emergency.

Their idea had been that the acquisition of Tongking would mean the aggrandizement of Saigon, that absorption of Annam meant a consolidated Indo-Chinese Empire, of which Cochin-China would be the metropolitan province and Saigon the capital. When it became apparent that there was no likelihood of its enjoying this access of dignity and advantage, but that Saigon was simply asked to sacrifice its free trade in the interests of symmetry and of French manufacturers, considerable opposition was manifested. The official programme was, of course, adopted; but not before the opposing views had been expressed with much force and clearness. The determining motive, however, it was explained, was the necessity for protecting French industry. The confession was humiliating, but it had to be made: "French industry required to be protected against its foreign rivals. In Saigon, as elsewhere, English and German products were taking the place of French products: without protection French industry was conquered beforehand; and that was why, appealing to the patriotism of Cochin-China, a sacrifice was asked from it, in order to help national industry and enable it to fight with equal weapons—at least in colonies acquired by French blood and treasure—against foreign industry."[1] It is difficult to appreciate the precise nature of the "equality" indicated: the idea would rather seem to be, to pit Frenchmen at scratch weights against foreigners with a heavy handicap. But the motive at any rate is clear enough, and it is needless to add that a consenting majority acquiesced in the Government scheme.

Having small belief in the efficacy of such attempts to help, by legislation, national industries that were unable to help themselves, British merchants connected with the East predicted that the measures resorted to were more likely to strangle what trade existed than to divert it into French channels. "Trade flows, they argue, between Hongkong and Tongking, because that is its natural course; because the articles required by Tongking are of Chinese production and come from Hong Kong, or of English production and stored in Hong Kong; and the prohibitive measures resorted to—instead of substituting

[1] The *Journal Officiel de la Cochin-Chine Française* of November 3rd, 1884, contained a full report of a meeting of the Colonial Council at which the subject was debated. The tariff adopted, under pressure from Paris, imposed duties varying from 5 to 10 per cent., with a deduction not yet fixed, but indicated at from 50 to 70 per cent., in favour of French products.

Saigon for Hong Kong as the commercial *entrepôt* of Cochin-China, or substituting French for English products in the Indo-Chinese market—are more likely to strangle what trade exists, and hinder the development which is looked forward to on the restoration of order." [1]

Judging, then, from the past, the prospect that France will get an adequate return for the blood and treasure she has expended do not seem brilliant. Military gratification she may find, and the satisfaction of possessing in the Far East a great territory, with prospects and possibilities of further extension. The interests will be served, too, of that propaganda whose spokesman Mgr. d'Adran constituted himself when putting forward his notable project, and whose views we have seen Mgr. Freppel defending, when supporting at the Tribune the policy of colonial extension. But of actual substantial recompense, in the sense in which Englishmen are apt to interpret the word, experience teaches us to be less hopeful. France seems to have lost—if we are to take the instance of Canada as proving that she once possessed—the knack of colonizing. She raises her flag in the hope that trade will follow, but it does not. That the delta of Tongking is fertile and may provide valuable material for export is certain, as it is that a certain amount of foreign goods would find their way into consumption under a settled and liberal *régime*. But experience tends to show that merchants other than French would be the principal

[1] Vide *London and China Express*, December 22nd, 1884.

instruments of that trade, if it were left unhampered, while the trade itself will be choked by the protective measures contemplated. Saigon is a capable colony, but what commerce exists is carried on chiefly by English, German, and Chinese firms: it is a Frenchman who once remarked that there are, there, so many officials governing each other! Nor is there reason to anticipate that things will eventuate much otherwise in Tongking. Of the mines, on which so much stress has been laid by advocates of annexation, it would be premature to say more than that the existence of metals seems clearly indicated, but the possibility of exploiting them profitably is a problem as yet unsolved. There remain, of course, the elastic possibilities of commerce with China, which suggested themselves to Baron two hundred years ago, and which form a prominent feature in the French programme of to-day. That such commerce has existed in a certain measure is certain, and that it may be considerably augmented, Dupuis' experience would seem to show; though the singular conditions of his adventure forbid us to accept it as precisely indicative of what might be expected from sober commercial enterprise. The Songkoi is no doubt a valuable stream; but its capacity as a water-way seems to have been exaggerated in the minds of those who first indicated the possibility of tapping South-western China by this route. It is certainly navigable for some distance—as far, according to Mr. Colquhoun, as Konence,—for steamers of light draught; but its upper waters "are impeded by sandbanks, rocks, and rapids," and are "impracticable from November to March, except for boats under four tons;" while above Laokai (near the Chinese frontier) the river "is useless for trade."

Annam proper seems to be comparatively poor and thinly populated; but we have the testimony of early visitors that Tongking was once a flourishing and populous kingdom. Populous it still is, if the estimate of 10,000,000 may be taken as approximately correct. Flourishing it may again become, if order and good government are restored to it under French auspices. But there is reason to apprehend that the very measures which are being taken to favour French trade will tend rather to hinder commercial progress.

III.

The protocol of Paris was followed (June, 1885) by a formal treaty, in which China recognized all the treaties concluded between France and Annam; agreed to join in delimiting the boundaries between Tongking and Chinese territory, and to permit trade across the frontier. Both powers promised to respect these frontiers, and to do their best to suppress the prevalent lawlessness and brigandage on either side. Subsequent conventions defined the terms on which trade should be carried on, and named Meng-tse in the province of Yunnan, and Lungchow in the province of Kwangse, as the stations through which it should pass: China was to post Customs' officers there, and France to appoint Consuls. The delimitation was accomplished, and Custom houses were opened in 1888. The latest reports of the officers in charge will indicate the degree of success that has attended the project of tapping the trade of Western China by this route. There passed through the station of Mengtze, in 1892, imports to the value of about 290,000*l.* (H.Tls. 1,149,000), and exports to the value of about 185,000*l.* (H.Tls. 736,865). The figures are not enormous, but neither are they contemptible. It should be noted, moreover, that they show a tendency to steadily increase. Each year's total has been greater than the last, and the foreign goods imported make their way, each year, further into the interior. It has been suggested that a lowering of the dues and the introduction of steam on the West River, which drains this region towards Canton, would prove that a portion of the trade which finds its way up the Songkoi is really diverted from the Si-kiang. But we have to deal only with the present situation. The *pourparlers* that have been going on with a view of inducing China to open up that channel of trade have not yet reached an issue; and trade may prove, after all, to prefer the Songkoi route. That merchandise to the value of nearly half a million sterling should find its way between Tongking and Yunnan by this channel shows that the glowing prophecies by which

France was led into the adventure were not baseless; but it proves, also, that they were very highly coloured, for the amount is certainly not commensurate with the language held, nor with the magnitude of the efforts involved. Still less do French manufacturers appear to have profited by the opportunity; for more than half (in value) of the entire import trade consisted of Indian yarn, which was almost exactly paid for by the export of 2000 tons of Yunnan tin; while the Commissioner's remark that "no steamers reached Laokai during the season of high water," seems to verify Mr. Colquhoun's estimate of the navigable capacity of the river.

We have been dealing, so far, with the trade route to Yunnan. But an opening had also been stipulated for, into Kwangse, by way of the famous city where Colonel Dugenne experienced his defeat, and from which even General Négrier was subsequently compelled to retreat. We have noted Mr. Colquhoun's impression that a railway is needed, even along the valley of the Songkoi. The need was quickly recognized as urgent, if anything were to be made of the route viâ Lungchow; and a railway was begun, two years ago, to facilitate transport by this route. The total length was to be seventy miles. The section from Phulang-Thuong to Bade was to have been completed in April, 1892, and the remainder in July, 1893. As a matter of fact, however, twenty miles only were opened last December. Some work has been done on the remaining fifty; but "no one," the Commissioner remarks "is willing to predict when the line will reach Langson." The total value of the trade which passed along this route last year, in the meantime, was 9000*l.*!

It would be incorrect, probably, to infer that the figures quoted represent the total trade between China and Tongking; because some merchandise, no doubt, finds its way along other than the regular roads. But they suffice to afford an estimate of the real value of the waterway which de Carné urged his countrymen to acquire at all hazards, and at the sacrifice of all scruple.

A word may be added as to the degree of success the French have attained in pacifying the country. It must be remembered that the incapacity and misgovernment of the Annamese officials and the insecurity of the waterways were the alleged excuses for intervention, at first, and for occupying the country in the long run. These were the pleas put forward by Garnier when he "placed himself alongside" the Annamese mandarins in 1874. They were the pleas alleged in justification of Rivière's expedition, and the eventual annexation of the province in 1884. It is perhaps scarcely surprising that, for a long time after that event, "anarchy" again "reigned supreme," as it did after Garnier's meteoric intrusion, but the French have had time now to prove the superior efficiency of their administration. Yet H.B.M.'s Consul at Saigon remarks, in his report on the trade of Indo-China for 1892, that "the almost daily reports of collisions in the interior [of Tongking] and the recent attack upon the Hongay coal mines point to a state of great insecurity." The remark is borne out by the language of the local press. The frequency with which we hear of piratical outrages and of punitive military expeditions seem, in fact, to forbid the inference that the French have, as yet, been much more successful than the Mandarins who had control at the time of Dupuis' expedition.

CHAPTER V.

CHINA AND HER TRIBUTARIES.[1]

THE prominence which has been given, by recent events, to the question of Chinese suzerainty over Annam, suggests a brief inquiry into the relations subsisting between the Great Empire and its neighbours. What is the real position in which the Emperor stands towards these so-called tributary states, and what the actual political value of the tribute he claims to receive? The case of Lord Macartney, who travelled through the whole length of the Empire, in happy ignorance that the words "Tribute-bearer" were inscribed on the flags floating above his barge, at once suggests itself in point. The idea seems ridiculous in our eyes; but it would probably have seemed equally ridiculous to a Chinaman, at that time, that a foreign emissary should dream of approaching the Emperor in any other capacity: the very term "Solitary Man," which is one of his alternative titles, precludes the idea of his being approached as an equal.

It would be a mistake, therefore, to ridicule the pretensions of China to suzerainty in Eastern Asia

[1] *The National Review*, June, 1884.

because she made the mistake, at first, of including Western nations in the same category as her neighbours. The argument would probably be more correct, that she made that mistake because her superiority over the countries with which she was acquainted was so manifest, that she conceived she was equally superior to the rest of the world. China was the "middle kingdom," surrounded by barbarian States permitted to exist by Imperial favour and to bask occasionally, in the persons of their envoys, in the sunshine of the Imperial presence. "As high as the heavens are above the earth," lately wrote an American naval officer, who had come much in contact with Chinese officials, "so high is his (the Chinaman's) conceit; as deep as the waters of the sea is the measure of his contempt for the outside barbarian." And no doubt this is, in a measure, still true. In spite of all that has passed, national vanity and contempt for foreigners hold their own in the mind of the great mass of the literati. Statesmen who have come much in contact with our representatives, and have seen evidences of our civilization and power, know better. Such men as Li Hung-chang, the great minister whose name figures prominently in every phase of Chinese politics, appreciate the real position of affairs; and—more or less, in proportion to their greater or less experience or ignorance—the idea of superiority is fading from the minds of his colleagues.

It was otherwise at the time of Lord Macartney's visit. From a Chinese point of view, all presents offered to the Emperor then were "tribute"; and we were set down as tributary accordingly, and enrolled as such, together with Portugal, Holland, and the Pope, in the pages of the *Ta-tsing Hwei-Tien* (an elaborate work[1] on Chinese constitutional law and polity), where the arrival and departure of our ambassador, his interviews, and his presents, find faithful record. It is noteworthy, however, that the last edition of this work issued was in 1820; and it is scarcely to be supposed that the Imperial Cabinet would take its stand, to-day, by the list of "tributaries" there published. Many things have happened since then, and it is likely the next editor will see reason to make many alterations. There exists, moreover, even in the Chinese mind, a subtle distinction between tribute and tribute. Everything presented to the Emperor is presumed to be offered by inferiors to a superior; but it may be merely a complimentary offering of the products of the country, or it may be an obligatory tender of articles definitely prescribed. Lord Macartney's embassy may be taken as an illustration of one extreme; the annual Corean embassies to Peking as an illustration of the other.

Quite apart, however, from any fanciful assumption, there exists a real preponderance and political superiority on the part of China, over her immediate neighbours, which it would be a mistake to ignore,

[1] The *China Review* of October, 1883, contains an interesting paper by Mr. G. Jamieson, of H.M.'s Consular Service, founded on this work, from which Mr. Jamieson translates many curious records of tribute sent and "tributary" visits paid.

because, in her ignorance and conceit, she has been guilty of wild exaggeration. Corea, Nepaul, Burmah, Annam, and the Liuchius, are distinctly tributary States; Thibet is a dependency, Tartary a portion of the empire; and, as already suggested, the very existence of this coruscation of satellites was calculated to foster the dream of universal superiority from which she has had to be rudely awakened. The degree of dependence of these several States varies, no doubt, in proportion to their importance and their distance from their giant neighbour; but all are more or less under the glamour of her influence. Corea is the most dependent; Burmah the least so; but even of Burmah it may be affirmed that the Chinese Governor-General of Yunnan was, at any rate till within the last few years, regarded as a greater magnate than the Viceroy of British India—a Power which had reft away half the country, and which held the rest in the hollow of its hand.

Recognition of the tributary status is shown by the payment of tribute, by the form of address (as from an inferior to a superior) and by acceptance of the Chinese Calendar; the more intimate dependents also receive investiture and a seal of office at the hands of a Chinese delegate; while in the case of the less intimate the ceremony is performed under the authority of letters patent. The nature of the tribute is fixed, as well as the times of despatch, and the route by which it shall be sent. The envoys of Corea come direct to Peking; those of Nepaul, by way of Chêntu, the capital of Szechuen;

those of Burmah, by way of Yunnan-foo, the capital of Yunnan; those of Annam, by way of Kwei-lin, the capital of Kwangsi; those of Liuchiu, by way of Foochow, the capital of Fohkien. And the governors-general of these several provinces are charged, respectively, with the conduct of all matters soever relating to each particular State. Corea sends tribute every year; Nepaul once in five; Burmah once in ten; Annam once in four; Liuchiu once in two. The character and amount of the presents are defined, and it is exacted that the accompanying letters shall be in the so-called "petitionary" form used by Chinese officials in addressing the Throne. Thus we find the Emperor Kanghi minuting with his own hand, on a letter from the King of Corea: "It lacks respect; let the Board of Rites examine and report;" —and the King was condemned to a fine of 10,000 ounces of silver, and to lose, during three years, the presents made by the Emperor in return for the annual tribute. While, on an occasion during the reign of Kienlung, when the tribute sent from Annam did not correspond with the amount which it was then customary to pay, the whole was sent back with orders that the mistake should at once be corrected. The acceptance of the Calendar, again, is one of those formulas which, in the East, have a meaning that seems extravagant to our ideas, but which cannot be disregarded with safety in intercourse with Asiatic sovereigns. The compilation of the Calendar is, in China, exclusively an imperial privilege, and every year it is formally promulgated and disseminated through the Empire. To receive it is to admit oneself subject and tributary; to refuse it is to place oneself in open insurrection.

Such appear to be the outward and visible signs of respect which China expects from her so-called tributaries; and it must be admitted that there is, in all this, something very different from the mere assumption of national vanity. Beyond, however, requiring the fulfilment of these conditions, she really interferes very little in their affairs, unless in case of invasion, or of some serious internal trouble where her help is sought or her own interests appear to be threatened. A brief glance at her historical relations with the several States on the list will serve to explain more clearly their several positions.

COREA.—The vassalage of Corea appears to date almost from the dawn of its history as a homogeneous kingdom. The first monarch who established an ascendency over the whole country recognized the overlordship of the Chinese Emperor, to whose help he had been largely indebted; and his successors have clung faithfully to the fortunes of their suzerains. Each change of dynasty in China has found the Corean ruler involved in the defeat of the falling house. When the Mings succeeded, at the close of the fourteenth century, in overthrowing the Mongol power, the reigning dynasty in Corea shared its downfall; and, similarly, we find Corea siding with the Mings in the war which resulted in the overthrow and supersession of the latter by the Manchus. A Manchu army then invaded the country, and dictated at the capital, in 1637, the treaty which continues to the present day to govern its relations with Peking. Under it, the king has to ask and accept investiture at the hands of a Chinese mandarin specially delegated for the purpose, whom he goes out of the city to meet on his arrival, and whom he receives and lodges with every mark of respect. He has to send a yearly embassy to Peking, with certain specified articles of tribute,[1] and receives certain customary presents in return.

Nor, on the other hand, has China been remiss when grave crises in Corean history have called for her intervention. At the time of Taiko-Sama's great invasion, in 1592, we find her exerting her whole might in favour of her dependent. Quite lately she has virtually imposed, by her influence, terms of intercourse with foreign powers; and, on the occurrence of an *émeute* and *coup d'état* caused by this violent change in the national policy, she sent soldiers to the capital, restored order, and carried off to China the father of the king, who was the leader of the revolt. Of course, it may be said she acted in her own interest, and in pursuance of her own policy: the Japanese invasion was directed beyond

[1] The following is a list of the Corean tribute:—100 oz. of gold, 1000 oz. of silver, 10,000 bags of rice, 2000 pieces of silk, 300 pieces of flax cloth, 10,000 pieces of common cloth, 400 pieces of hemp cloth, 100 pieces of fine hemp cloth, 1000 rolls of large paper, 1000 rolls of small paper, 2000 knives, 1000 buffalo-horns, 40 painted mats, 200 lbs. of dye-wood, 10 bushels of pepper, 100 tiger-skins, 100 deer-skins, 400 beaver-skins, 200 blue squirrel-skins.

Corea, against China; and the foreign treaties are designed to safeguard Corea, as an outlying bulwark of China, against Russia. But, as was shown lately in the case of Tongking, their capacity to act as buffers in warding off hostile contact is, in the eyes of China, not the least useful function of the petty States which surround her.

In the case of none other, however, is her authority so directly exercised as in that of Corea. Of the extent to which it stretches, and the minutiæ to which it descends, an appeal from a Corean king (in 1694) for permission to change his queen may be quoted as an amusing instance. Childless for a number of years he had, he writes, at length a son by a concubine.

> His birth caused me incredible joy. I at once took for queen the mother who bore him; but I made herein a mistake which has caused many suspicions. I compelled Queen Min-chi, my wife, to withdraw into a private house, and I made Chang-chi Queen in her stead. Now, I reflect that Min-chi has received the patent of rank from your Majesty, that she has ruled my house, has assisted me in the sacrifices, has served both my grandmother and my mother, and wore mourning for three years for them with me. According to the laws of nature and justice I ought to have treated her with honour, but I allowed myself to be carried away in my imprudence. After the thing was done I regretted it extremely. Now, in order to conform to the wishes of the people of my kingdom, I desire to restore to Min-chi the dignity of Queen, and to replace Chang-chi in the rank of concubine. Thus the government of the family will be in order, and the foundation of good morals and the welfare of the State will be rectified.

His Majesty goes on to apologize, on these grounds, for venturing to trouble the Emperor several times about such a matter, and ends by begging a consent which it is gratifying to know was accorded: delegates were sent to re-crown Ming-chi, with presents of splendid robes and all due formalities.[1] It will be admitted, however, that a prince who cannot crown or uncrown his wife without the Emperor's approval is somewhat dependent.

NEPAUL.—Chinese influence over Nepaul has probably waned, of late, in proportion as British power in India has waxed; still, the Rajah continues to send the prescribed missions. The actual terms of the present tribute appear to have been imposed after the Goorkha invasion of Thibet, in 1792. Warren Hastings had been endeavouring to open up commercial relations with Lhassa, and the Thibetan Minister is said to have shown himself more favourably disposed than was pleasing to the Chinese.[2] However that may be, it is clear that, soon after the last British Envoy's departure, he conceived it wise to take refuge with the Rajah of Nepaul; and the latter, soon after his arrival, invaded Thibet and overran the country. China, however, sent an army which defeated the Nepaulese in two battles, penetrated their country, and compelled them to purchase peace by restoring all their plunder and paying tribute to the Emperor. The Chinese general is said to have been a former Viceroy of Canton, and hostile to the English. At any rate, he closed the frontier

[1] "Histoire de l'Eglise de Corée." Par Ch. Dallet, Paris, 1874.

[2] *Narrative of the Mission of G. Bogle to Thibet*, by Clements R. Markham.

by establishing a chain of posts along the southern border of Thibet and Bhootan, and this isolation has ever since been maintained. The Nepaulese appealed to their conquerors for help, not long after, on the occasion of a dispute with the British about some territory which we claimed but which they refused to surrender, and it is fair to say that the appeal was promptly answered. Three Chinese mandarins were sent to Khatmandu, and an army after them. Letters were interchanged between these and the Governor-General, the former repeating what the Nepaulese had stated, and asking explanations which the latter gave. Presents were shortly after sent by the Commissioners, saying they were satisfied, and the incident closed. The most noteworthy sentence in the correspondence, for our present purpose, is in reply to a proposal by Warren Hastings that the Emperor should station an officer at Khatmandu to act as referee in case of trouble. "Be it known to you," the Commissioners replied, "that the Goorkha Rajah has long been a faithful tributary of the Chinese Government, and refers himself to it whenever occasion requires."

Quarrels between Nepaul and Thibet have somewhat ruffled the current of intercourse at times; and Sir Jung Bahadoor was credited, some years ago, with a threat to break off the relationship altogether. It has, however, endured, and we find in the *Peking Gazette* of the 20th May, 1876, a memorial from the Chinese resident at Lhassa, announcing the receipt of the usual "petition" from Nepaul, requesting information as to the period for sending tribute, "couched in language reverentially submissive, and expressive of the most devoted loyalty."

He (the Resident) accordingly makes report thereof for the Imperial information and, looking upwards, asks of the Celestial Grace whether permission may be granted to send the tribute offerings at the regular date. . . . He has to add that the King aforesaid makes mention of the birth of a grandson, which he thinks it his duty to report. He (the Resident) has expressed congratulation in reply, and has sent back an Imperial donation of two rolls of embroidered satin, to which he has added on his own account a roll of wide satin, by way of congratulatory largess, in furtherance of his Sovereign's desire to cherish tenderly the foreigner with a liberality that knows no bounds.

THIBET.—Thibet scarcely comes within the category of feudal states, as it has ceased, since 1746, to have an independent existence. Up to that period, a native sovereign owning fealty to the Emperor still held a more or less nominal sway over the country. But a revolt which broke out in the reign of Kienlung led to its complete subjugation, and to the placing of the entire government in the hands of the Dalai Lama,[1] assisted by four ministers of his own choosing, under the supreme control of two Chinese Residents who became in reality Regents of Thibet.

Very little is known as to the degree of control China really exercises at Lhassa; but the assump-

[1] "Illustrations of the Lamaist System of Thibet," by W. F. Mayers. Vol. iv. of the *Transactions of the Royal Asiatic Society of London*, 1869. Mr. Mayers' paper was designed to illustrate the method in which the Lamaist succession in Thibet is perpetuated, and is full of curious information on the subject.

tion would probably not be far wrong that her influence is considerable, but her actual power slight. Settling difficulties with the border States would seem to be one of her chief functions: we have already seen her intervening once or twice in case of Nepaul; and bickerings between Thibetans and Nepaulese seem to be frequent causes of trouble. There have been published recently, in the *Peking Gazette*, several memorials from the Chinese Resident, about a fresh quarrel arising out of the plunder of some Nepaulese traders, at Lhassa, which threatened at one time to lead to war. It was composed, however, eventually, under Chinese mediation, by Thibet undertaking to pay compensation and to punish the robbers.

It was China, as we have seen, which closed the Himalayan passes in 1792; and, on the several occasions when British-Indian officials have tried to re-open them, the Thibetans have usually expressed themselves willing but have averred that the decision lay at Peking. The Chinese, on the other hand, locate the difficulty at Lhassa, and plead Thibetan timidity and opposition. They have, however, ended by accepting the responsibility: the (Chefoo) Convention negotiated with China by Sir Thomas Wade, in 1876, contained a special article, sanctioning the despatch of a British mission of exploration—either from China by way of Szechuen and Thibet into India, or from India by way of Thibet and Szechuen into China; and a memorial in the *Peking Gazette* of the 18th of June,

1877, from the Resident at Lhassa, shows that the import of the negotiations was promptly communicated to the Thibetan authorities. The memorialist had, he said, received a communication from the Board of Foreign Affairs, "stating that Europeans have stipulated for entry into Thibet;" it was therefore "indispensable that the officers filling the various Commissionerships should be intelligent and active persons, without which it would be difficult to maintain authority and order. . . ." He accordingly advises that two Imperial Commissioners in Western Thibet, whose term of office had expired, be retained in their posts for another term.

It is evident, from the Resident's expression, that the Chinese expected immediate effect to be given to the stipulation; and that they interpreted it in a sense wider than the words implied. The intention was, in fact, to pave the way for renewed commercial intercourse between India and Thibet; but the Commissioners must have had a weary time if they were retained in office as proposed, for circumstances long delayed execution of the project. The point which concerns us, however, is the assertion of control and acceptance of responsibility implied in the agreement.

Burmah.—The connecting tie in the case of Burmah is probably slighter than in that of any other of the neighbouring states. Tribute is due only once in ten years, instead of at the much shorter intervals we find prevailing where the dependence is more marked; and, instead of being, as in the case of Annam, a natural result of cognation, the relationship, such as it is, has been imposed and enforced by war. Colonel Burney has taken the trouble to compile, from the chronicles of the Kings of Prome and Ava, a narrative[1] of the various wars between Burmah and China, which throws much light on the relations between the two countries, and has the advantage of giving the Burmese view of the question.

The claim to tribute would seem, from this story, to have arisen about the middle of the eleventh century, as a consequence of a Burmese invasion of China, undertaken to obtain possession of a Buddha's tooth. The relic is alleged, by the Burmese chronicle, to have refused to quit China—probably because the Burmese were not strong enough to take it. King Anauratha, however, is said to have had a meeting with the Emperor, though under what circumstances is not stated. What does seem clear is that he entered into some engagement, or committed himself in some way which the Chinese interpreted to mean an acceptance of tributary relations. The Burmese version of the tale is that the Emperor supplied him with food dressed in various gold and silver vessels, which he, on his departure, delivered to the Emperor's religious teacher, with directions to dress food in them daily, and make offerings of it to the Sacred Tooth. However this may be, it is clear that the

[1] "Some Account of the Wars between Burmah and China, etc." By Lieut.-Colonel H. Burney. *Journal of the Asiatic Society of Bengal for* 1837, vol. vi.

proceeding – whatever it was—induced subsequent Emperors of China to demand presentation of the same kind of vessels, as tribute due. It is equally clear, however, that the position has not always been acquiesced in by Burmese sovereigns. A refusal of tribute, at the close of the thirteenth century, led to the great invasion by Kublai Khan, which is described in remarkably varying terms by Marco Polo and the Burmese chroniclers, Marco Polo declaring that the invading army was composed of the gleemen and jugglers[1] of Kublai's Court, while the Burmese speak of 6,000,000 of horse and 2,000,000 of foot; and declare that these had to be repeatedly reinforced before ultimately achieving victory! The main facts appear to be that the Chinese Emperor sent to demand the customary gold and silver vessels; but the King, instead of complying, slew the whole of the embassy, whereupon the Emperor sent an army which overcame the Burmese and occupied their capital (A.D. 1284). A fresh invasion is recorded in the year 1300—in pursuance, this time, of a legitimate function of suzerainty, the object being to restore a king who had been dethroned by rebels. In 1442 we find the Chinese again sending "to demand vessels of gold and silver, which they declared King Anauratha had presented as tribute;" and in 1477, another similar demand led to the verge of war. There appears, according to

[1] The idea of an army composed of gleemen and jugglers appears so extravagant that the thought suggests itself whether Marco was thinking of the remarkable athletic performances which characterize Chinese drill, and which might not unnaturally suggest the idea of mountebanks.

Chinese admission, to have been a breach of relations from the reign of Kiatsing in 1522 to that of Kienlung in 1721, when the arrival of a Burmese mission at Peking is again recorded. The resoldered connection, however, was soon again disturbed. The last and probably the hardest fought of the many international wars broke out in 1765, and lasted four years, ending in a treaty dated December 13th, 1769, which has since secured peace and commerce between the two countries. The Burmese claim to have had the best of the long struggle, in that they successfully kept out the Chinese invaders; and they declare that the ultimate proposals for peace came from the Chinese. There is a decided flavour of the traditional claim to tribute in the words: "If the sun-descended King sends presents we shall send presents in return," which are said to have been used in the Chinese overture, as that is precisely the usual course of procedure exacted. But the treaty (as translated by Colonel Burney) certainly disguises the obligation under language as little distasteful as possible to Burmese pride, merely stipulating that "the princes and officers of each country shall move their respective sovereigns to transmit and exchange affectionate letters in gold, once every ten years."

So much for the question from the point of view of Burmese story. We have, here, little evidence of what was done during the long intervals of peace; but we have evidence of a claim to tribute asserted by China for 800 years, and enforced, at times, by invasion when Burmese kings were willing to repudiate the obligation. It may be interesting, in conclusion, to illustrate the actual practice at the present day, by extracts from one of those "affectionate letters," as printed in the *Peking Gazette* of December, 1874. Communication between the two countries had been interrupted for some time on account of the Mahomedan rebellion in Yunnan; but at the close of 1874, the Governor-General of that province reported that a Burmese official had made his way to the provincial capital, "bringing a letter to the effect that the King, having heard of the restoration of order, had sent him to ask what arrangements should be made about tribute and other matters." He was instructed "that action should be taken according to the existing rules," etc., etc.; and then we have one of those tit-bits of Chinese officialism which serve, better than an essay, to illustrate the national vanity. After dilating on "the glorious influence exerted by the sovereigns of the present dynasty in securing the tributary allegiance of Burmah after an interruption of two centuries," the Governor-General goes on to observe that, although the language used in the despatch "is respectful and submissive in the fullest degree, without a word of self-assertion or arrogance, still the King has not described himself by name and surname,[1] and has made use of much that is improper in the enumeration of his titles. It is to be feared, consequently, that the rules of propriety might be transgressed in the address to the Throne which will

[1] This has reference to the Chinese custom which exacts that an inferior official, addressing a superior, shall describe himself only by name, and not by his rank or official status.

be presented with the tribute;" and it is asked that a "proper form" may be supplied from Peking, to replace that which was lost among the official archives destroyed during the rebellion. It must be admitted that the King's letter (as translated into Chinese), when the tribute-bearers actually started, goes far to justify the pretension. It is couched in terms of extravagant humility and adulation:—

"As the sun-flower bows before the sun, so does all mankind turn with adoration towards your imperial person. . . . Recently, owing to war and rapine on the borders, communication had long been interrupted; but the horrors of strife are now happily over, and the universe returned to tranquility. This letter has, consequently, been respectfully drawn up," and is accompanied by the articles stated.[1] The whole are placed in charge of an envoy, "who is charged to respectfully convey them to the palace gate, and to humbly crave that his great Majesty the Emperor will deign to receive the offerings, and will further graciously lend ear to the feelings of obedience, respect and submission entertained by your vassal."

The mission thus heralded crossed the frontier on

[1] The following is a list of the Burmese tribute: One letter in gold; a Burmese stone image of the God of Longevity; five tame elephants; a pair of ivory tusks, weighing 90 catties (120 lbs.); three jade-stone articles, weighing 210 catties (280 lbs.): eight gilt-frame and inlaid mirrors; two red jewel gold rings; two more gold rings; eight pieces of yellow, red, and green Spanish stripes; ten pieces thick heavy shirtings; ten pieces of foreign crape; ten fine handkerchiefs; twenty foreign carpet rugs; 10,000 sheets of gold leaf; 10,000 sheets of silver leaf; eight catties of sandal-wood; nine catties of red sandal-wood; ten bottles of scent; ten bottles of pomade; four No. 4 size ornamented boxes; fifty No. 5 size ornamented boxes; five pictures of elephants; fifteen peacocks' tails.—Vide *Peking Gazette*, 15th May, 1875.

February 1st, 1875, and left Peking on the return journey on November 18th of the same year.

ANNAM.—The interest of China in Annam, or Annan as it is called in Chinese records, is said to date from 214 B.C. About that period, according to Chinese story,[1] the Emperor Tsin-chi-wang overran the region now known as Tongking, and transplanted thither 50,000 Chinese families, who spread and multiplied, as is the Chinese wont, and gradually introduced the Chinese written character, customs, religion, and entire system of government and politics. The new territory at first formed an integral portion of the Chinese Empire, under the name of Ngan-an; but it is not surprising that so remote a province should eventually seek its independence, and this appears to have been so far accomplished, after a severe struggle, about 875 A.D., that a native prince was left in possession of the throne, on condition of sending tribute every three years. It would be tedious to enter into details of the next 900 years. The story is full of wars and rebellions and Chinese inroads—sometimes to "restore order," sometimes to replace a dethroned king. The native sovereigns appear to have resisted the Mongol conquerors of China in the thirteenth century, but were forced to submit; and the Emperor (Kublai Khan) recognized the reigning family on condition, as before, of a triennial tribute, which was to consist of gold, silver, precious stones, medicine,

[1] *Lettres Edifiantes.* Tableau historique de la Cochin-Chine.

ivory, and rhinoceros horns; a Chinese Resident being imposed on the court.

A further measure of independence seems to have been acquired under the Mings; and the Annamese princes seem to have been loth to recognize the subsequent ascendency of the Manchus. It was not, in fact, till some years after North China had been subdued that these invaders succeeded in establishing their ascendency in the South. The reign of the first Manchu emperor is commonly dated from 1644, but it was not till 1661 that the King of Annam "sent a letter submitting his allegiance;" nor does he seem to have been very fixed in his ideas, even then, for it is only in 1664 that he "applies to be invested as king." He was ordered, in reply, to hand back the patent and seal of office which he had received from the emperors of the last (Ming) dynasty, when "his application would be considered." Finally, in 1666, the formalities are completed. "The hereditary Prince of Annam, Le Wei-shih, sent the Ming patent and seal, whereupon a mission was despatched bearing the imperial letters patent and a camel-knob silver-gilt seal, in order to instal him as king." Seventeen years later, Le Wei-shih has been succeeded by Le Wei-cheng, who applies for investiture in turn; and again, in 1761, emissaries are sent to invest Le Wei-jui, nephew of the preceding, carrying with them a new seal made of silver inlaid with gold and inscribed with Manchu characters, for his use.

Le Wei-jui seems to have been, practically, the

last of his house; for now comes the record of the convulsion which overthrew the Le dynasty and resulted in the elevation of Bishop Pigneau's *protégé* to the throne. His grandson seems to have been installed, but the ceremony can hardly have been completed before he was expelled from Tongking. "In 1789," runs the entry, which I am tempted to quote at length from Mr. Jamieson's interesting translation, "there was internal strife in Annan. Le Wei-chi threw away the seal and absconded, and the people of the country put forward Yuen Kwang-ping as chief. He respectfully continued the former allegiance, and begged to be allowed to come in person to Peking to see the Emperor."

China seems to have acquiesced in the proposal. The provincial treasurer of Kwangsi was instructed to convey letters of investiture, a new seal was issued, and in the following year the visit was paid. The motive was to congratulate the Emperor Kien-lung on the attainment of his eightieth year, and on the day of the ceremony, the King "was assigned a place next below the princes of the first order." He was received with high favour, and an extraordinary number of presents was showered upon him. The opportunity seems to have been taken, also, to suggest certain alterations in the incidence of the tribute. A vassal going to visit his suzerain, in Europe, under such conditions would probably have asked to have it lightened. But the King of Annam wants the dates made more frequent; and so a decree (1792) orders that "Annan shall send tribute, henceforward, every two years instead of every three as formerly, and a mission to Peking every four years instead of every six." And these modifications were continued when, ten years later, the founder of the present dynasty sent to ask for investiture in turn; for Yuen Kwang-ping's term was short. In 1802, "Yuan Fu-ying (Nguyen-Anh) attacked Annan, whereupon the reigning king abandoned the seal and absconded. Yuan Fu-ying subdued the territory of Annan and sent messengers with tribute to ask for investiture. He also prayed that a new name might be given to his kingdom. In reply, it was ordered by decree that the name of the country should be changed to Yueh-nan, and, in conformity with the regulations, letters patent were granted conferring upon him the rank of king. A new seal was also issued, and the Lieut.-Governor of Kwangse was instructed to proceed to the country and invest him." [1]

We have seen that the Annamese tribute is held to be due biennially; though, on account of the great distance from Hué to Peking, two quotas are permitted to be sent simultaneously. Every four years, accordingly, may be seen, in the *Peking Gazette*, a record of the arrival and departure of the Annamese Mission with its stated tribute and imperial presents in return. The last was in 1881, and it may not be

[1] This was the outcome of the French episode. The investment of Yuen Kwang-ping and Yuen Kwang-tsuan seem to point to the successful invasion of Tongking by Nhac, and the temporary ascendency of the (Nguyen) prince whom he placed on the throne.

uninteresting to quote the King's letter to the Emperor, on that occasion :—

My nation, a tributary state from time immemorial, has been graciously confirmed in its possession by You. It has been ordained that the tribute day shall recur once in four years, without change. On each occasion offerings have obediently been sent. On the 8th day of the first moon of the 6th year of Kwangsü, the appointed time having come round, I requested, through the Governor of Kwangsi, Your permission to start, and I received an answer from him, appointing the 1st day of the 9th moon for admission across the frontier. When I received these commands, I was filled with thankfulness and awe. That the hills and streams of my country enjoy security and rest is because I have obeyed your behests; and we have not failed, generation after generation, to send our bounden tribute. Now the day is at hand once more, and I am again permitted to send my offerings. Truly this is because You have deigned to consider my loyalty and love, and the hearts of my subjects are satisfied and grateful. As is the duty of a vassal prince, gazing from afar at the Heavenly Abode, I have entrusted to my envoy Yuan-shun, and others, various offerings[1] to be presented to you. In all humbleness I await your acceptance of them.

It may be added that the *Peking Gazette* of March 20th contains the usual report that the mission had passed the frontier and reached the provincial capital, where the governor entertained them at a banquet.

[1] The following is a list of the Annamese tribute: 2 elephants' tusks; 2 rhinoceros horns; 45 catties (=60 lbs.) of betel nuts; 45 catties of grains of paradise; 600 ozs. of sandal-wood; 300 ozs. of garroo-wood; 100 pieces of native silk; 100 pieces of white silk; 100 pieces of raw silk; 100 pieces of native cloth.—In addition to the regular tribute, there are extraordinary occasions, such as marriages, birthdays, coming of age, coronations, etc., when the Court of Hué is bound to send two pairs of elephant's tusks, four rhinoceros horns, 100 rolls of each of three different kinds of satin, and 100 rolls of cotton cloth.

His Excellency adds, moreover, that having noticed that "the mission was ill-supplied with clothing, insufficient, indeed, to supply changes for so long a journey, he presented them with a further supply of silk and fur clothing at his own expense!"

We have seen that a notable feature in the tributary relationship is the acceptance from the Emperor of a seal of office; and it is not a little curious to observe that, when signing the new treaty imposed on him by the French, the King gave up to M. Patenôtre the seal so held by his predecessors, which the French forthwith destroyed.

The nature of China's connection with what she now calls the Kingdom of Yueh-nan may be judged from the above outline; and it may be judged also with what degree of truth the French could pretend to regard the connection as having only a legendary interest.

THE LIUCHIUS.—The little group of islands known as the Liuchius are the subject of a mixed claim, which recently brought China and Japan to the verge of war, and which still remains unsettled. Lying midway between the two countries, they have not unnaturally fallen under the influence of both; and the manifestation by Japan of an inclination to annex them altogether, gave the signal for an angry protest by China.

The suzerainty of China seems to date from the accession of the Ming dynasty, towards the close of the fourteenth century, when Hung-wu, the first Ming emperor, persuaded them to acknowledge dependency; and these relations, once established, have continued to be acknowledged to the present day. Successive princes have received investiture at the hands of an Imperial delegate, and sent the customary tribute [1] to the Celestial capital.

At the same time, however, the islands seem to have fallen under the influence of Satsuma, and were regarded as so clearly an appanage of that principality that, on the abolition of feudalism and assumption of power by the Mikado, they were reorganized on the same footing as the rest of Japan, and made a prefectural district.

Whether of their own motion or under Chinese inspiration it would be difficult to determine, the inhabitants petitioned China against this undisguised absorption, and China remonstrated energetically on behalf of her *protégé*. The dispute reached an acute stage, and was more than once nearly escaping from the hands of diplomacy. It was, however, brought back within the paths of negotiation under the advice of General Grant, at the time of his visit to the East; and Japanese and Chinese plenipotentiaries were duly commissioned to bring about an agreement. This took the simple form of dividing the property, Japan taking the northern and China the southern half; and on this basis everything seemed settled; the day was even fixed for the exchange of ratifications, and for entry on possession

[1] The Liuchiuan tribute consists of 126 peculs of sulphur, 30 peculs of copper, and 10 peculs of white tin.

of the respective islands, when suddenly the Chinese backed out. They had, they said, been instructed to negotiate terms of agreement; but the terms, when come to, had necessarily to be submitted for the Emperor's instructions, and he desired to consult the Grand Superintendents of Trade before deciding. Considering this a deliberate slight, and failing to hold the Chinese to their bargain, the Japanese withdrew from the negotiation, and declared the agreement null. The question was thus blown back into the air; but the Japanese remain in possession.

SIAM.—Siam is also classed by the Chinese among tributary states, but the Siamese themselves deny the impeachment. Looking at the facts from an Oriental point of view, however, it is difficult to escape the conclusion that there is ground for the Chinese pretension; and that the simple fact is that Siam, alone among the Celestial satellites, has thrown off her traditional allegiance. It seems beyond dispute that, for several centuries, the Siamese rulers sent triennial embassies with presents to Peking; though they have now, for thirty years, given up the custom, and are willing to minimize its original import. We may quote, from the archives of Peking, two instances in illustration of the practice. In the twelfth year of Kanghi (A.D. 1673), "the kingdom of Siam applied for investiture. The imperial patent and a camel-knob silver-gilt seal were issued to the tribute messengers." And when, a century later, a new "chief of Siam named Chinghwa sent messengers with tribute, carrying a letter asking to be enrolled as a feudatory,"[1] the Chinese Cabinet again sent him letters patent and a silver-gilt seal, in accordance with this precedent.

Two documents, published some years ago in the Shanghai press,[2] enable us to obtain a fuller insight into the facts of the case. There appeared in the *Peking Gazette*, towards the close of 1869, a translation of a memorial from the High Officials of Fohkien, stating that a request had reached them from Siam to be permitted to resume the despatch of tribute, which had been interrupted then for eighteen years owing to the disturbed state of the empire during the Taeping Rebellion. Her rulers had expressed to a Chinese official, who was sent to Bangkok to buy wood for the Foochow Arsenal, her wish to resume more intimate relations; and he undertook to be the bearer of a so-called "petition," which the memorialists now sent up for the Imperial decision. This document, as translated in the pages of the *Peking Gazette*, was to the following effect:—

"Our depraved rulers have, from generation to generation, been invested by the Celestial Sovereigns, and have paid tribute without intermission. During the second year of Hienfung, however (1852), an embassy returning from Peking, whither it had pro-

[1] The customary Siamese tribute (we learn from Mr. Jamieson's excerpts from the Ta-Tsing Hwei-tien) consisted of elephants, rhinoceros horns, elephant tusks, cardamoms, laka wood, lucraban seed, cassia lignea and sandal wood, ebony and sapan wood, cutch, gamboge, sulphur, camphor, kingfishers' skins and peacocks' feathers.

[2] Vide *North-China Herald*, 11th December, 1869, and 12th April, 1870.

ceeded to pray for an investiture, was attacked and spoiled in the neighbourhood of Yung-cheng, in Honan. The principal linguist was killed, an envoy wounded, and the imperial presents were lost. . . . In the second year of Tungchih, the Governor-General of Canton notified that the requests preferred by that embassy had been acceded to, but that no steps had been taken to return thanks for the imperial favour thus displayed. On this, my principal Ministers drew up a petition setting forth that the Rulers of Siam have respectfully and loyally rendered tribute to the Celestial Sovereigns from generation to generation, and that their duties as subordinates have been faithfully discharged. Since the second year of Hienfung's reign tribute had not, however, been forwarded, owing to the disturbed state of the Celestial Empire rendering its safe transit impossible. . . . Were it, however, allowable to forward the tribute to Tientsin, an embassy could be specially formed." To this application no answer had been received, and as (continued the king) "I, who have lately ascended the throne, am anxious to pay tribute as has been customary, I respectfully pray your direction as to how I shall proceed."

It must be admitted that if this version of the despatch can be trusted, the admission is complete of the various points required to establish tributary relationship. The embassy in question was on its way to solicit investiture; the periodicity and continuity of the tribute are admitted, and the request for permission to change the route is an admission of the existing rule.

However that may be, the publication of these documents evoked from Bangkok a semi-official protest against the assumption of China and the inference drawn, to the following effect:—

Burmah and Cochin-China were tributary, yes! and both had endeavoured to throw off their allegiance, but had failed. But Siam had never come into collision with China, and never had occasion to pay tribute. What had happened was simply this. In the year 1350, the King removed his capital to Ayuthia (on the Meinam), and Chinese ships came and traded. The Siamese wished to join in the trade; and the King accordingly sent an ambassador to go and ask for friendly relations with China. The Emperor acquiesced, and opened the port of Canton; but the Chinese exacted such heavy duties that the Siamese traders lost. The King then sent another ambassador "in charge of a royal letter, with a request to give annual presents to China in order to save the duties." This request also was granted. "An ambassador was permitted to go once in three years, and Siam obtained privileges for the vessels which conveyed him. . . . The Emperor gave a great amount of presents in return; and the Siamese, perceiving this to be to their advantage, continued to send presents as a uniform practice; but they did so out of a desire to secure the advantages of trade, and for that purpose only."

And so again with reference to the alleged application for investiture. "A new sovereign having ascended the throne, royal letters were despatched to all nations in friendly treaty relations —to China the same as to other countries; although, no presents having been sent for eighteen years, it was not clear whether the Government of China would receive them; so a letter was written asking to send an ambassador with presents by the nearer route of Tientsin." The Chinese refused, replying that "to allow the ambassador to go by Tientsin would be contrary to custom: let him be sent by way of Canton, as formerly! The Siamese Government received this intimation with regret," as they had wished to send an embassy *viâ* Tientsin in the hope that it would be "treated somewhat in the same manner as those which had been sent by western nations." As it was, the matter had been dropped "until the Government of China was willing to receive them in what the Siamese Government considered a proper manner."

The explanation is plausible, and the attempt to put the present-giving practice in a light favourable to Siamese intelligence and independence, ingenious; but we can hardly blame the Chinese for regarding these periodical missions as tributary in their degree. It is not essential that a nation should be conquered to become tributary; and Siam appears, for her own purposes, to have fulfilled certain requirements—until, having broken through the custom for a while during the Taeping Rebellion, she concluded to reject it altogether, and try to place her relations on the same footing as those of western powers. As a matter of fact, the Government has since acted in accordance with the purpose here expressed. That is to say, not only has it taken no further steps to re-open political intercourse, but, when China sent an envoy to Siam, to require that the despatch of tribute should be resumed, he is said to have encountered a peremptory refusal. Nor, curiously enough, do the Siamese appear to have lost anything by their recalcitrance. Ships flying the white elephant of Siam are admitted into the Chinese ports open to foreign trade, on the same footing as those of other nations having the most elaborate treaty rights.

We have now glanced, in succession, at the various kingdoms which really fall under the shadow of the Great Empire. We find the dependence implicit in the case of Corea and Annam; slighter and more vague in the case of Burmah and Nepaul; while Siam has altogether broken off tributary relations, and the Liuchiu Islands are a subject of dispute between China and Japan. The origin of the relationship may have been different in different cases. In that of Annam it grew out of colonization; in that of Burmah it seems to have been imposed by military force; while Siam sought it for purposes of commercial advantage. But it is hard to escape the conclusion that nations which are held bound to send given presents, by given routes, at given intervals, and which conform to the obligation, are "tributary"; or that rulers who are held bound to address the Emperor with nearly the same form of respect that would be used by a Viceroy, are "dependent," in the sense which the Chinese claim. And not only so, but—with the exception of Siam, which, as we have seen, has thrown off the yoke, and Nepaul, which probably yields to the pressure she feels on her northern frontier—there is reason to believe that, so far from feeling the obligation irksome, they have thought it a high privilege to be allowed to bask, at given intervals, in the sunshine of the Imperial presence. How far that sentiment may be affected by recent events is a question difficult to answer. It seems hardly possible the Empire should escape, with undiminished prestige, from an ordeal making manifest its inability to protect its vassals. But custom has, in the East, a wonderfully enduring force; and China has for centuries loomed so large in the eyes of her neighbours, that her influence will probably survive, with little apparent injury, the effect of her discomfiture.

CHAPTER VI.

FRANCE AND SIAM.

THIRTY-FOUR years have passed since Napoleon III. was persuaded to utilize the Expeditionary force then on its way back from Tientsin, to conquer Cochin-China and found a French colony at Saigon. There were great potentialities in the enterprise, and the "forward" school of politicians were not slow to make them evident. It was discovered that Cambodia had been tributary to Annam as well as to Siam, and that the duty devolved upon France of assuming the responsibilities and privileges of her new acquisition. Then the dual suzerainty was found inconvenient; and negotiations were entered into which resulted in the cession, by Siam, of the sole protectorate to France—with the reservation, only, that Cambodia should never be incorporated as a Cochin-Chinese province. Then an expedition sent, under M. de Lagrée, to explore the Meikong, detected advantages that would result from planting the French flag along its banks; and when Dupuis had proved the practicability of reaching Yunnan by way of Hanoi, it occurred to certain people in Paris and at Saigon that it would be well to occupy Tongking. The desirability had now become evident of strengthening the Central Power whose outlying dependencies had been detached, and the blessings of civilization in the shape of a French protectorate were conferred upon Annam.

It seemed now, for a moment, that the natural limit of things had been reached. The Annamese empire had been once more compacted, and the mountains which separate it from the valley of the Meikong form an admirable scientific frontier. But historical students discovered that the kings of Cambodia had once owned a much larger territory than they now possessed, and that former kings of Annam had collected tribute in the Meikong valley. France clearly inherited all rights and duties this might be held to imply; and the potential claim was worked up till M. Ribot was moved to declare, two years ago, in the Chamber of Deputies, "that all the countries lying eastward of the Meikong, from the point where it leaves China, should belong to France." Now, the bearings of this observation, like an equally famous one of Captain Cuttle's, lie in the application of it. English interest is keenly concerned in the maintenance of Siam as a buffer State between Burmah and French territory. That interest might remain languid so long as French activity was confined to the lower Meikong; but it might conceivably become acute if the claim were pushed to its potential limits; for it not only involves the annexation of a region somewhat larger than Annam itself, which Siam alleges to have been under her own jurisdiction for more than a hundred years, but it would involve the alignment of France with our own frontier in the north, and the absorption of territory which the Anglo-Burmese Delimitation Commission has just ceded to Siam. It will scarcely be wasted time, therefore, to review certain facts that bear upon the French claim. Political boundaries in the Far East are frequently ill-defined; and in the Indo-Chinese peninsula, especially, warfare seems to have been well-nigh constant and the tangle of races to have become well-nigh inextricable. Certain historical outlines are, however, perceptible, and history is always useful in throwing light on modern development.

French relations with Siam date back, as is well known, to the days of Louis XIV.; and though the episode forms a well-known chapter of Oriental history, the details are sufficiently curious to deserve recapitulation at a time when Republican statesmen seem bent on reviving the policy and projects of the Great Monarch. Many strange things were done during those early days of European adventure when Holland and Portugal and France and England were striving with jealous rivalry to obtain concessions and commercial privileges along the coast-line of Southern Asia; but it would be hard to find an incident surpassing in eccentricity the attempt made by the French to convert and dominate Siam. They were curious times, in many ways. Nations that were hostile to each other in Europe carried their quarrels to India and Indo-China. Sects that were in rivalry at Rome carried their differences to China and Japan. Individual adventurers were carving out for themselves careers that led to power and fortune. Intrigue was rampant, diplomacy little scrupulous, and the propaganda overbearing in fanatical activity and aggression. One of the most dissolute of kings was finding salvation under the seductive influence of Madame de Maintenon and Père la Chaise: Colbert was trying to push French commerce; and both were willing to establish French influence in Siam, with a view to the advancement of the Church, the extension of trade, and the exaltation of the monarch who conceived himself the impersonation of France. When, therefore, Mgr. Pallu, who had been hospitably entertained by King Phra Narai, returned to Europe with projects of ecclesiastical, political, and commercial adventure, he gained a ready hearing at the French Court.

Phra Narai, who was then King of Siam, seems to have been constitutionally liberal. He had not only admitted the English and Dutch to trade in his dominions, but had sent to Goa to invite commercial relations with the Portuguese. There was, therefore, nothing surprising in his willingness to receive the French; though it is by no means unlikely that political motives may have predisposed him to welcome relations with a country which stood out as a rival to Holland. The Dutch Power loomed large, at that epoch, in the Eastern seas, and a king of Siam might think it wise to cultivate good relations with the Sovereign who had just concluded the Treaty of Nimeguen. The missionaries naturally took every opportunity to extol his greatness, for the firmer the foothold France could gain the stronger would be the position of the Church in Siam. When, therefore, the *Vautour*, bringing letters and presents from Louis XIV., arrived off the mouth of the Meinam (in September, 1680), Deslandes-Boureau was allowed all the commercial facilities he could desire, and Phra Narai was persuaded to send a responsive Embassy. Three Siamese officials and a suite of twenty persons, accompanied by a French priest as conductor and interpreter, set sail in the same year. But the ship which carried them was lost, with all on board, in a hurricane off the coast of Madagascar; and it was not till three years later that a Siamese Embassy put in an actual appearance at Versailles.

The broad outline of the ensuing episode forms, of course, a well-known chapter of Oriental history; but its details were hidden away in the French Colonial archives till M. Lanier[1] had the happy thought of disinterring them at a moment when French interest in Indo-China had received a fresh impulse. Confirmatory researches at the Quai d'Orsay subsequently enabled M. Marcel[2] to add some quaint particulars to the narrative; and we are

[1] "Relations de la France et du Royaume de Siam, &c." Versailles, 1883.

[2] "L'Expédition de Siam en 1687." *Révue de l'Etréme Orient*, October-December, 1884.

indebted to these writers for a story of romantic adventure, of unscrupulous intrigue, of pretension on the part of France, and resentment and eventual rebellion in Siam, that might tax our credulity if it were less well authenticated by extant records. The records, however, are there—French as well as Siamese: letters from kings and ministers, from envoys and missionaries, from military officers and commercial agents—and they have enabled the picture to be reproduced with circumstantial detail. Greek and Jesuit, abbé and factor, ambassador and mandarin, assume their places upon the stage, and afford a curious picture of the motives which prevailed in the French Court and disturbed the Eastern world during the closing years of the seventeenth century.

By one of those romantic chances to which the times were favourable, a Greek named Phaulkon had found his way to the Siamese capital, and had succeeded in attaining a position of considerable wealth and power. His commercial talents had recommended him to the Prime Minister, who had, in turn, recommended him to the King; and both seem to have trusted him largely in the management, at least, of foreign and commercial affairs. This man appears to have thrown himself heart and soul into the French interest. If it is often difficult to gauge the character of living statesmen in days of complete publicity, it is much more difficult to appreciate the motives that influenced a Greek adventurer holding a difficult position at an Oriental Court, two centuries ago. Messrs. Lanier and Marcel appear to concur in regarding him as an unscrupulous intriguer, careless of the interests of a too confiding master. But the surmise may be admissible that his motives were less wholly selfish. The elevation of a foreigner could hardly fail to excite the envy, hatred, and malice of Siamese courtiers, and Phaulkon might well feel the want of exterior support. It is by no means unlikely that in forwarding French interests, in protecting French missionaries, and admitting French soldiers, he may have been influenced measurably by a desire to make powerful friends. But it is not unreasonable to suppose that he was actuated, also, by a wish to secure political support for Siam. The Power which had just annexed Bantam was importuning for concessions on the coast of Tenasserim, and Phra Narai seems to have been in full accord with Phaulkon's policy of setting up France as a counterpoise to Holland. If the Most Christian King aimed at wholesale conversion where Phaulkon contemplated toleration, and at military and political predominance where he contemplated alliance, it is not fair to hold the Greek altogether responsible. Whatever his defects, he appears to have promoted commerce, inspired wise laws,[1] and helped the King to hold at bay the Burmese, who were soon to settle the question of Tenasserim by reaving it once for all from

[1] Mrs. Leonowens tells us that he is still remembered by his Siamese name of Vicha-yen (cool wisdom); that traces of his handiwork are still visible in the laws, buildings, and fortifications; and that all marvellous works are still attributed to gods, genii, devils, or to the Vicha-yen!—"The English Governess at the Siamese Court." London, 1871.

the Siamese grasp. He fills, at any rate, such a remarkable place in the narrative that it was necessary to fix attention upon his personality, in order to appreciate one of the principal forces in the political game.

It has been noted that the first Siamese Emissaries were engulfed before reaching the Cape. But the news had not reached Ayuthia three years after the event. Mgr. Pallu had, in the meantime, been again to Europe and brought back fresh letters from Louis XIV., which Phra Narai was persuaded to acknowledge by sending other envoys—personally conducted, again, by a French priest. The fact that this Mission sailed in an English ship may serve to indicate that the French Company had not yet availed itself very largely of the opening offered; and this comparative subordination of the commercial to the clerical element is a leading feature in the entire episode. The religious idea, as Deschamps has pointed out,[1] was in the ascendant. In the charters of the West India as well as of the East India Companies—under Richelieu as well as Colbert—the duty of promoting Christianity is connoted with the extension of commerce; and it is evident from the records before us that the idea dominated Louis XIV. in his dealings with Siam. Colbert and de Seignelay might see the wisdom of encouraging commerce, and of competing with Holland for the wealth which enabled her to hold out against France in Europe; but Père la Chaise

[1] "Histoire de la Question Coloniale en France." Paris. 1891.

evidently had a hand in shaping the course of negotiations. A return Embassy was decided on. A converted Protestant named de Chaumont and a converted rake named de Choisy were selected as its chiefs; and the following extract from their instructions will explain, better than any dissertation, the objects it had in view:—

"The principal object [writes de Seignelay] which His Majesty had in resolving to send an embassy to Siam is the hope, which the missionaries have given, of the advantage that religion would derive; and the hopes they have conceived, on sufficiently plausible grounds, that the King of Siam, touched by this mark of esteem, would finally make up his mind (acheveroit de se detérminer) to embrace the Christian religion for which he has already shown much inclination. His Majesty relies with the greater confidence that his intention in this respect will be executed, as he knows that the Sieur Chaumont makes particular profession of piety.

"His Majesty wishes also, in this voyage, to procure all possible advantages for the commerce of his subjects in the Indies."—etc., etc.

The French had, in the meantime, evidently been placed on a most friendly footing: the missionaries had been allowed to institute stations and establish hospitals; while Deslandes had been given every facility for commerce, and had only his superiors to thank if the English and Dutch were allowed to do the bulk of the business. De Chaumont had a gorgeous reception, in which every possible concession was made to European custom. The misfortune was that the whole edifice was built upon illusion. While Phra Narai wanted a defensive alliance, and Phaulkon wanted support and Colbert wanted commerce, Louis wanted the *éclat* of a grand diplomatic conversion. And so, while the King talked about Holland, and Phaulkon talked commerce, de Chaumont talked conversion, about which Phra Narai had never dreamed. The Greek did his utmost, as interpreter, to round off the edges of the conversation; but eventually the shock came. To a direct question by de Chaumont, the Siamese monarch replied drily that he saw no reason for abandoning a religion which his countrymen had exercised uninterruptedly for more than 2000 years!

The disillusion was terrible; and the envoys appear to have realized that the conclusion of a treaty[1] giving ample facilities to missionaries and remarkable concessions to the Company could not be expected to compensate, in the eyes of the Most Christian King. The view of the Siamese, "that heaven was a great palace which could be reached by many roads," would be simply incomprehensible to the monarch who was about revoking the Edict of Nantes; and Phaulkon met blank inattention when he broached the question of an offensive and defensive alliance to which all these concessions had doubtless been intended to lead up. The resources of Greek subtlety were not, however, exhausted. Foiled in his attempt to come to an understanding with the French Envoy, he looked about for other means, and found in a Jesuit named Tachard a congenial ally. The disciples of Loyola have always

[1] Signed at Louvo (the King's palace) by de Chaumount and Phaulkon, 10th December, 1685.

been willing to mix politics with religion; and have often mixed them, in the East, to their own detriment. In erudition and suppleness Tachard seems to have been a typical member of the order. He threw himself into Phaulkon's plans; and de Choisy frankly admits that he and de Chaumont became, thenceforward, mere puppets on the stage.

It was resolved to carry the negotiations to Paris; and Phra Narai was persuaded to despatch a fresh Embassy, of which, it need hardly be added, Tachard was to be the inspiring genius. Failing a dramatic conversion, political pre-eminence might conciliate the vanity of the French King; and a Jesuit might persuade Jesuits that more gradual methods would be more likely to result in success: the missionaries had ample opportunities to preach, and proselytize if they could; and Phaulkon offered to admit French garrisons into the ports of Mergui and Bangkok. The bait took. The Siamese were received with distinction at Versailles; and a responsive Embassy was sent, under La Loubère and Céberet de la Boullaye, accompanied by a detachment of troops under Des Farges who was to take possession of the proffered ports. Louis was willing, perhaps, to procure the Compagnie des Indes some compensation for the loss he was inflicting on it by forbidding the importation of Indian cottons, which were found to compete inconveniently with French manufactures. It seems, moreover, to have been impressed upon him that the establishment of commerce would best conduce to the execution of his other purposes; for the Envoys are instructed to "mettre les Français en estat de faire tout le commerce de toutes les Indes"; remembering always, however, that the promotion of religion is the ulterior object which his Majesty has in view! La Loubère, accordingly, was to inform himself about the politics, resources, military strength, and general condition of the country; Céberet was to negotiate a commercial treaty; while Des Farges was to fortify himself in the promised positions, with the aid of workmen whom he was to require from the King of Siam.

The Envoys set sail from Brest on March 1st, and reached the Meinam on September 27th, 1687. But again the divergence between the pretensions of Louis and the intentions of Phra Narai became quickly apparent. The ideas of France were the exaltation of the Church and military occupation and predominance in Siam; but Phaulkon declined to hand over the promised fortresses unless the French took an oath of fidelity, not only to the King but to himself! "Au Roi de Siam, passe encore," was the not unnatural exclamation; "mais à Phaulkon jamais." Rather than go back empty-handed, however, they consented to the exigency, though the event was to prove that the obligation lay lightly on their minds: and the Greek then fulfilled his portion of the compact. French garrisons under Des Farges and Du Bruant were admitted into Bangkok and Mergui; ample privileges were given to missionaries; and Céberet was enabled to conclude a treaty which gave the Company complete freedom of trade, with civil and criminal jurisdiction over its servants, the right of establishing factories where it pleased (en quelque lieu que ce soit du royaume), the promise of an island near Mergui—a treaty, in fact, which gave something like a monopoly of foreign trade with every conceivable facility for carrying it on. La Loubère, however, kept harping on the question of religion with a persistence that may well have seemed inexplicable in face of the large toleration that had been promised and decreed. It was difficult, indeed, for anyone who retained a measure of common sense to realize the fatuous credulity of Louis about this royal and national conversion, which the missionaries dangled before his eyes and which the Ambassadors were instructed to press for as a sort of diplomatic concession. If [wrote La Bruyère]—

> "If one assured us that the secret motive of the Siamese Embassy was to induce the Most Christian King to renounce Christianity, and give free course to Buddhist priests who were making their way into our houses to commend their religion to our wives and children and ourselves, who had built pagodas in the middle of our towns and set up metal images to be adored—with what laughter and contempt should we not receive such an extravagant proposition! Yet we go 6000 miles over sea to make seriously, to all those peoples, propositions which must appear to them equally foolish and ridiculous."

Even that picture fails to represent the full extravagance of the situation, for "those peoples" were actually permitting what would have appeared so monstrous if the situation had been reversed! But that was not enough. If Phaulkon pointed to the toleration afforded, the Envoys rejoined that mosques and Hindu temples were tolerated also; and desired that the King should be told, in so many words, that Louis' object was the advancement of Christianity!—not tolerance, in fact, but intolerance—the imposition on Siam of the *régime* which he was imposing on France. No wonder the worldly-wise Tachard could scarcely veil his contempt under a hint that the Apostolic Missionaries did not understand enough Siamese, and that they must wait till the Jesuits had mastered the language to see the King brought round!

An interchange of letters was going on, all this time, with Versailles; and the utterances of the French Court might almost tempt one to believe that Dumas' romance of the substitution of one twin for another erred only in supposing it to have been defeated by D'Artagnan's perspicacity. While the successor of Colbert writes politics and commerce, the priests invoice church furniture; while Seignelay instructs Des Farges about his fortifications, Louis orders him to exact from his soldiers the observance of Friday fasts, proper behaviour in church, a respectful bearing towards ecclesiastics, and abstinence from "berlands, académies, et autres lieux de débauche." Such an atmosphere of cant and cross-purposes could hardly fail to be redolent of intrigue. Phaulkon set himself to attach Des Farges to his own interests. Tachard schemed for the advancement of the Society of Jesus over the missionaries who had preceded it in the field. Veret, who was officiating as local agent for the Compagnie des Indes, hated Phaulkon and was ready to conspire against him and his Jesuit ally. The populace were angered by the indiscipline of the French troops, who conducted themselves as though they were in a conquered town. The jealousy of the Notables had been excited by the foreign leanings of the King and the aggressive attitude of the intruders; and it is not a little curious to find the Siamese Envoy, who had been the object of so much flattery at Versailles, among the chief leaders of the reaction which was to overthrow the political edifice and whelm stage and performers in a common ruin.

Phaulkon was too familiar with the Siamese not to perceive the dangerous nature of the forces that were at work. It was in a despairing effort, no doubt, to induce Louis to modify his attitude and to send a more supple Representative, that he persuaded Phra Narai to despatch another Embassy and to accredit, again, his ally Tachard. The failure to effect more sweeping conversions had to be palliated and explained; and both Tachard and Phaulkon agreed in throwing the onus on the bishops and the Missionaires Apostoliques. The discretion of the Jesuits, on the other hand, was lauded; and Tachard was commissioned to assure not only Louis XIV., but Pope Innocent, of Phra Narai's full intention to protect the Christians in his kingdom. He met a favourable reception at Rome; and, with Père la Chaise near the height of his influence, found the way smoothed for him at Versailles. Negotiations with Seignelay resulted in a fresh agreement, which may remind us of the famous treaty negotiated by Bishop Pigneau, a hundred years later, that paved the way for the assertion of French interests in Cochin-China. Its drift may be inferred from the fact that Louis sent with it, as a proof of goodwill, fifty French gentlemen to act as a Royal Guard, under the command of the Marquis d'Eragny who was to have supreme control over all French interests in Siam. M. Lanier scarcely exaggerates, in fact, when he thus sums up the situation :—

"Louis XIV., with the complicity more or less unforeseeing of Phaulcon, designed to complete by these measures the conquest of Siam. He occupied the approaches at Bangkok and Mergui. The troops under Des Farges overawed Siamese discontent, and closed the mouth of the Meinam against foreign enemies. The Marquis d'Eragny, installed at Court master of the Palace and the person of the King of whom he was instituted guardian,—at once captain, councillor, diplomat, and chief judge,—was to exercise under the guise of an obedient servant, a real protectorate disguised under the name of friendship, and impose if necessary by force, the suzerainty of the great Western King on this Asiatic vassal thus tardily undeceived."

It had been realized, however, before Burns, that "the best-laid schemes of mice and men gang aft aglee." All these beautiful arrangements were to be defeated by the unreasonable objection of the people for whose benefit they were designed. Before the expedition could set sail, a revolution at Ayuthia had swept away King, Greek, and garrison.

A dangerous feeling of irritation had, as we have seen, been long brewing at the Siamese capital.

Phra Phret Raxa, an official who seems to have occupied the position of Master of the Horse (and Elephants), placed himself at the head of the malcontents. The Dutch were evidently ready to give them something more than moral support; and the personal jealousies at which we have hinted were to exert a paralyzing influence on French action. Getting wind of the danger that was brewing, Phaulkon appealed in hot haste to the French garrison for support. But, after marching as far as Ayuthia, Des Farges allowed himself to be dissuaded by Veret and the missionaries, and returned to Bangkok, where he remained deaf alike to entreaty and reproach. The conspirators, accordingly, found their way clear. They surrounded the Palace; overcame, easily, what little resistance was offered; and accomplished their revolution with ridiculous ease. A certain obscurity shrouds the fate of Phra Narai, though native report credits him with suicide when he saw that his enemies had triumphed: Phaulkon was tortured and put to death with every species of contumely; and Phra Phret Raxa laid hold on the reins of power.

Too late, then, Des Farges decided on resistance. French interests had been bound up with Phaulkon and Phra Narai; but it was not, seemingly, till they were dead that he began to realize the fact. He refused to evacuate Bangkok, and held out against the efforts of the Siamese helped, it is alleged, by the Dutch—till provisions began to fail. Compelled, then, to surrender and accept the offer of transport to Pondichery, he tarnished his reputation by giving up Phaulkon's widow, who had thrown herself on French protection. It was part of the agreement that Mergui also was to be surrendered; but that had been already accomplished. Constrained by want of water, the garrison had cut their way out, and taken refuge on board a French ship in harbour. It was consistent with the romantic nature of the episode that they should be wrecked on the coast of Pegu and rescued by a Siamese vessel. It was consistent also with the curious obliquity of perception which characterizes too many of the actors in the drama, that Des Farges should return from Pondichery, occupy an island off Mergui and write, thence, to make fresh overtures which, it is hardly necessary to add, the Siamese promptly declined.

It seems to have been perceived in France, if it had not been apparent to Des Farges, that the death of Phaulkon meant the close of the opportunity. The expedition which had been destined for Ayuthia was diverted to Pondichery, whence the Siamese Envoys were forwarded to Mergui. Informal negotiations seem to have gone on, from time to time, during the next ten or fifteen years; but they were only the flickerings of the candle before it went out. The Siamese were willing to admit French commerce pure and simple; but the Great Monarch could conceive no status other than that of military occupation. We find, accordingly, an opening which had been effected, in 1697, by the irrepressible Tachard, closed because Louis wanted to occupy the forts at

Mergui. The son and successor of Phra Phret Raxa showed himself willing, six years later, to accept intercourse with France on the same terms as with other nations; but Louis still wanted advantages, and so got nothing. The whole matter then dropped; and it was not till 150 years later that another French Envoy was to open negotiations on a basis more in accord with modern ideas.

At the time these events were taking place on the Meinam, a Laotian Power was enthroned in the Meikong valley, with its capital at Wien-chang, nearly in the heart of the peninsula; and a Dutch Mission, which ascended the river in 1641, mentions that the Cambodians were being compelled to retire before its unceasing attacks. Soon after, however, according to Garnier,[1] it split into two principalities; and the Siamese and Annamese began a struggle for its heritage which ended, eventually, in favour of Bangkok. The Siamese affirm that the Annamese and Cambodians were expelled, about a hundred years ago, by the founder of the present dynasty; and claim to have held the country—loosely, no doubt, but to the exclusion at least of rivals—ever since. The conditions have not been those of a Roman Peace: there was a great revolt in 1829; there have been incursions of Chinese banditti in the north, and there has been fighting with Cochin-China about Cambodia in the south. A map published[2] only last year, by M. Fauvel, shows the Annamese

[1] "Voyage d'Exploration en Indo-Chine."

[2] In the *Révue Française.*

boundary of 1838 as overpassing even the Meikong; but it is difficult to resist the impression that this must represent, at the best, a temporary circumstance, even if it have any other foundation than the probable truth that the Laos have occasionally paid tribute to Hué as well as to Bangkok. The persistency with which French writers refer to this date seems indeed to indicate that they regard it as important to reduce the unassailable fact of Siamese occupation within the briefest possible limits. Their contention would seem to be that the suppression of the Laos revolt indicates its real origin; and M. de Lanessan twits the Siamese, in his famous work,[1] with only having been in possession of the disputed territory for fifty years. But even if this contention were admitted, the French claim would not be perceptibly strengthened, for it is at least an admission that Siam had been in possession for half a century at the time he wrote; and the map of Europe would be seriously disturbed if a general attempt were made to re-arrange it with reference to a date prior to 1836. There was no doubt, at any rate, about the state of things in 1866; for we find M. de Lagrée calling upon the Siamese authorities at Stung-treng and Khong for the boats and accommodation which "they had been ordered to supply, from Bangkok;" and Garnier admits incidentally that Siamese jurisdiction extended up to the Annamese mountains, as far as Attopeu, "which was the farthest eastern possession of Bangkok." He perceives, certainly, very

[1] "L'Expansion Coloniale de la France." Paris, 1866.

excellent reasons why the French flag should be hoisted at various trading centres along the river bank, with a view to fostering and developing the commerce that was to spring up under its shade; but the population is Laos and the Authority is Siamese.

The motive of de Lagrée's expedition was to examine the navigability of the Meikong and the commercial capabilities of the region which it drains. It was hoped that it might prove a practicable channel of intercourse with Yunnan, besides offering facilities for trade with the country along its banks. And that hope seems still to inspire French colonial policy, notwithstanding that it is now known to be broken by impassable rapids, and that the prospects of local trade appear slight and unpromising. Garnier's own observations point inevitably to these conclusions, though his sanguine temperament enabled him, as Mr. Archer [1] suggests, "to see the colours of the rainbow in a grey sky." Mr. Archer, however, was free from any such hallucination, and his sober conclusions can hardly fail to command interest at the present crisis:—

"The prospects of French trade in the Mĕ-kong Valley have of late years been vaunted to such a degree that I must take this opportunity to state that it seems to me impossible for a candid observer to conceive how French commerce can compete with the present trade of the country or find a profitable field in these regions. French goods are not suited to the people, and must

[1] *Report on a Journey in the Meikong Valley.* By W. J. Archer, H.M.'s Consular Service in Siam. Siam (Blue Book) 1 of 1892.

naturally be too expensive for them. It is hardly necessary to say that France cannot export piece-goods, yarn, or ironware, as cheap as Manchester and Birmingham, and it is precisely such goods that the people will buy. Communications in all the country east of Luang Prabang are so bad that to bring goods from Annam or Tonkin it would be necessary to incur an enormous outlay on improving the means of transport. Even were this done, I doubt whether Manchester or Birmingham goods such as the people require, subject to a high protective tariff and to the cost of transport by road, railway, or steamer, could undersell the imports from Bangkok. The only serious attempt that could be made to dispose of French goods in these regions would be (say) to prohibit all other imports. On the whole, this would not be quite an undesirable consummation, for it would restrict the people to their own manufactures, which are of better taste and stronger texture than any imported goods; and it would tend to preserve the industries of the country, which are threatened extinction by increased facilities for obtaining foreign goods. However, I am convinced that the present trade of Luang Prabang need not fear French competition; but, anyhow, it is so inconsiderable, and has so little room for development, that it is hardly worth making efforts to improve it. The plain facts are that Luang Prabang and its sister provinces on the north-east are a mass of mountains with hardly any soil available for plain cultivation, and with a sparse population, chiefly nomadic, that tends to emigrate westward to the richer territories of Nan and Chiengmai."

And again, with regard to the prospects of navigation:

"I do not in the least believe that steamers can ever be advantageously employed on this river for trading purposes. No steam-boat could safely make head against the treacherous current up the rapids or shoot them on the way down. . . . The regions of rapids in the Më-kong below Luang Prabang may be roughly placed in the following separate localities: Tha Düa, Chiengkhan, Kemarat, Khon, and Preatapang. Granted that steamers could be brought above these different rapids and navigated in the still reaches between them, how is the transport between the principal towns on the river to be effected? Are there to be unloading and reloading stations, and roads made past the rapids? If so, what is likely to be the cost of transport of small quantities of goods from Cambodia to Luang Prabang? It hardly requires a practical mind to make the proper answers to these questions; and I think I can do no better than quote the remark of the Commissioner at Luang Prabang, who, when a French traveller was trying to convince him of the practicability of bringing steamers up to Luang Prabang, silenced him by saying that he would undertake to build wharves for them at his own expense as soon as they arrived. But the absurdity of a scheme for the navigation of the Më-kong, from a commercial point of view, may be judged best by comparing it to a similar undertaking on the Më-nam. If a regular steam service up a large river from a port like Bangkok, that feeds the whole of the rich, populous valley above it, is hardly profitable, it is inconceivable that it should be more so up a difficult river, through a poor, mountainous, and sparsely-populated country. The high expectations recently raised of the navigability of the Më-kong can only come from those who have their own purposes to serve in leading the French commercial classes to suppose that there is a great possible market for French goods in a country that offers absolutely no such prospect. . . . It appears to me that the perusal of M. Garnier's work must necessarily bring an impartial observer to the conclusions that the Më-kong is difficult of navigation, the population small, and the trade insignificant. Trade naturally finds the route best suited to it, and that to Bangkok is the only one of any importance for the Më-kong Valley from Cambodia to Luang Prabang; but when, moreover, the Siamese Government completes the construction of the railway to Korat, which it is about to undertake, neither Cambodia nor Annam can have any chance of competing with Korat for the trade of the Më-kong Valley. Korat is the natural feeder of that country; and there can be no doubt as to its importance as a trade centre, nor as to the necessity for railway communication with Bangkok."

Mr. Archer did not extend his journey to the Lower Meikong. He quitted the river at Chieng-khah (about 18 N.), where it makes its second great easterly bend; but Garnier's observations and recent experiments confirm his statements as to the impracticability of the lower rapids. Khong and Stung-treng, which the French have recently occupied, are the capitals, respectively, of the provinces next above Cambodia. Stung-treng, which stands on the east bank of the Meikong, contained at the time of Garnier's visit about 800 inhabitants, all Laotians. What commerce it possessed was in the hands of Chinese, who brought up betel nut, sugar, salt, and silk and cotton goods, and took back cardamom, wax, lacquer, ivory, skins, and trifling articles of native manufacture. Both provinces lie to the left of the Meikong; but the town of Khong stands on an island in the river bed, just above the rapids of Khone, which have so far been found impassable by steam. Gunboats are accordingly being sent out in pieces, to be put together above the rapids; and the Colonial Government has voted a subvention of $20,000 for the purpose of placing a cargo steamer on the upper reach, which is navigable to Kemaret and possibly farther during a certain period of the year. In point of commercial importance Khong seems about on a par with Stung-treng. Garnier is emphatic, however, in his declaration that the French flag must be hoisted, not only on the island but on the right bank, "to protect the transshipment of merchandise at the cataract." It is true, the right bank is Siamese; but so, as we have seen, was the whole region. That, however, is a trifle: it had once been Cambodian! And M. de Lagrée returned from an exploration of the Tonly Repou, a little river which falls into the Meikong on the west, with a conviction that France ought also to acquire the province of that name, which she might fairly claim on Cambodia's behalf as Siam had only gained possession of it, a generation or so previously, through the rebellion of a Cambodian Governor who had thrown himself on the protection of Bangkok! It is true the Siamese describe the event in question as an appeal for Siamese protection during one of the chronic invasions of Cochin-China; but that only shows the perversity of the Siamese! And so on up the river. The protection of the French flag was equally required at Bassac, "whose natural advantages point it out as one of the points in the Lower Laos where French influence should be most solidly planted."

The records of the expedition seem, indeed, to have been a sort of Peter the Great's will, tracing a scheme of French adventure. But even Garnier, to do him justice, does not appear to have dreamed of anything so sweeping as the annexation of the region between the Meikong and the Annamese crest. Those who have read his monumental work will not need to be reminded that it contains two maps, one of which was compiled from the best sources at his disposal, before setting out, while the other was the result of careful survey and inquiry elucidated by all the help the Siamese could give, during the course of his journey; and it is significant that, while the former makes the Siamese boundary run along the crest of the mountains, the latter brings it only a very little farther to the west. The maps, therefore, constitute a pertinent admission of the state of things in 1866-8.

Nothing, indeed, is more curious than the French complaints of "encroachment," by Siam, in a region where Garnier found her officials established, and where her authority is alleged to have been predominant for more than a hundred years. The complaint seems based, mainly, on alleged breaches of an agreement to maintain the *status quo* pending definite delimitation. An agreement to that effect appears to have been proposed by Siam herself, when French claims upon the eastern half of the Meikong valley began (about 1888) to take official shape. Siam asked then, and has repeatedly asked since, that the frontier should be surveyed and delimited. Pending such a settlement, she proposed the observance of a neutral zone, 30 miles wide, between the 13th and 19th degrees of latitude. This was, she considered, already a concession, as the whole tract was under her jurisdiction and it was for the French to disprove her claim. There does seem, however, this much ground for the charge—that both parties failed to observe, strictly, the limits of the neutral zone. Siam declares that the Franco-Annamese began encroaching on their side, and that she was driven to advance on hers if she would not see the territory occupied in her despite; while a recent article in the *Révue Française* accuses the Siamese of having taken up positions close to the Annamese slope and of having, in one case, even passed the watershed and approached within thirty miles of Hué. This is the muddying of the water which excited so much indignation in the French Press, and which the French representative at Bangkok was instructed to terminate, once for all, by asserting a claim to the whole left bank of the Meikong, and by demanding that Siam should evacuate all her military posts to the east of that river.

The storm had, as we have seen, been long brewing. The idea that French "rights" might be made to stretch to the Meikong found casual expression soon after the extension of the Protectorate over Annam and Tongking. Neïs, Pavie, and other travellers began, at first casually, and afterwards systematically, to explore and map out the whole Laos country. The subject was discussed by M. de Lanessan, the present Governor-General of French Indo-China, in the work written after his visit to the peninsula in 1886, and has been kept alive by the Deloncles and politicians of the adventurous colonial school. But it was when Siam decided to make a railway to Korat that it took form and substance, and was elevated into a political maxim. In the work already quoted, de Lanessan had gone so far as to urge that that project should be thwarted by every possible means. French interests lay in trying to drain the commerce of the country south-eastward towards Cambodia and Cochin-China, while the Korat railway, as we have seen with Mr. Archer, would encourage its tendency to flow south-westward to Bangkok. It was time to do something if that conclusion was to be defeated; and hence, apparently, the resolve to obtain timely possession of the rival channel. On March 1st last, 206 years exactly after de Chaumont set sail from Brest, M. Develle announced that he had come to an understanding with the Colonial Department as to the measures to be taken to ensure French rights. The occupation of Khong and Stung-treng by a Franco-Annamese contingent quickly followed. Another force, marching across the mountains farther north, descended the valley of the Se-bang-hien, pushing the Siamese before them, to the banks of the Meikong opposite Kemaret. A telegram, dated June 3rd, announced that the post of Kham Muon, on the river Kading, had been vacated at the summons of M. Luce; and a further telegram, dated ten days later, stated that all posts occupied by the Siamese in the territories between Kham Muon, Houten and Nong Kay had been evacuated, and that the Siamese had recrossed the Meikong to the right bank. The occupation of these places would, in fact, complete the clearance of the Lower Laos, as distinguished from the northern or Luang Prabang region; and France was, doubtless, well assured that no one would contest her progress so far.

It is above the parallel of 18° N. that English and Chinese interests tend to become acute; and it remains to be ascertained how much farther she will be allowed to advance along the upper reaches of the river. Even the territory claimed by M. Ribot—the left bank up to frontier of Yunnan—would hardly satisfy the more eager politicians. M. Demanche[1]

[1] *Révue Française*, June 15th, 1893.

urges, for instance, that Annamese domination once extended nearly up to the crest of the watershed which divides the Meikong from the Meinam; M. de Lanessan has, himself, expressed aspirations after the basin of the Se-moun, while a work entitled *La France et L'Angleterre en Asie*[1] contains a series of maps suggesting various divisions of the peninsula, ranging from the preservation of a diminished Siamese kingdom in the south to a complete partition in which even Yunnan is coloured French! These may be taken as the irresponsible conceptions of irresponsible writers; but there has been just published, under official auspices, a splendid map[2] which all available information has been utilized to complete—except that it leaves the question of frontier absolutely blank! It would have been satisfactory to infer that this implied a willingness to consider the dispute open to negotiation and settlement by historic proof: nothing could be fairer than the Siamese proposal that both sides should bring forward evidence in support of their respective claims, and that resort should be had to arbitration in case of inability to agree. The high-handed action of the Government, however, quickly precluded any such supposition; and France can hardly complain if the world choose to suspect her of inability to substantiate her claim.

[1] Par Philippe Lehault. Paris, 1892.

[2] Carte de l'Indo-Chine dressée sous les auspices du Ministre des Affaires Etrangères et du sous-Sécrétaire d'Etat des Colonies; par les Capitaines Cupet, Friquegnon et de Malglaive, Membres de la Mission Pavie, etc.

CHAPTER VII.

ENGLAND, CHINA, AND SIAM.

We have seen that Siam met the French demand that she would recognize Annamese rights on the left bank of the Meikong, by expressing a willingness to do so as soon as they were defined, and by proposing that a Commission should be appointed to examine the merits of the contention. We have seen, also, that the French Government apparently ignored the proposal, and confined itself to insisting on its claim. The facts that Garnier found the Siamese dominant throughout the Meikong valley, that de Lanessan is constrained to admit they had been established there for at least fifty years, and that Chaigneau, who carries us back to the beginning of the century (he having lived at Hué many years prior to 1820) expressly affirms that Annam was then bounded by the mountains which extend down its western frontier—seem to have been ignored or treated as of no account. It has been shown, in previous chapters, that the project of enlarging their possessions at the expense of Siam had been long present in the minds of French politicians, and the time had arrived for putting it in execution. La Fontaine only stereotyped a familiar fact, in noting that pretexts are seldom lacking when quarrel has been determined on. The facts that a French official and his escort were killed while conducting the Siamese magistrate out of Kham-muon, that a French officer was captured by local levies who objected to the occupation of Khong, and that certain French gunboats were fired on while ascending the Meinam in defiance of the treaty and of their own instructions, were as good pretexts as any other for pressing matters to an issue. The *Intransigeant* admitted: "We are going to Siam under pretence of avenging an insult, but really with the idea of making a new conquest."

At a Cabinet Council held on July 18th, it was resolved, accordingly, to present an ultimatum in the following terms:—(1) Recognition of the rights of Annam and Cambodia to the left bank of the Meikong and the islands; (2) evacuation of the posts held there by the Siamese within one month's time; (3) satisfaction for the various aggressions against French subjects in Siam and French ships and sailors in the Meinam; (4) punishment of the culprits and pecuniary indemnities to the families of victims; (5) indemnities of two million francs for various damages inflicted on French subjects; (6) immediate deposit of three million francs as a guarantee for these claims or, in default, an assignment by way of security of the revenues of Battambong and Angkor. Should these terms not be accepted, the French Minister would leave, and the coast be blockaded forthwith.

The reply of the Siamese Government was admirable. It again regretted that no precise definition had ever been given of what it was to understand by the expression "rights of the Empire of Annam and of the Kingdom of Cambodia on the left bank of Meikong." It had always been ready to abandon any territories over which those rights could be proved, and had proposed, five months earlier, to submit all contested points to international arbitration. Yielding now, however, to the pressure of circumstances, it consented to delimitation on the following terms: "All territory on the left bank of the Meikong south of a line drawn [practically along] the eighteenth degree of north latitude, to be regarded as Annamese and Cambodian territory; the river below this point becoming the line of separation, and the use of the islands in the river being common to the three conterminous States." For the rest, reparation would be made as demanded, and 3,000,000 francs would be immediately deposited to cover the griefs enumerated; though—"believing that, after proper inquiry, this sum would be found to exceed the amount of indemnities claimable—the king relied upon the justice of the French Government to refund any balance that might remain available after the settlement of the different cases."

The French, however, declined any such qualified concession, and ordered the immediate institution of the threatened blockade. What was perhaps more serious—a cry for the occupation of Battambong and Angkor made itself heard; and the king, feeling that hesitation would only open the door to further requirements, supplemented his answer by an expression of unreserved acquiescence.

Even this failed, however, to satisfy the growing exigencies of the French Government. Accepting the submission in a tone which seemed to imply that the contumacy shown might have entailed unknown penalties at the hands of a less benevolent Power, M. Develle went on to formulate additional conditions as guarantees for the execution of the first demands. (1) France was now to occupy the port and river of Chantaboon, pending the evacuation of the left side of the Meikong by Siam; (2) No Siamese troops were to be allowed within 25 kilometres of the Meikong; (3) Siam was to have no armed vessels on the Great Lake; (4) The French were to have a right to establish consulates at Nan and Korat.

The idea of imposing a second ultimatum, as a guarantee for the execution of the first, is so remarkable that the thought occurs whether a certain section of French politicians were not disappointed that the Siamese surrender placed a limit to their enterprise. It is, as we have seen, patent that the recent aggression is the outcome of a long-planned design; and it is equally certain that the provinces of Battambong and Angkor have long been objects of envy to French colonial politicians.

Writing several years ago, the present Governor-General of Indo-China recorded his impression of this region in the following terms:

> "The Great Lake has not merely a great economic importance; it has also an immense political value. The entire possession of that great depression and of the basin which it drains is one of the most important *desiderata* of the work which we have hitherto pursued in an empirical way, but which we can and should accomplish henceforth systematically. The western part of the lake especially—namely, the part which our too ignorant or too careless diplomacy ceded to Siam with the provinces of Battambong and Angkor—is one of the vital points of the peninsula, from whatever point of view, commercial, political, or military, we regard it."

And again:

> "All the efforts of the Government of Indo-China should be directed towards repairing the injuries inflicted by the deplorable treaty of 1867. It may be said that the interest of Siam is also at stake. In assuring to her the protection of her independence, which is destined to be constantly threatened by England, we might easily obtain, without striking a blow, a modification of the treaty of 1867, which would secure for Cambodia not only the whole of the Great Lake, but also the provinces of Battambong and Angkor, which ought to constitute, in this point of the Indo-Chinese peninsula, the limit of our reasonable ambition."

It was the known existence of these aspirations that caused the stipulated lien on the revenues of Battambong and Angkor to be viewed with so much apprehension; and it is by the light of these aspirations that we must judge the proposal to occupy Chantaboon when it seemed likely that Siam would be able to prevent the execution of that clause. Chantaboon is the second port in point of importance in the Siamese dominions, and is situated in the Gulf of Siam, on the river of the same name.

The trade is carried on chiefly by Chinese, though a British company holds a concession for working the deposits of precious stones for which the neighbouring mountains are famous. But what is more significant is that it is the port of Battambong; and here is what M. de Lanessan has to say regarding it:

> "Battambong communicates by a march of five or six days with Chantaboon, a port in the Gulf of Siam, inhabited principally by colonies of Annamese and Chinese. This route has now acquired much importance in consequence of the working of the sapphire mines of Payrinh, and it is by this way that arms and munitions of war are introduced into Cambodia. If we succeeded in utilizing our new position in Annam so as to demand from Siam the protection of the Annamese, who are very numerous throughout the whole of the Lower Meinam, on the coast, and especially at Chantaboon, we should necessarily be led to place a vice-consul at the port, which interests us in many ways, and at which no one could dispute the preponderant influence of our agent."

It is scarcely surprising, in presence of these remarks, and of the obvious superfluity of the occupation as a guarantee, that apprehension should be felt lest there lurk behind the demand a possibility of further complications that might indefinitely retard the withdrawal of the occupying force. It is true that all this was written when the author was in a position of greater freedom and less responsibility; but the very fact that he does now hold the post in which, of all others, he may be supposed able to influence French policy in Indo-China must tend to confirm the apprehension with which these ancillary demands are viewed. The *République*

Française has indeed admitted, with the frankest cynicism, that Siam is not out of the wood. "After satisfaction has been obtained, we must (it says) give the king to understand that at the first outbreak on his part we will seize two of his provinces as security." Which those two provinces would be, we may now be able to infer. Nor should the fact that these are only side issues, appearing as it were incidentally among French demands, be allowed to obscure our perception of their gravity; for they clearly constitute a possible danger to the integrity of Siam in which England has avowed a vital interest. The French Government has committed itself to an explicit declaration of its intention to respect this integrity, and Lord Rosebery has doubtless "taken note" of the assurance; but a more definite understanding will be desirable, to strengthen the treaty of 1867 in respect to provinces which constitute a vital portion of the kingdom.

The language of the ultimatum regarding the Meikong was judiciously vague. It demanded recognition of the rights of Annam and Cambodia to the left bank of the river and the islands, without indicating at what point those rights began. But M. Ribot had previously defined them as extending from the frontier of Yunnan to the sea; and some less responsible politician, inebriated apparently by the exuberance of his own imagination, was found to affirm that they extended up to 23° north. Seeing that this would carry them well within the frontier of Yunnan, it is scarcely surprising that the

Chinese representative should have taken occasion to call at the Quai d'Orsay and remark that Siam had no territory to cede, so far north as the parallel indicated; while England no doubt hinted that there existed, even two degrees lower, territory lately belonging to Burmah which she had yielded to Siam on the express condition that it should not be ceded to another Power.

Siam offered, as we have seen, in her first reply, to yield everything up to 18° north. That would practically mean giving up the eastern half of the old kingdom of Wien-chang, which she finally extingushed in 1834, and which is now commonly known as the Lower Laos. There would remain the principality of Luang Prabang and the States of Kiang-cheng and Kiang-hung. The interests of England and China will presumably safeguard the two latter. It remains to be ascertained, only, where the boundaries should be fixed; and how far the "buffer" principle may be held to permit, or hinder, the partition of Luang Prabang.

A good deal has been said about feudal relations between China and Siam. It was announced by telegram, from Tientsin, that China was preparing to take up the cause of her tributary, and was preparing even to come to her help. The statement emanated, doubtless, from a Chinese source; but it must, I think, have originated in exaggeration or misconception, in so far as it expressed a thought of championing the whole cause of Siam.

China has, apparently, tributary rights over the

province of Kiang-hung, which lies astride the Meikong immediately below Yunnan: but Kiang-hung is not Siamese. She has also, undoubtedly, great interests in Siam. She is interested in the territory along the left bank of the Meikong as far south as Luang Prabang, through which her caravans pass from Yunnan on their way to traffic with the Shan States and Burmah. She has also the great interest implied in the residence at Bangkok and, indeed, throughout the whole country, of immense numbers of her subjects who are occupied in various industrial pursuits and do the greater part of the retail trade. M. Gaston Rautier estimated, some years ago, in the *Révue Française*, that there are in Siam as many Chinese as Siamese. Taking the total population at 10,000,000, he estimated that it is made up of nearly one-third Chinese, one-third Siamese, with Malays, Laotians, and Cambodians in about equal proportion, for the rest. The Chinese are, he says, all over the country, in every rank of life, competing in every occupation, and tending to absorb the whole trade. The Government revenues, even, are often farmed to them. And he proceeds to argue that this preponderance of Chinese is a political danger, because the time may come when they may refuse obedience to Siamese laws.

It is obvious, at any rate, that the presence in Siam of such a vast number of her subjects must give China an immense influence, if the interests of the Empire impelled her to stir up a political movement. But, far-reaching as that influence may be, I do not think China would be disposed to assert, or Siam to admit, the existence of tributary relations between the two Courts. That such relations have existed in the past seems beyond dispute; though they were far from being of the intimate nature that characterized those with Annam. Chinese statements about tribute require to be taken with reserve, for every envoy who approached the Emperor was spoken of as a "tribute-bearer," and every present which he brought, as "tribute." But there was, as we have seen in a previous chapter, a difference between these vague pretensions and the precise relations by which vassalage was really defined; and Siamese kings do appear to have complied, from time to time, with certain prescriptions which justified China in considering them tributary, in a different sense from the European nations whose occasional embassies flattered her pride.

The Court records[1] of the Manchu dynasty speak of Siam under the name of Sien-lo, and say that it sent an envoy requesting to be enrolled as tributary, in the reign of Shun-chih, though it was not till several years later, in the reign of Kanghi, that a patent and a seal of office were issued (1673), investing the ruler as king; and it is curious to note a contemporary decree providing that, as the Siamese ships have to come a long sea journey, any article of tribute that may have been damaged during the journey need not be replaced. A century later,

[1] *Vide* "The Tributary Nations of China." By G. Jamieson. *China Review*, 1883.

again, a new "chief of Siam" sent "messengers with tribute;" and it is interesting to note, this time, a reference to the wars between Burmah and Siam. In the year 1766, the record runs, "the country was broken up by the attacks of Burmah, and the dynasty changed to that of a family named Cheng." But the new ruler "sent a mission of tribute in 1786, and obtained investiture as king; a silver-gilt seal of office being handed to the envoys, together with the patent of investiture, to carry back." It would be tiresome to multiply quotations; but one more instance may perhaps be noted, as showing that the Siamese were disposed, from the first, to assert a superiority over some other dependents of the Empire. In the very first year of his reign, the great Emperor Kien-lung was called upon to decide a grave question of etiquette arising out of these aspirations. The Siamese envoy had, it would seem, asked to be treated on the same terms as Corea; that is, by being invited to sit down and have tea in the Audience Hall. But it was decided that this favour was allowed Corea because her envoys were nearly on a par with ministers of the Empire, which was not the case with other tributaries such as Annam and Siam: only in case these states sent a brother or son of the reigning prince, as envoy, could the favour sought be accorded.

At what time precisely these relations lapsed no one knows, probably, but those concerned. But it may be taken as unquestionable that the letter[1] addressed

[1] See *ante*, chap. v. p. 143.

twenty years ago to the *N.-C. Herald* represents the attitude of the Siamese Government at the present day. China, we know, is conservative; she interferes very little with her tributaries—especially with distant ones; and means were, I believe, taken, subsequently to that letter, to convey to the Siamese Court that things would be made easy for it if it would fall back on the ancient ways. The king was, however, obdurate in refusing to send envoys otherwise than by way of Tientsin, and so the matter dropped. It might have been better, perhaps, if he had been less punctilious; for, though China did not succeed in saving Tongking, she was the means of causing its conquest to be so costly that France might have hesitated to plunge into a similar enterprise if she had avowed as much interest in the Meikong as she avowed in the Songkoi.

As matters now stand, China will not interfere, and never dreamed, probably, of interfering, to protect Siam from loss of territory on the Lower Meikong; though she was undoubtedly disturbed by the French advance, and her anxiety might become more acute if the Meikong were overpassed and French "interests" were found to extend to the watershed of the Meinam. She has asserted, however, and England is understood to admit, her interest in Kianghung. It has been shown in a previous chapter that, by M. de Lanessan's own admission, Siam was in possession of the Lower Meikong, at any rate, fifty years ago. Even that is a fairly long title as things go, in a quarter of the world where perpetual warfare between Annamese and Siamese, Laos, Khmer, Burman and Shan seems to have been the normal condition as far back as we are able to penetrate; and we have, curiously enough, the unimpeachable testimony of an English officer to the position of affairs in Kiang-hung at that very date. The Journal of the Asiatic Society of Bengal for 1837 contains an account of a journey made by Lieut. MacLeod from Maulmain to Kiang-hung, which has exceptional interest at the present crisis.

MacLeod's object was to open up trade with that region, and to persuade Chinese and Shan traders to prolong their journeys to British territory. He made his way first to Zimmé, which was then, as now, under Siamese authority, where he found Chinese merchants residing, and where a Chinese caravan arrived during his stay. The Siamese wanted him to go on by the left bank of the Meikong, being moved by jealousy of the Burmese whose authority prevailed in the State of Kiang-tung through which he would have to pass if he persisted in a northerly route. The Chinese, however, advised him that the way through Kiang-tung was the best; so he persevered, and was allowed to proceed.

He found Kiang-tung governed by a native (Shan) Tsawbwa, from whose revelations we gain a curious glimpse of the turmoil into which the country had been thrown by the constant warfare between Burmah and Siam. He was, he told MacLeod, one of six brothers who had rebelled thirty years previously against the Burmese and placed themselves under the protection of Siam. His brothers were still interned at Zimmé; but he, seeing reason to distrust Siamese promises, had broken back to his native place and again become tributary to Ava, though he seemed to have little affection for one, more than for the other, of his neighbours.

Pursuing his journey through a region which had been lately overrun by the Siamese, and seemed to be slowly recovering from the ruin which Oriental incursions usually leave behind, MacLeod made his way next to Kiang-hung; and it is his observations on the political position there, that have special interest at the present moment. The town stood in 21·58° N. and 100·39° E., on the face of a hill on the right bank of the Meikong which varied, here, from 300 to 650 feet in breadth according to the season. It was, he found, the capital of a large province. It was tributary to Burmah, to which it "made certain offerings of submission and dependence once in three years," and which had a representative there to look after its interests. But it was also tributary to China, to which "it paid a regular land revenue and other taxes, to collect and regulate which an establishment of Chinese officers and clerks was kept." At a dinner given him at the palace, he found not only the Tsawbwas but the attendants clad in Chinese costumes and the dinner completely Chinese. It is interesting to note, moreover, that the Shans seemed thoroughly well affected towards their Chinese overlords: these insisted on the regular payment of taxes, and wrote long letters about a few farthings, but they never took or kept any sum they were not entitled to.

MacLeod wanted to continue his journey to Szumao, the frontier town of Yunnan; but was restrained from doing so until permission could be obtained from the Chinese authorities. He caused these to be informed accordingly; but he might have spared himself the trouble. The Chinese have, as we have seen, but one idea in regard to foreign envoys: they all bring tribute, and are all bound to travel by a given route. "British ships," ran the answer, "daily visit Canton; and that was the proper route for an officer deputed on a mission to go: they had consulted their historical records, but could not find any precedent for an official coming that way; if he insisted in doing so, it would be necessary to refer the matter to Peking!"

MacLeod next proposed to cross the Meikong and return by the left bank; but if there is one thing which an Oriental dislikes, it is change. He had come by way of Kiang-tung, and he must go back by way of Kiang-tung. Besides, the Burmese were as anxious to get him back as the Chinese were to prevent his going on. He returned accordingly by the way he had come, little dreaming that his narrative would be appealed to, fifty-five years later, as proof of Chinese "rights" against the pretensions of France.

So much for Kiang-hung. Shan by nationality, it appears to be Chinese by political affinity; and England, as the heir of Burmah, is understood to purpose yielding her interest to China, in the course of the frontier rectifications that are now in progress along the Burmo-Chinese frontier.

The adjoining province of Kiang-cheng is in a somewhat similar case, except that Burmese claims were here shared with Siam. Like Kiang-hung, it sits astride the Meikong; and England yielded it to Siam, in the course of frontier delimitation between the two States, on the understanding that Siam should not cede it to any other Power. She was, therefore, in a position to object to its cession to France, and to insist on its being upheld as a buffer between French and British territory. She had, also, ulterior interests, which were no doubt present in the minds of our diplomatists when arranging for its future safety. Kiang-cheng figures prominently in the scheme of railway communication with Yunnan which Mr. Holt Hallet has so warmly advocated, and upon whose advantages Lord Lamington dwelt in a recent address to the London Chamber of Commerce. Mr. Hallett's scheme involved a Siamese trunk-line, from Bangkok to Szumao, which England should tap at Raheng by a branch line from Maulmain. Siam does not seem to have fallen in with that idea, and is confining herself, at present, to a line from Bangkok to Korat which she purposes, or did purpose, extending to Nong-kay. This, she appears to conceive, will best meet her own requirements; and extensions towards China may be left to international enterprise. If these extensions are ever made, it is through Kiang-cheng and Kiang-hung that they would have to run; and as the Siamese and Chinese tariffs are only five per cent., while the French impose heavy duties on everything that is not French, we may be pardoned for preferring that Kiang-cheng and Kiang-hung should continue, respectively, Siamese and Chinese. It may be taken, probably, that England and China have expressed that wish with sufficient definiteness during recent negociations; and that the only remaining question is to ascertain the area over which these provinces extend. That is the problem with which diplomacy is at present concerned. It would be premature, therefore, to do more than indicate a river called the Nam-u, which runs into the Meikong near Luang Prabang, and a mountain range on the N.E. which seems to constitute its watershed, as affording, possibly, the requisite materials for its solution.

There remains the principality of Luang Prabang which used apparently to be independent, in the days when the Laos ruled in the Meikong Valley, but which has long since become a dependency of Siam. The Lower Laos may be taken as having passed, now, under the dominion of France. How far the Upper Laos is to undergo a similar fate is a question upon which no decisive statement has yet been made, but in regard to which grave apprehensions are entertained. There is no doubt that the French are extremely anxious to acquire this region. The town of Luang Prabang, which is situated at the corner of the second great bend, has already been designated on French maps as the objective point of a line of railway from Tongking. Mr. Archer speaks of it as "a large straggling village of bamboo huts interspersed with brick temples." He describes the river valley here as narrow, with very little plain country. The people live, like the Chinese, mainly on fish, rice and pork. Fever is very prevalent, and even the Siamese troops quartered there are said to consume inordinate quantities of quinine. Possession of Luang Prabang, however, would carry with it possession of all the territory comprised in the elbow of the first great bend; and it is for that reason so much interest attaches to this section of the French claim. A map which was drawn by Mgr. Taberd, then Bishop of Cochin-China, in 1838—a date to which the French are fond of referring—though asserting an Annamese claim to the Middle Meikong, excludes Luang Prabang and, indeed, all west of 104°. MacLeod also remarks that Luang Prabang was distinctly tributary to Siam, to which it paid tribute "of ivory, eaglewood" and other produce; and the tendency has certainly been to convert vassalage into implicit subjection, and to strengthen the exercise of Siamese jurisdiction, in the interval. He adds, however, that it "is said to be also tributary to Cochin-China and China,[1] to the former of which it sends presents triennially, and to the latter once in eight years."

[1] It is curious to find mention made in the Chinese Court records of a Laos state, named Nan-chang, sending tribute for the first time (A.D. 1730) during the reign of Kienlung. The country is described as lying south of Yunnan, and adjoining Burmah. *V. China Review, ut supra.*

It would be difficult to find a more perfect object lesson of the confused relations between these border states, out of which France has evolved such exaggerated claims. Lower Cochin-China, Annam, and Tongking have formed, for centuries, one dominion; Siam and Burmah were equally sovereign states looking up, in a greater or less degree, to the preponderant mass of China; but all the petty states along their borders seem to have paid tribute to each more powerful neighbour. The French Protectorate over Cambodia was evolved out of the fact that it paid tribute to Cochin-China as well as to Siam. It is quite possible that the Lower Laos was once in similar case. Writing of the basin of the Se bang-hien, M. de Lanessan says, "up to 1830, the Annamese administered these provinces either directly or through the intermediary of the local chiefs, collecting tribute and taxes. About 1830 they were driven back by the Siamese to the chain of mountains which border the Meikong valley, and have not since been able to recover the lost ground." Siam contends, as we know, that the alleged possession merely implies that the Annamese intervened during an insurrection. The incident may, however, serve to explain the political instability and unrest which led these states to make presents, indiscriminately, to neighbours so much more powerful than themselves. It does not necessarily follow that the tribute meant, in each case, an acknowledgment of equal rights. A kingdom can no more serve two masters than a man, though both may be willing to propitiate a powerful friend. The influence of Siam was unquestionably predominant in Cambodia, though tribute was also paid to Annam. Kiang-hung was mainly Chinese, though it had tributary relations with Burmah; and Luang Prabang is essentially Siamese, even if it has had secondary relations with Annam. The Siamese authorities, who were unwilling that MacLeod should travel through Kiang-hung because it was Burmese, were willing that he should travel along the east bank of the Meikong because it was Siamese. When the so-called Hôs burst into the country, after the French invasion of Tongking, it was the Siamese who restored order. French surveyors on the Upper Meikong have travelled, quite lately, with Siamese assistance. It is scarcely surprising, therefore, that the Siamese should have challenged the French to produce proof of the claims which they so confidently advanced—nor, perhaps, that the French should avoid debating the issue.

We may be in a position, now, to estimate with tolerable accuracy the rival forces and interests that are at work in this much-vexed region. Siam was precluded, as we have seen, from appealing to China as her overlord, because she had protested her independence and had refused to acquiesce in relations that might wear a tributary aspect. She was precluded, similarly, from appealing to England, because she rejected an English Protectorate when it was offered her, I believe, some years ago; before its assertion would have involved acute antagonism to the still inchoate projects of France.

She could appeal, however, to both England and China, as interested parties; and it lay with those Powers to define where their interests began. The interests of China in Indo-China are, as we have seen, enormous: there is an immense Chinese population in Siam and, indeed, throughout the whole peninsula—in Burmah and the Straits Settlements as well as in Tongking and Saigon. It would be in her power to foment a rebellion that would shake the French position to its foundations, and to help it by pouring troops across the frontier of Yunnan into the Meikong valley, as she poured them out of Kwangtung through Langson into Tongking. China, however, prefers peace; and so long as her frontiers are guarded at Kiang-hung, and her caravan routes are protected through Kiang-cheng and Luang Prabang, she will let sleeping dogs lie. She will do well, however, to assert her influence and her power with more emphasis in time of peace, if she would exercise the weight to which her position entitles her, in the councils of the Far East. There was a time when people were disposed to smile at the power of China; when they were disposed, in fact, to smile at everything Chinese. But she is becoming recognized as a substantial fact, and she must resolve to sustain her *rôle*. She cannot, consistently with her dignity, disavow ulterior interests in a country where so many myriads of her subjects are domiciled; and she would do well to declare that interest by exhibiting the dragon flag, occasionally, in the Meinam.

England is in somewhat similar case. Her possessions are conterminous with those of Siam throughout the whole length of the peninsula; and she naturally prefers the neighbourhood of a peaceful and commercial people to that of a restless military power. The commercial interests of France in Siam are infinitesimal. The last report by H.B.M.'s Consul at Bangkok showed that eighty-seven per cent. of the whole shipping that entered and cleared at that port, in 1892, was British. 1,242,000*l.*, out of 1,386,000*l.* worth of the exports went to Singapore and Hongkong, while 1,172,000*l.* out of 1,296,000*l.* worth of imports came from those two British colonies. French interests, on the other hand, were represented by one steamer which runs monthly between Saigon and Bangkok, and which carried, last year, cargo to the value of 8000*l.*—less than ½ per cent. of the total trade.

It has been pointed out that the tendency of trade with the interior is to flow towards the mouth of the Meinam; and that it was, seemingly, the inception of the Bangkok-Korat railway which fired French resolution to get possession of the Meikong. We can sympathize, in a measure, with France. Much was hoped, at first, from Saigon, at the mouth of an important branch of the Meikong: then it was found desirable to go a little further, and take in the Cambodian delta: then it was revealed to Garnier, during his celebrated expedition up the Meikong, that the French flag should be hoisted at Stung-treng and Khong and Bassac, and other stations which might serve as depôts for the trade of the Laos: then the discovery was made of the river connecting Yunnan with the Gulf of Tongking which de Carné advised his countrymen to acquire at all hazards, with the certainty that its possession would eclipse British efforts to open up trade with Yunnan. Well! Saigon had been annexed, Cambodia had been annexed, Tongking had been annexed; and still the demand for French manufactures had not come. Garnier's project should be tried! It signified nothing that rapids, falling little short of a cataract, barred the ascent of the river at Khong: a Decauville railway might be made to transport goods past the obstacle, and steamers sent out in pieces to be put together above it. The river was certainly navigable between Khong and Kemmaret; and there was hope that Luang Prabang might be reached during four months of the year. All this had been resolved on, when Siam finally resolved to make a railway from Bangkok to Korat.

No one was better aware than the present Governor-General of French Indo-China what that meant. Let railways be constructed, he wrote, some years ago, and "neither the Meikong nor the Tongking route could struggle against them:"[1] the greatest efforts should therefore be made to prevent that consummation, and endeavour to deflect the commercial current towards French possessions. The effort having failed, apparently, if it was ever made —the Korat railway being in course of construction

[1] "L'Indo-Chine Française," p. 478.

—nothing remained but an effort to annex the Meikong. Not only the mouths, but the channel and the valley of the great river would then be under French control; and Manchester goods could be hindered by the application, to them, of the same methods by which it had been endeavoured to exclude them from Tongking.

The probability is that the attempt will succeed in about the same degree. Manchester goods pass in diminished quantities through the French Customs nets; but the perverse Indo-Chinese cannot, somehow, be persuaded to take an equal quantity of Rouen manufactures in their stead. Commercial possibilities serve as a lure to draw the French nation continually on to further aggression. Rouen is being perpetually assured that it will be able to "best" Manchester, if just this one more province, this one more river, this one more valley be brought within the scope of the French protective tariff; but the result usually disappoints expectations, and it is possible that the chief result of this new attempt to develop French commerce will be to increase the number of functionaries whom a clear-sighted Frenchman once described as being principally occupied *à s'administrer eux-memes.* Neither a Consul at Korat nor a Consul at Nan is likely to succeed in diverting commerce from the channel which experience has shown to be most convenient, and which the projected railway will increasingly develop. But French consuls at Nan and Korat might conceivably excite a feeling of unrest that might facilitate further political adventure. A river is a bad frontier, even if it marks an ethnical division; but the Meikong constitutes no such divison. All the states in its valley appear to sit astride it. Nan sits astride it; and even when the French have reft away half its territory the population of the two halves will remain the same. It is easy to conceive that the consul at Nan might, under these circumstances, become a disquieting influence, just as a consul at Chantaboon might exert a disquieting influence over the Annamese section of the inhabitants of that important town. Korat is on the Se-moun, which is an affluent of the Meikong; and M. de Lanessan has frankly indicated the basin of the Se-moun as within the scope of French aspirations. Some years ago, M. Deloncle tried to obtain, from the King of Siam, a concession to make a canal across the isthmus of Kra between the Bay of Bengal and the Gulf of Siam. The project failed, as the project of obtaining a footing in Burmah failed, about the same time; but M. le Myre de Vilers is said to have instructions to revive it while negotiating the new treaty that will be required to consecrate recent changes. If the canal were constructed, British shipping would certainly profit by it most; yet England would probably look askance at the acquisition, by a French company, of a broad belt of land exactly at the point where Siam is spliced, as it were, with Tenasserim.

These are among the reflections which occasion anxiety as to the future course of French policy.

Declarations of a purpose to respect the integrity of Siam would carry more conviction if we had a distinct assurance where that integrity begins. It is to be hoped that pending negotiations will result in defining the position, and in a clear understanding that both China and England would resent any further advance. Events are tending to show more clearly, every year, that the interests of the two nations in Eastern Asia are closely allied. The same great military Powers press on the frontiers of each; and it is conceivable that a situation might arise in which each might be able to render the other effective help. I am not one of those who apprehend that China will some day overrun the world; but the immense numbers of frugal and hardy men whom she can pour, and continue pouring, across her borders in any given direction would make her a valuable ally in the conceivable event of our being concerned, simultaneously, to uphold a common interest.

RUSSIA AND CHINA.

CHAPTER VIII.

THE KULDJA DIFFICULTY.

FEW questions would have seemed, at a first glance, more easy of adjustment than that which arose between Russia and China, in 1880, regarding the occupation of Kuldja and Ili; yet it was allowed, by the unskilful diplomacy of the Chinese at the outset, to grow into the dimensions of a serious quarrel which reached, at one time, the verge of war, and continued for a whole year of uncertain issue. The incident is so characteristic of the diplomatic habits of the two nations, and deals with such a curious episode of Central Asian politics, that it may be worth while to take a retrospective glance over its origin and history.

The Mahomedan uprising in Chinese Turkestan that resulted in the erection of a considerable district of Central Asia into an independent State, with which the Governments even of India and of Russia thought it worth while to open direct negotiations, will be fresh in the minds of our readers;[1] and no further reference need be made to Yakoob

[1] *Times*, April 18th, 1881.

Khan and his short lived power, than to indicate that uprising and the subsequent struggles between Andijan and Tungan as the first origin of the Russo-Chinese difficulty. It was during the anarchy that accompanied the progress of the insurrection, and when Tso Tsung-tang had barely commenced the work of reconquest, that Russia declared herself obliged to occupy the town and district of Kuldja, in order to maintain quiet and ward off disturbance from her own frontiers. Recognizing, however, the fact that it was Chinese territory, she notified the Peking Government of the step she had taken, and undertook to yield up possession whenever the latter was in a position to reoccupy it and re-establish settled authority. Cut off from her dependency by the Desert of Gobi and by the insurgent provinces she was trying to subdue, China, whether satisfied or not, was obliged to acquiesce till she had succeeded in her task; but when Kashgaria, exhausted by its wars and deprived by death of the leadership of Yakoob, had collapsed, and she had been able to re-occupy the revolted districts of Turkestan, she promptly reclaimed the gage.

Established in Kashgar, Aksu, and the other cities of the Altishahar, the Chinese general proceeded to demand fulfilment of the Russian promise. He was on the frontier, prepared to garrison the town and re-establish the Imperial rule: let the Russians retire! The request was not refused; but neither did Russia show herself disposed to surrender, so easily and unconditionally, territory which she had perhaps thought, as did other on-lookers at the commencement of the struggle, that China would never be in a position to reclaim. Difficulties were raised, and conditions put forward which the Chinese Government strenuously resisted. Russia had, they said, occupied the district for her own and not for Chinese convenience, avowedly for the purpose of maintaining order. China was now in a position to resume occupation and maintain order herself; and they expected, or professed to expect, that her claim to do so would be frankly recognized.

Failing to bring about a satisfactory settlement with the Russian Ambassador at Peking, the Empresses-Regent and their advisers sent Chung-how, a mandarin of rank and a connexion of the Imperial family, as Minister-Plenipotentiary to St. Petersburg, to urge their claims; and—making every allowance for the wide difference between preferring a request and procuring its concession—it is easy to appreciate the disappointment and irritation of the Imperial Cabinet at the result of his mission. So far from obtaining a recognition of the Chinese claims to a surrender pure and simple of the Kuldja territory, Chung-how entered into a contract by which he agreed to receive a part instead of the whole of the disputed country; and, in addition to engaging to pay five millions of roubles for expenses of occupation, he rectified frontiers and granted commercial privileges with a liberality which the Russians must have deemed truly Oriental. Instead of ratifying this treaty when presented for their approval, the

Empresses-Regent utterly repudiated it and threw Chung-how into prison, under sentence of death. Resenting this conduct, and in response to the hostile attitude assumed by China, Russia began to prepare for war. The Government of the Czar sent considerable reinforcements of ships and men to the Chinese coasts and frontier; while China, on her side, began to look to her defences, made large purchases of munitions of war, and hurried additional troops towards the possible scenes of conflict.

This was the position of affairs, and the outbreak of hostilities seemed imminent, when one more attempt was made to bring about a peaceful solution. The Marquis Tsêng, Chinese Ambassador at the Court of St. James's, was ordered to St. Petersburg to endeavour to amend the action of his predecessor; and Colonel Gordon, in response, it is understood, to an indirect invitation from the Imperial Government, went personally to Peking and threw the weight of his great personal influence into the scale of peace. The efforts of both were so far successful that the danger of immediate collision was staved off. The energetic representations of the Marquis Tsêng induced his Government to refrain from an act of punishment which would have been condemned as barbarous, and would have alienated the sympathy of every civilized Power; while wiser counsels seem to have calmed the excitement of the War party, and induced a clearer perception of possible consequences. Chung-how was reprieved and subsequently pardoned, and Russia agreed to re-open negotiations.

Breathing time was thus gained, during which a peaceful solution might be found for what had, however, grown into a serious international difficulty. If two men who are on the point of fighting can be restrained for a few moments and induced to talk over the matter in dispute, the chances are that, even if the quarrel be not made up, they will part without a blow being struck. If the grievance be tangible, it will be referred to a court of law; if it be sentimental, the greater portion of their rage will evaporate in strong language, and time will do the rest. But quarrels between nations are, unhappily, not so easily settled. The principle of international courts has not yet met with universal acceptance, and if the demands made are such as either thinks cannot be yielded without sacrifice of national honour, there is nothing left but the arbitrament of the sword. No nation willingly surrenders territory which it regards as an integral part of its possessions; and China is to the full as conservative in this respect, as Russia is acquisitive. The latter is little prone to yield what she has once grasped, and China can with difficulty be brought to give up what she regards as her own. The problem was, therefore, to find a solution by which the national pride of China might be saved, while the demands of Russia were still partially satisfied. It must be admitted that the task thus imposed upon the Marquis Tsêng, of amending a position rendered more difficult than it was originally by the action of his predecessor, was neither easy nor enviable; nor was the position of affairs at his own capital such as to lighten the difficulty. For the crisis found the leading Chinese statesmen separated into two distinct camps, and seems to have accentuated their differences. The Reactionary and War party was headed, at Court, by Prince Chun, father of the present Emperor, and among the great provincial satraps by Tso Tsung-tang, the Governor-General of Eastern Turkestan; while the Moderate Progressist party, headed by Prince Kung and the Grand Secretary, Li Hung-chang—more keenly alive, perhaps, to the danger of the situation—desired to maintain peace.

The circumstances which led to the installation of the present occupant of the Imperial Throne will be remembered by all who have followed the course of Chinese politics; but a few words of recapitulation may help to elucidate the situation. The natural course, when the last Emperor, Tung-che, died childless, would have been to elect from among the members of the Imperial clan a child who should be adopted as his son, and during whose minority the newly-widowed Empress would govern as Regent. But the Empresses Dowager of Hienfung, who had enjoyed the sweets of power during the long minority of Tung-che, saw an opportunity, too good to be passed by, of regaining the position they had lost. Overruling the claims of other aspirants in favour of a child of four, they adopted him as a son to Hienfung, and thus brought the new Sovereign under their own tutelage instead of that of their daughter-in-law, whose subsequent early death removed all further danger of opposition or intrigue. Now Chinese custom requires that the father of a child so elected should hold entirely aloof from politics and from interference in his son's affairs, the extreme parental authority which is so marked a feature in Chinese polity being obviously incompatible with the equally complete subservience due by a subject to his ruler. So far, however, from regarding this theory, Prince Chun seems to have succeeded in gaining at the capital an influence overshadowing that of his brother, Prince Kung (whose name is familiar as the Prime Minister and leading statesman of China after the death of Hienfung), and to have had, moreover, the powerful support of the Regent Empress who takes the most active part in State affairs. It was, indeed, to this support, which gave them the virtual use of the Imperial name, that the War party were greatly indebted for the influence they enjoyed. For, though Li Hung-chang had infinitely more friends than his rival, Tso, in the ranks of the mandarinate, and reckoned the Governors of the chief provinces of the Empire as relatives or political allies, he and they were powerless in opposition to the Imperial mandate, unless prepared to break out in open rebellion.

This, then, in the spring of 1880, seems to have been the political position at Peking. Prince Chun and the Empresses-Regent were eager for war; and Tso Tsung-tang, with the tattered legions which had never dared to meet the army of Yakoob Khan, vainly believed himself able to cope with the Russian forces; while Li Hung-chang and other great satraps who, with a juster appreciation of the relative strength of China and Russia, desired peace, were dominated by the power of the Imperial name. There is no need to dwell on the circumstances of Colonel Gordon's visit, or on the intrigues which attended his advent. It is enough to say that he paid a visit of several days to the great Viceroy with whom he had acted in the days of the Taeping rebellion; and, both to him and subsequently to the high authorities at the capital, urged every argument in favour of peace. Exposing the weakness of their forts and ships, and the unwieldiness and imperfection of their whole military organization, he is said to have warned the Chinese that the outbreak of hostilities at Kuldja would be followed by an invasion of Manchuria from the Amoor, and that they might expect a hostile army, within two months, before the gates of Peking. He left, moreover, with Li Hung-chang, at his departure, a memorandum on the military power of China and how that power can be best developed, which should be read at length by those who have been inclined to accept the Chinese at their own value, and to estimate them as a possible factor even in European politics. It may be sufficient to say, here, that it advises them to retain their own military system as best suited to their capacity, and warns them against essaying pitched battles with foreign troops in which they would almost certainly be broken up and defeated. They should cultivate skirmishing; utilize their faculty for throwing up earthworks; rely on the capacity for quick movement given by the absence of kit and baggage, to harass and worry the enemy while avoiding close conflict; depend chiefly on breech-loaders, and eschew heavy artillery; lay themselves out, in fact, for the irregular warfare in which their numbers, frugality, and hardihood would give them an advantage, instead of attempting to emulate the solid organization and expensive armaments of Western nations. The same with ships, the same with torpedoes; plenty of them, but small and cheap. And "China needs," wrote her adviser, "no Europeans or foreigners to help her in carrying out this programme: if she cannot carry out what is here recommended, then no one else can do so." The memorandum hinted, even, at the removal of the Emperor to one of the cities of the interior; Peking being too vulnerable, owing to its proximity to the sea. But the answer to this suggestion is said to have been prompt and emphatic: removal from Peking would mean the downfall of the dynasty and was, therefore, beyond the pale of consideration.

Short as it was, then, the visit of such an outspoken adviser seems to have been an important factor in bringing about a more intelligent view of the position, among the statesmen in power; but Gordon's counsels were, no doubt, powerfully aided by the representations of their own Ambassador at the Russian capital. One of the first acts of the Marquis Tsêng was to procure the reprieve, and ultimate release, of his unfortunate predecessor. The following edict, which appeared in the *Peking Gazette* of August 12th, 1880, was significant of the change that circumstances were combining to bring about:—

"A decree was issued some time since temporarily remitting the sentence of decapitation which had been passed upon Chung-how, but ordering that he should continue to be kept in prison. Tsêng Ki-tse (the Marquis Tsêng) was also called upon to act with due care and attention in the matter of the treaty that had to be discussed. The Tsung-li Yamen now report that they have received a telegram from Tsêng Ki-tse to the effect that he is now discussing the settlement of the various matters under dispute, and that he begs the Yamen to appeal on his behalf to the Throne for the exercise of clemency. As an act of special grace, we command that Chung-how be released forthwith."

Sanguine politicians saw room for hope that statesmen who could find such excellent reasons for complying with the requirements of Russia in this case, without mentioning their real motive, would be successful in rounding the corner of the more serious difficulties that awaited solution. The long interval which had elapsed without a settlement being reached showed that there was, at least, a growing willingness on either side to avoid a conflict, though it also showed that the differences which had arisen were by no means easy of adjustment. But neither were there wanting those who believed Russia willing to avail herself of the opportunity to extend her frontiers in a direction remote from Kuldja, and to make the valley of the Ili a stalking-horse for assumed designs on the seaboard of Corea. The alleged project was openly discussed in the Eastern

Press, and a writer in Japan drew the following glowing picture of the advantages to be gained:

"Admiral Lessofsky's own forces are in themselves equal to the conquest of the peninsula and to the permanent occupation of its strategic points. But if the attack were combined with an invasion of Russian troops from the side of Manchuria, Corea would in a very short time become Russian territory, and Russia would then possess a magnificent Pacific coast line, with noble harbours, open water, unsurpassed sites for dockyards, arsenals, and naval establishments, and unparalleled positions for dominating Japan on the east and Northern China on the western side. The conquest would be so easy, the gains, both political and strategic, so valuable that we have no doubt the reports which have reached us both from Europe and China are correct, and we may expect to see the seizure of Corea during the commencement of the spring."

There is little use in discussing schemes that, whether present or not at any period in the minds of Russian statesmen, certainly never appear to have been put forward by them. It may well be that, at St. Petersburg as well as at Peking, opposing counsels were striving for the mastery, and that the same spirit which occasionally dictates the annexation of large tracts in Central Asia, in defiance of orders from the capital, urged the present opportunity for the extension of the Russian sea-board on the Pacific. Nor is it unlikely that, if war had ensued, the integrity of Corea would have been seriously jeopardized. The risk was, in any case, averted, and the task of persuading the little kingdom to admit foreigners within its coasts and borders reserved for more peaceful efforts. We have only to deal with the situation as it must have presented itself to the Chinese Envoy on his arrival at the Russian capital; and that was, fortunately, not complicated by the introduction of any such extraneous difficulty.

The ultimate issue remained, as it was, long uncertain; and those who best understand the Chinese character will probably attribute the preservation of peace, at a time when the least false step would have precipitated war, mainly to the prompt action of Russia in preparing for the latter contingency. It is probable that the appearance of a Russian squadron, weighing on their coasts, powerfully seconded the efforts of the wiser Chinese statesmen to hold at bay the party who seem, for a time, to have paralyzed the Government and constrained it to act in a manner that must have rendered successful diplomatic action almost impossible. It will be fortunate for the future destinies of the Empire if the more intelligent Chinese realize that it is to those restraining influences, and to the mutual good sense and forbearance of those who influenced and conducted the prolonged negotiations, that the preservation of peace is due. China had everything to lose by war, for which she was utterly unprepared: the outlay would have been ruinous to her already straitened exchequer; while defeat would not only have entailed loss of territory and a heavy indemnity, but would have shaken the dynasty to its foundations. We should, ourselves, have suffered from the disorganization of a great trade, of which by far the larger portion falls to our share, and other nations would have suffered in proportion to their lesser interests. The assurance is, indeed, said to have been given that, in the event of hostilities, Shanghai and the other Treaty ports south of Pechili would not be included in the Russian scheme of operations; and it is likely that the Czar would have been anxious to avoid complications with other Powers through interference with the great trading stations on the Yang-tse and the Southern coasts. But trade is affected by other influences than direct blockade; and not the least injurious among these would have been the increased exactions to which China would have been driven to resort, and which would probably have lasted, as in the case of the Taeping rebellion, long after actual hostilities had ceased.

The Marquis Tsêng and his advisers deserve, therefore, hearty congratulations upon the successful result of their diplomacy. By the Treaty of St. Petersburg, Russia consented to give back nearly the whole territory originally in dispute, including the important Tekkes Valley (the surrender of which was the principal offence of the former Envoy), and the command of the passes in the Tien-shan. And that the Marquis Tsêng should have succeeded in gaining this important point, under infinitely greater difficulties than those which induced Chung-how to yield it, testifies to the intelligence which guided his negotiations, and proves the justice of the allegation that it was the unskilfulness of Chinese diplomacy, at the outset, which allowed a question so capable of adjustment to grow into the dimensions of an international difficulty.

Nor is that all. The Treaty of 1881 revives stipulations, for the right of navigation on the Manchurian rivers, which had been omitted from the Russo-Chinese Treaty of 1860, and which may well become of first-class importance in future eventualities. Some modifications are made, in accordance with the wish of the Chinese, to lessen the number of Consulates which Russia was empowered to institute for the purpose of facilitating commercial intercourse; and certain conditions are laid down for the future control of the trade which it is anticipated may grow up over the vast region in which the possessions of the two empires are contiguous. It is not surprising, on the other hand, that the pecuniary indemnity which was required in the Treaty of Livadia should bear larger proportions in the new agreement: for not only was the Russian occupation of Kuldja considerably prolonged by the refusal of the Chinese Government to ratify that Treaty, but the cost of the occupation was naturally enhanced by the uncertainty of the political position.

CHAPTER IX.

COREA.[1]

BY a combination of circumstances, not the least curious of which is that the weight of China was thrown into the scale of progress, the last kingdom in Asia to maintain a policy of seclusion was persuaded, in 1882, to open its gates and have intercourse with the outside world. In the spring of that year, Admiral Schufeldt on behalf of the United States, Admiral Willes on behalf of Great Britain, and the commander of the *Stosch* gunboat on behalf of North Germany, signed, at a village on the banks of the Han river, treaties by which Corea agreed to open certain of her ports, for purposes of commerce, to foreign ships, residents and visitors. The project had been long incubating—frequently essayed, and as frequently defeated. The persistency of its seclusion, the almost ludicrous tenacity with which it was defended, had thrown a gleam of romance over the little Hermit Kingdom, and helped to invest it with an interest altogether disproportioned to what was known, or assumed, of its population or political importance. It may not be amiss, therefore, before

[1] Written in July, 1884.

the halo is altogether dispersed, to glance back at its early history and at the chain of events which eventually decided it to enter the modern political arena.

There is always a disposition to invest the unknown with something of the marvellous, and Corea has come in for its full share of curiosity and romantic legend. Horses three feet high, hens with tails three feet long, hills of pure silver, and kings buried in golden coffins, have been among the tales told of the remote peninsula. The rigidity of the seclusion of course made accurate information, regarding either the country or its inhabitants, difficult to obtain; and, although they can certainly not be said to have no history—for they have a very chequered one—the Coreans have done their best to realize that condition by leaving it unwritten, and throwing us on Chinese and Japanese sources for what facts we may glean regarding it. Through the medium of Chinese merchants returning to Newchwang from the great fair held annually near the "Corean Gate;" through the medium of the embassy which comes once a year to Peking with tribute to the Emperor; through the mouth of some shipwrecked mariner, who made his way back to civilization with quaint tales to tell of a people among whom he was, at any rate, generally treated with kindness—information more or less reliable occasionally filtered. But to the adventurous pioneers of the Church of Rome a more intimate knowledge was vouchsafed of the strange land and its inhabitants; and to them we have largely been indebted for the chief facts known regarding it.

Separated from Chinese territory by the Yaloo river on the north-west, and from Japan by a hundred miles of sea on the south-east, the peninsula is sufficiently isolated by Nature to favour its independence, but too near both countries to escape their interference. The earliest glimpses of its history reveal a state of almost continual warfare among divers tribes of Tartar origin, who eventually consolidated themselves into the three States of Sinla, Petsi and Kaoli; and these again, for centuries, appear to have been almost perpetually at war either among themselves or with China and Japan, varying the internecine programme only by an occasional alliance against a foreign adversary. It is not till the eleventh century that we find the whole country united into a single kingdom, which took the name of Kaoli from the tribe that finally acquired the ascendency. It was natural that the new State should at once feel and admit the ascendency of its great neighbour. The first king recognized the suzerainty of the Chinese emperor; and the relationship seems to have been, from the first, of a very close character. So intimate indeed was it that when, three hundred years later, the Chinese succeeded in overthrowing the Mongol power, the Corean dynasty shared its downfall. The first Ming emperor dethroned the reigning king, whom he had found fighting in the hostile ranks, and replaced him by a Chinese partisan whose family have now for five hundred years retained possession of the throne. The new king drew closer his relations with the suzerain State, and organized a system of government very much after the Chinese model, which has remained in force to the present day. He divided the country into provinces and districts; removed the capital to nearly the centre of the kingdom, where it is better situated for purposes both of administration and defence; and consolidated his power by a tributary agreement with China, and an alliance of friendship with Japan.

Two hundred years of comparative peace followed the wise measures of this able Sovereign, during which the people had time to become accustomed to an orderly and settled life. At the end of that time, however, the calm was disturbed by the most terrible invasion the country had yet suffered. In the year 1592 Fidejosi, then Tycoon of Japan, having rendered himself undisputed master at home, resolved to turn his arms against China, and poured an army of 200,000 men into Corea, which he designed to use as a stepping-stone towards its neighbour. This was a time when the influence of Christian missionaries in Japan was nearly at its height, and the Tycoon is said to have had a double motive for his adventure. Disliking the Christians, but unwilling to persecute them openly, he is said to have recruited the invading army principally from their ranks, and placed at its head Christian princes whom he designed to keep henceforth in practical banishment, compensating them with Corean territories for those which they were never more to revisit! Curiously enough, we are indebted to the enterprise of an early English publisher for a translation of the first authentic information which became available, of the fate of the invaders. "Three severall testimonies concerning the mighty kingdom of Coray . . . collected out of the Portugale Iesuites yeerely Iaponian epistles," printed by Hakluyt in the year 1600, give a curiously interesting account of this great expedition which, failing utterly in its object, exercised nevertheless a material influence on Corea. The project seems to have been unpopular in Japan, which was already impoverished by internal wars and could ill support the crushing expense. So feared, however, was the Tycoon, that no one dared oppose him; and we are told—to give an idea of his power and splendour—some curious particulars of a grand sporting expedition in which he indulged his nobles before the start, when "his game had so good successe that he caught above 30,000 fowles of all sortes;" though it is distressing to learn that, "for his greater recreation, and for the more solemnitie of the game," he was imposed upon by the addition of "many dead fowles, which the Iaponians with certain poulders or compositions know how to preserve sweete in their feathers a long time."

The preparations were carried out upon a scale commensurate with the importance of the undertaking. The vanguard of the invading force, sent forward to effect a landing, was completely successful; the Corean "gunnes of 2 spannes and ½ long, which instead of bullets discharged with a terrible noise woodden arrowes headed with forked points of yron," proving no match for the "brazen ordinance" of the Japanese, who carried the principal fortresses by assault and quickly overran the country; driving the king himself to seek refuge in China. It is noteworthy that the prince who led the attacking force, and achieved this brilliant success, was a Christian; and the missionaries fail not to congratulate themselves, in the quaint language of the translator, that it "had pleased his diuine maiestie to lay the honour of all this warre upon Christian lords." The Japanese had, however, by no means an easy time thereafter; for the Coreans, abandoning the open country to the invaders, took refuge in the woods and mountains, whence they carried on a guerilla warfare while their ships harassed the smaller vessels of the Japanese. Nor, although Corea lay at his feet, could the Tycoon advance a step farther in his projected invasion of China. The Coreans had, of course, called on their neighbours for assistance; and the latter, menaced as well in their own safety, collected troops on the banks of the Yaloo, which they commanded with their war junks so effectually that they were able to transport an army into Corea and attack their would-be invaders. The Japanese were victorious in two pitched battles that ensued; but the Tycoon, though successful in the field, seems to have realized that the conquest of China was a task beyond his power,[1] and eventually withdrew a great portion of his troops.

The lull was, however, only temporary. With characteristic assumption, the Chinese appear, three years later, to have sent an embassy to Japan with proposals for tributary relations, which so enraged the Tycoon that he again poured his troops into Corea, and began fresh preparations for an invasion of China—to which his death shortly put an end. The Chinese again crossed to the assistance of their allies, and appear this time to have succeeded in breaking up the invading army. Many of the Japanese were killed; some returned to Japan; many are said to have settled in the southern districts of Corea, where the local dialect testifies to the influence of Japanese intercourse. Terms of peace were eventually agreed on (in 1615), by which the Japanese acquired the island of Tsusima, and the right to keep a garrison of 300 men at Fusan (a port in the south-east corner of the peninsula, immediately opposite that island), which they retained and exercised for 260 years. Though by no means the only occasion on which Corea was made a battle-ground by the Japanese, this was the most serious and the last of their invasions. The remains of fortified camps in various parts of the country still

[1] Two years after the outset of the expedition, in 1594, Father Organtino Brixiano, speaking of the Tycoon's usual success in war, says, "This late warre of China onely excepted, which far surmounted all his forces. Howbeit, in the kingdom of Coray he maintaineth yet great garrisons, as well to keep his honour, as to constraine the Chinians to sue for peace."

testify to the completeness of their occupation, and the Coreans are said to admit that the best firearms they possess are those left behind by the Japanese.

The somewhat severe experiences which had attended, and partly helped to effect, the consolidation of Corea into a nation, were now drawing to a close. The same fidelity to the fortunes of the suzerain dynasty which had brought down upon it the wrath of the Mings, was to subject it to one more invasion when the latter fell before the attack of the Manchus; for a Manchu army invaded Corea and dictated at the capital, in 1637, the terms which continue to govern its relations with China to the present day. It would be superfluous to describe, here, the forms and ceremonies, and the articles of tribute, which constitute the outward and visible signs of Chinese overlordship. Suffice it to say that, while exacting implicit recognition of her own preponderance, China seems practically to leave her tributaries to manage their own affairs, unless her help is sought or her own interests appear to be threatened. We have already seen her hand shown, on more than one occasion, under these circumstances; and we shall see her taking action, with vital effect, in the dramatic scenes which mark the awakening of Corea to international life.

Since the conclusion of that treaty, Corea has been at peace with both her neighbours and able, till within the last twenty years, to maintain the seclusion she so much desired. Until the beginning of the present century—when the doctrine preached by Roman missionaries in China began to filter across the frontier, and to provoke a fitful and uncertain intercourse between them and the few Coreans who had been attracted by the new religion—the only fresh glimpse we obtain of the interior of the country and its inhabitants is afforded by the well-known story of Henry Hamel,[1] who was wrecked off the Corean coast in 1653, and detained there twelve years as a prisoner at large. As a source of information his narrative has of course passed out of date, but as a record of remarkable adventure, and for its quaint account of the people and their customs, it well deserves a passing notice. Hamel sailed in a ship which left Texel for Japan on January 10th, 1653; and, after calling at Taewan to land a new Governor for the settlement which the Dutch then claimed in Formosa, was caught in a typhoon and wrecked on the Corean island of Quelpart, where thirty-six only, out of a crew of sixty-four, succeeded in landing. They were received so kindly by the local magistrate that, in the words of the narrator, "we may affirm we were better treated by that idolater than we should have been among Christians;" but they were soon to learn that their prospects were not altogether so bright as this experience might have led them to infer. They were astonished, after some six weeks of this hospitable detention, to find themselves one day in presence of another foreigner who had become an unwilling object of Corean

[1] *Vide* Pinkerton's "Collection of the best and most interesting Voyages and Travels," vol. vii.

hospitality. He was, he told them, also a Dutchman, by name Wettevree, and had been sent by the king to interpret, as soon as news of their arrival had been received at the capital. He had been five-and-twenty years in the country, having been captured with two others who had been sent ashore for water from the Dutch frigate *Ouderkes*; and there was, he feared, no chance of escape. As a matter of fact, at the end of nine months they also were carried before the king, who refused their request to be sent to Japan, saying it was not the custom of Corea to suffer strangers to depart out of the kingdom, but promised to provide them with all necessaries, and enlisted them in his life-guards, with an allowance of 100 lbs. of rice per month as wages! One or two attempts to escape were frustrated, and an appeal to the Chinese ambassador seems to have been especially disastrous. They had been ordered not to stir out during his visit: two of of them did so, notwithstanding, and caught hold of his bridle to ask protection, but were seized, imprisoned, and died. The rest were banished to a distant spot, and were so hardly treated that they were reduced to begging, to get clothes. At the expiry of nine years their numbers were reduced to twenty-two; and these, in consequence of a terrible famine which supervened, were distributed among three different cities to facilitate their maintenance. Eventually, in 1665, a few of the survivors contrived to buy a boat with a little money they had been able to earn, and made their way to Nagasaki, where they found themselves again among their own countrymen.

It would lead us far to enter into Hamel's quaint description of the country, which was still suffering from the recent Japanese and Manchu wars, and groaning under the exactions the latter had entailed. The political relations with China are clearly and accurately sketched; and what is said of the trade with China and Japan would have been almost equally applicable, twenty years ago. The system of military service is also well described. A sketch of the punishments in vogue speaks more highly for the ingenuity than the humanity of a people who could tolerate them. The following tale, at any rate, could scarcely be surpassed in the records of the Holy Office which was practising, at that period, in the West:—

> The king having desired his brother's wife, who was excellent at her needle, to embroider him a vest, that princess, bearing him a mortal hatred, stitched in between the lining and the outside some charms and characters of such a nature that his Majesty could enjoy no pleasure nor take any rest while he had it on. At length, suspecting the matter, he had the vest ripped, and found out the cause. Hereupon the king ordered her to be shut up in a room, the floor whereof was of brass, and ordered a great fire to be lighted underneath, the heat whereof tormented her till she died.

And when a high official ventured to remonstrate against so cruel a sentence, the king ordered him to have twenty strokes on his shin bones, and to be decapitated. The punishments for marital offences were equally severe and ingenious. If a woman killed her husband, she was buried alive up to the shoulders in a highway, and an axe laid by her, with which all passengers who were not noblemen were obliged to give her a stroke on the head till she died. Gay bachelors caught infringing the sanctity of the domestic hearth were liable to be stripped to their drawers, to have their faces daubed with lime, an arrow run through each ear, and a little drum fastened on the back which was beaten at all the cross-streets—the whole ceremony winding up with a flagellation.

We come now to events nearer our own time, in which the propaganda of Rome and the proceedings of its emissaries begin to play a prominent and interesting part. In the year 1784,[1] a young Corean named Le, who had come to Peking in the suite of the tribute-bearing embassy, applied to the Roman Catholic Mission for books and instruction in the science of mathematics, of which he was naturally fond. The missionaries profited by the occasion to lend him books on religion, which awakened his interest and led to his eventual conversion. As usual in such cases, the neophyte set himself, directly on his return, to propagate the new creed he had learned, among his relations and friends; and with so much success that, in less than five years, he had, according to Mgr. Govéa, gained 4000 adherents. As may be imagined, however, the doctrine acquired

[1] *Lettres Edifiantes.* Relation de l'établissement du Christianisme dans le royaume de Corée. Par Mgr. Govéa, évêque de Pekin, 1797.

from a convert who had had only a few months' instruction, and disseminated again at second-hand by men who had caught the crude idea from his conversation, was of a somewhat obscure description; and it hardly needed a special appeal, to persuade the Bishop of Peking that it was time to send a more qualified teacher. The frontier was, however, guarded with extreme jealousy, and careful precautions were necessary. It was arranged that a missionary should proceed to a certain spot, at a given date, in the following year, and should there be met by converts who would guide him through the Corean lines. The priest was punctual to his appointment, but not so his intended hosts, and, after waiting fruitlessly for a given time, he returned to Peking. The blank continued. Neither letter nor news was received from the Corean Christians for more than two years; but two converts made their way to Peking, at the close of 1793, with news of a severe persecution which had occurred in the interval.

The trouble had arisen from the same cause which had produced a similar effect, at a moment when there seemed a prospect that Christianity might gain a hold in China. It is unnecessary to expatiate, here, on the nature of the reverence paid by the Chinese and cognate races to the memory of their dead, or to recapitulate the arguments for and against toleration, which were terminated by a decree from Rome condemning the practice. Suffice it to say that the question had also been asked by the first converts in

Corea, whether it was permissible to erect ancestral tablets, or to keep those already in existence; and the Bishop of Peking, as in duty bound under Pope Clement's Bull, had replied in the negative. Two enthusiastic brothers had at once acted literally on this opinion, and burned objects which were held sacred in the eyes of their relations and neighbours. A tremendous outcry was naturally raised, which had compelled the interference of the Government and led to measures of persecution which had terminated, for the present, in the torture and execution of the two offenders.

The tenacity of the Roman Church finds admirable expression in the courage, perseverance, and self-sacrifice of its emissaries; and, whatever we may think of a system which seems to prove more often a firebrand than a message of peace, we cannot withhold admiration from its devoted exponents. A footing once gained is never abandoned; and after the fiercest persecution there always remain some enthusiasts, over whose head the storm has passed, ready to welcome a new pastor. Corea has been no exception to the rule. No sooner had the persecution which followed this act of iconoclasm subsided, than a priest was successfully introduced across the frontier, to instruct and impart new life to the converts. Nor, it is affirmed, has the flock ever since been left unguarded. Persecution has followed persecution; but from Jacques Velloz, the first missionary to cross the frontier, who suffered martyrdom in 1800, to Mgr. Ridel, who has returned to

Europe with health shattered by the anxieties and hardships undergone during the latest outbreak, there have always been some priests alternately tolerated or hiding in the country, and the spark lighted by the young Corean attaché has never been quite extinguished.

We come now to the first link in the chain of events which have tended gradually to bring Corea within the sphere of modern politics. On July 7th, 1866, a Roman Catholic missionary arrived in a Corean boat at Chefoo, with a tale of dire persecution. Two bishops, nine priests, and a number of Christians of both sexes had been massacred, many of them after judicial tortures of atrocious cruelty. Three members of the mission only survived, and M. Ridel had been chosen to carry the news to China, and endeavour to procure assistance. It was to the French authorities, naturally, that he addressed himself; and both Admiral Roze, the Commandant of the French fleet in Chinese waters, and M. de Bellonet, then chargé-d'affaires at Peking, lent a sympathetic ear to his protest.[1] The Chinese Government, which was first appealed to, as suzerain, for redress, declined any responsibility in the matter; though the missionaries learned afterwards, in Corea,

[1] M. de Bellonet, indeed, was moved by his indignation to pen a sentence of deposition against the Corean king, which subsequent events made rather ridiculous:—"The same day on which the king of Corea laid his hands on my unhappy countrymen was the last of his reign. He himself declared its end, which I, in my turn, solemnly declare to-day."—*Vide* "U.S. Diplomatic Corresp.," vol. ii. for 1867, p. 424.

that it had written to the king, condemning the persecution as calculated to bring him into trouble with the French, whose power he could not hope to oppose. An expedition was accordingly resolved on, and Admiral Roze assembled at Chefoo, for that purpose, a squadron comprising the *Guerrière* frigate, the corvettes *Laplace* and *Primanget*, the despatch-vessels *Deroulède* and *Kienchan*, and the gunboats *Tardif* and *Lebrethon*.

The receipt of this news in Corea had one notable result. There had arrived at Chefoo, within a few weeks after M. Ridel, the crew of a small American schooner which had been lost on the eastern shore of the Yellow Sea. They had been twenty-five days in Corea, fed and well treated by the authorities, and forwarded overland to China. The same thing had happened in the case of another shipwrecked crew, a few months previously; and the contrast between this kind treatment of shipwrecked sailors and the massacre of resident Christians had given rise to significant comment among foreign residents in China. Whether news of French threats at Peking and of the hostile preparations at Chefoo had influenced the change of conduct, or whether the Corean Government were alarmed at the indications of a desire to open up commercial intercourse shown in the recent visits of one or two foreign ships to the coast—a vessel despatched by Admiral Roze to survey the approaches to the capital learned that another American schooner (the *General Sherman*), which had gone ashore a month previously in the Pieng-an river, had been burned as she lay, and all hands murdered.

The city of Han-yang, more commonly called Söul "the capital" of Corea, was found to be situated in 37·30° N., and 124·30° E., on the banks of a river named the Han, which flows into the Yellow Sea. The channel seemed navigable, for steamers of moderate draught, to within a short distance of the walls. The entrance was protected by fortifications on the island of Kang-hwa, but these did not appear to be garrisoned. Having obtained this information, Admiral Roze started from Chefoo with the expeditionary force on October 11th, arrived off Kang-hwa on the 14th, and occupied it, after a merely nominal resistance, two days later. The Coreans were apparently taken by surprise, having perhaps thought that the danger had passed with the withdrawal of the surveying expedition. The forts along the banks of the river were found ungarrisoned, and Kang-hwa itself, a considerable fortress containing large stores of munitions of war, was practically undefended. A letter was received, a few days later, inviting Admiral Roze to come or send delegates to Söul, to talk over matters in a friendly spirit; but he replied that, if the Corean authorities wished to treat, they had better come to Kang-hwa. This attitude was meant, no doubt, to be impressive, but the event proved it to be slightly premature. So far all had gone well; but the expedition was about to collapse with a suddenness contrasting remarkably with the expectations raised by M. de Bellonet's denunciations and Admiral Roze's hauteur.

It may be well to explain, with reference to the present and subsequent complications, that the reigning King of Corea is not the son of the last Sovereign, who died childless; but, like the reigning Emperor of China under similar circumstances, was adopted into the royal family from a remote branch. He was still a child at the time of these occurrences, and the Government was administered by his father who, under the title of Regent, exercised nearly despotic power, and seems to have been the incarnation of the spirit of exclusion that had characterized his country. The persecution was ascribed mainly to his influence, and he now ordered a general levy to resist the invader. Parties of soldiers began to appear on the banks of the river, in the neighbourhood of the French position, and spies brought news that an attack was intended. A party sent out to reconnoitre along the road leading to Söul was surprised and severely handled; and, though the sailors succeeded in driving the Coreans from the earthworks behind which they had been concealed, the reconnaissance was not pushed farther. Shortly after, news was brought that 300 soldiers had effected a landing during the night on the island of Kang-hwa itself; and that the process was to be continued until a sufficient force had been gathered to make an attempt on the French position. Another reconnaissance was accordingly ordered, with an even worse result. The party, of about 150 men, had reached within 120 yards of the fort, when suddenly the walls were manned and a volley was fired which killed three and wounded thirty-five of their number. A sortie of the garrison was repulsed, but the French judged it wise to retire and carry back their wounded to camp. The disastrous termination of these two movements appears to have persuaded Admiral Roze that the force at his disposal [1] was insufficient to prosecute the enterprise to a successful issue, in face of Corean hostility. It was no longer a question whether he should go to Söul or the Coreans come to him: the expedition was at a deadlock. He had rejected the first overtures, and was not strong enough to impose terms.

A retreat was accordingly decided on. The city of Kang-hwa was burned, with its public offices and royal palace; the munitions of war which it contained were destroyed; its library of 300 volumes, a number of curious specimens of native industry and art, and silver ingots to the value of some 8000*l.* were carried off; and the troops re-embarked. An intention of returning in the spring was expressed, but was never carried out. Mexican affairs were causing the French Government much trouble at the time, and Corea was allowed to fall into oblivion. It is satisfactory to know that Messrs. Féron and Calais, the two other surviving members of the mission,

[1] *Vide Moniteur*, 27th December, 1866, and 7th January, 1877. Also M. Ridel's narrative in "L'histoire de l'Eglise de Corée," vol. ii. pp. 578 *et seq.*

succeeded in escaping to China; but the persecution of native Christians, as was to be expected, broke out with renewed fury after the departure of an expedition which had been powerless to coerce, and able only to cause injury and irritation. Left to himself, with the conviction that he had fairly repulsed his assailants, the Regent grew more and more despotic, and more confirmed in his hatred of foreigners and in his policy of exclusion.

A vein of comedy runs through the story of the next attempt to enter the Forbidden Land, though the attempt itself was held sufficiently grave to involve the leaders in serious difficulty with their judicial authorities. Royal remains, stolen calves, defeated treaties, silver bullion, grey shirtings and golden coffins combine to form the elements of a tale worthy the pen of a Cooper or an Edgar Poe. On July 7th, 1868, a subject of the United States named Jenkins was indicted before his Consul at Shanghai, for having,

> together with others not amenable to the jurisdiction of the American Consulate, entered in and upon the steamer *China* on a scandalous and unlawful expedition to Corea, for the purpose of exhuming for his own profit the body of a deceased Sovereign of Corea, to the evil example of others, and against the peace and dignity of the people of the United States.[1]

The object of the defence was, naturally, to tell as little as possible of a story about which no one but they could know the full particulars; but sufficient came out to give a tolerably clear idea of the adventure, and that has since been supplemented by the

[1] *Vide North-China Herald*, July 11th, 1868.

published narrative of Mr. Oppert,[1] one of the "others" referred to in the indictment.

The patent facts were that Oppert had chartered the steamer with money advanced by Jenkins, that an unusually large crew of over 100 Manila-men and Chinese had been engaged, and that a quantity of arms had been taken in at Nagasaki, *en route*, which were distributed on board. The further impression seems to have been, that a French missionary had told the adventurers of the whereabouts of a grave containing a gold coffin, in which lay the remains of a former king of Corea; and that these gentlemen had undertaken an expedition with the view of possessing themselves of that curious property; that they had carried out their purpose so far as making the voyage to Corea, but had failed in their ulterior design and got into a more or less serious row with the natives. Jenkins was acquitted, chiefly it would seem because there was a doubt as to the jurisdiction of the court. Oppert, who was called as a witness at the trial, spoke of a treaty which he had hoped to negotiate with Corea, and of possible contracts for grey shirtings, as among the objects of the trip; while the owner of the steamer hinted at silver bullion, as an element which he had expected to find in her return cargo. But the bearing of these remarks was not made clear, at the time, to the minds of the audience, and it is to the pages of Mr. Oppert's book that we must look for the key of the riddle. We agree with

[1] "A Forbidden Land, &c." By Ernest Oppert, London, 1880.

him that "the circumstances are so exceptional and unusual, and the character of the voyage itself is so out of the common," that it is desirable to give a clear statement of reasons and motives.

It should be premised that Mr. Oppert had already made one tentative voyage to Corea, in the hope of opening up commercial intercourse, and was known to be much interested in the country; so that he naturally became intimate with the missionaries who, as we have seen, had fled to China from the recent persecution. It appears, then, that Père Féron, one of these gentlemen, came to him one day and said:—

> "I have always looked to you as the one person able and willing to help us. If I now place the means in your power to bring the Regent and his Government to submit to the demand for opening up the country, and sign treaties to that effect with foreign powers, will you undertake another voyage to put this in execution?"

Somewhat astonished, as he well might be, at this overture, Mr. Oppert nevertheless expressed willingness, provided the scheme looked feasible; and M. Féron went on to unfold it in the following terms:

> "The Regent, a person of very superstitious disposition, laid great store upon the possession of some old relics which had been in his family for long years, and which were kept guarded in a secluded place belonging to him. The possession of these relics was thought to ensure the fortune of himself and his family, and they were accordingly much treasured, and looked upon with a kind of superstitious awe." [So much so that M. Féron's Corean friends advised him that] "the temporary possession of these objects would be tantamount to investing their holders with an

almost absolute power, and equivalent to having possession of the capital itself."

Whether these "relics" (? *reliques*) really consisted of the golden coffin of the Shanghai legend, or what was their exact nature, is not definitely stated. But M. Féron appears to have so convinced himself, and so convinced Mr. Oppert, of the importance attached to their possession, that the attempt was resolved on, in the belief that they could be used to extort whatever conditions were wished from the Corean Government. That one of these conditions would have been an agreement to tolerate Christianity and missionary enterprise, may be taken as beyond doubt. Whether possibilities of ransom and concession of commercial privileges may explain the vague allusions, at the trial, to grey shirtings and specie freight, must remain uncertain; for the attempt, as we know, failed.

The difficulty of the undertaking seems to have been commensurate with its eccentricity. It was necessary to ascend an inlet which was only navigable during thirty hours, once a month, at spring tides; and the locality in question was distant some four hours' good walking from the landing-place. This spot was successfully reached in a steam-launch, and a number of the crew, carrying arms and tools, set out on a march into the hills in further prosecution of the search. The relics, whatever they may have been, were found enclosed by an immense mound, which was penetrated with much difficulty and labour, only to find a further obstacle in the shape of a huge stone slab which they had neither tools nor time to remove. Many hours had passed, the return march was before them, and the tide must be caught. Reluctantly, therefore, the project was abandoned, and the "relics" were left in peace in their native soil.

No opposition seems to have been offered to this remarkable journey of armed strangers through the country, and a collision which did occur at the place of embarkation is attributed by Mr. Oppert to the indiscreet appropriation of a calf, by one of his followers, rather than to any general feeling of hostility to the intrusion. Such is the history of this curious adventure, as told by its leader and chief; and so abortively ended the second grand attempt to open up intercourse with the Forbidden Land.

Moved, no doubt, by the destruction of the *General Sherman* and her crew, the Government of the United States next resolved to try to open negotiations with this jealously guarded country. Mr. Low, then United States Minister at the Court of Peking, was entrusted with the task; and Admiral Rogers, commanding the United States naval squadron in Chinese waters, was instructed to accompany him on the mission, "with a display of force adequate to support the dignity of the United States Government." While given the means, however, of upholding this dignity if necessary, Mr. Low's instructions were far from being of a warlike character. In language of studious moderation, he was told to try to secure a treaty for the protection of shipwrecked mariners; but, while maintaining firmly the right of the United States to this end, "to exercise prudence and discretion, and avoid a conflict by force unless it could not be avoided without dishonour."[1] He was also told to endeavour, as M. de Bellonet had done, to enlist the influence of the Chinese Government to further his designs. But the latter again declined interference, and consented only to forward a letter from Mr. Low to the Corean Government, announcing the expedition and explaining its object.

In May, 1871, the American fleet, comprising the *Colorado* (flagship), *Alaska* and *Benicia* (second rates), and *Monocacy* and *Palos*, gunboats, assembled at Nagasaki preparatory to the start; and on the 29th of that month it anchored off the mouth of the Söul river, at the same spot which Admiral Rozo had selected four years previously. Immediately on its arrival, certain officials presented themselves, who were assured of the friendly purpose of the visit, and informed that the Admiral intended making a survey of the river but would wait a few days, before starting, to enable his object to be fully explained and understood. On June 1st, accordingly, four steam-launches, followed at a convenient distance by the two gunboats, set out on the proposed expedition. Two hours' steaming brought them to the island of Kang-hwa, which the French had occupied during

[1] Despatch from Secretary Fish to Mr. F. F. Low, dated April 20th, 1870.

their brief sojourn, and which was destined to prove the limit of progress of the new visitors. In 1866 the batteries had been found empty, and the fortress only slightly held. This time, both were fully garrisoned; and, as the launches were being swept past by the tide, a fire was opened on them from some seventy pieces of artillery which the Coreans had thought, with pardonable vanity, must inevitably sink everything within range. The bad gunnery of the artillerymen, however, and poor character of the projectiles defeated their object; and the boats swept, almost unscathed, through the *feu d'enfer* that had been prepared for their reception. Opening fire in their turn, they were soon able to shell the Coreans out of their position, and clear a way for return to the fleet, where the sound of the firing had created a not unnatural anxiety.

Admiral Rogers seems to have considered that this incident left him no option but to obtain an apology or chastise his assailants. He had come with quite friendly intent, but if the Coreans persisted in treating as enemies everyone who approached their shores, they must pay the penalty of their mistake. Ten days were let pass, to give time for the Government to explain what might possibly have been an unauthorized act of the mandarin in command; but, as no message of any kind was received, it was resolved, at the expiry of that period, to destroy the fort in order to punish the insult to the flag. This was successfully effected by a landing party of 650 men, supported by the armed launches and gunboats of the fleet. A plucky resistance was offered by the garrison, but the superior arms and discipline of the Americans prevailed. The fort was carried by storm, with the loss of an officer and two privates killed and six wounded: the magazines were exploded; and on the following day the party returned to the fleet anchorage. But if the insult to the flag had been avenged, nothing had been done, either by peaceful message or forceful chastisement, towards gaining the objects of the expedition. The Corean Government remained impervious and uncompromising in its refusal of intercourse. The following characteristic letter, addressed by the Corean authorities to Admiral Rogers, tersely expresses their attitude of resolute isolation:—

> In the year 1868 a man of your nation, whose name was Febiger, came here and communicated and went away; why cannot you do the same? In 1866 a people called the French came here; and we refer you to them for what happened. This people has lived 4000 years in the enjoyment of its own civilization, and we want no other. We trouble no other nation—why do you trouble us? Our country is in the extreme east, and yours in the extreme west: for what purpose do you come so many thousand miles across the sea? Is it to inquire about the ship destroyed (the *General Sherman*)? Her men committed piracy and murder, and they were punished with death. Do you want our land? That cannot be. Do you want intercourse with us? That cannot be, either.

To an offer to parole the wounded and prisoners, it was answered: "Do as you please; if you keep them too long, they will suffer heavy punishment from us when released." What was to be done with such a people? The American Minister and Admiral wisely decided to withdraw, for the present, from an expedition they could not hope to prosecute to success with the force at their disposal, and report a position of affairs which had become too serious to be dealt with under their instructions. As a matter of fact, the American Government appears to have resolved to abandon a project which promised no result equal to the difficulties in prospect; and, once again, the Coreans were left to their isolation, and to the conviction, no doubt, that they had successfully repelled the attempted invasion of another barbarian power.

Still, notwithstanding the bold front shown, the barriers were really tottering to their fall. The Japanese were the first to establish formal relations. Having been, themselves, only recently brought to conclude treaties with Western Powers, they seem to have thought they would like to negotiate one on the same model with Corea; and the Coreans, disturbed no doubt by recent events, but disposed rather to accept as allies than repel as intruders a neighbouring and well-known nation, acquiesced in the proposal. On February 26th, 1876, there was signed accordingly, at the now familiar island of Kang-hwa, a treaty of peace and friendship by which the interchange of ambassadors, the appointment of consuls, and the opening of certain ports in Corea to Japanese trade, were regularly provided for. And this was followed, eighteen months later, by a supplementary agreement laying down regulations for trade and making certain additional provisions, among which it is only worth while to particularize a clause stipulating for the kind treatment of shipwrecked foreigners, of the exact nature the Americans had wished to dictate. The end, however, was not quite yet. This acquiescence in the overtures of Japan by no means implied a willingness to enter into relations with other foreign powers. The Japanese, as we have seen, were old acquaintances; and they appear to have attained their end rather by flattering the spirit of isolation than from any tendency on the part of the Corean Government to relax its vigilance. The Duke of Genoa, who paid a flying visit to the country in the Italian frigate *Vittor Pisani*, in the summer of 1880, found the old spirit still in force; and was persuaded that the Japanese not only subserved the Corean policy, but were tending, by their brutal treatment of the people, to intensify the feeling cf hostility to foreign intrusion.

The Duke's visit seems to have been undertaken as much out of curiosity as any other motive; but an expressed desire to thank the Corean Government for kind treatment of an Italian sailor, who had been wrecked two years previously on the island of Quelpart, afforded an excuse for trying to approach the officials at the ports visited. The new Japanese settlements of Fusan and Gensan were selected, as affording the easiest means of access; but the Duke had been warned that, though he would certainly receive courtesy, he would hardly have the real assistance of the Japanese in his efforts to open up intercourse; and the result seems to have justified this prediction. He failed, at any rate, to obtain an interview with, or even to get a letter transmitted to, the prefect of Torai, which embraces the port of Fusan; and only succeeded better at Gensan, by threatening to send the letter with an escort of Italian marines if he could get no Corean to carry it. Such as it was, however, his intercourse with the people seems to have been friendly and interesting. He was accompanied by Mr. Donald Spence, a member of H.B.M. Consular Service and an excellent Chinese scholar, as interpreter; and the difficulty seems to have been to answer the questions sufficiently fast, rather than to get into conversation at all. The Corean spoken language is totally different from the Chinese; but Mr. Spence found that every one, even among the poorest classes, could read and write the Chinese character; and communication was kept up by tracing characters in the air, on the sand, or on the hand as opportunity offered. The prefect of Yung-hing even brought himself to pay a visit to the *Vittor Pisani*, under the threat mentioned; and an amusing account is given, in Mr. Spence's report,[1] of the scene that took place in the cabin of the frigate on the occasion. Conversation was carried on by writing, or in dumb show; the crowd of attendants, in the meantime, eating, drinking, and smoking everything that was offered them or that they could lay hands on, and carrying off empty bottles and biscuit tins as valuable mementoes of their visit and specimens

[1] Report by Mr. Spence of his visit to Corea, with H.R.H. the Duke of Genoa: dated Shanghai, September 9th, 1880.

of foreign art. The prefect could not, however, be persuaded to undertake the responsibility of forwarding a letter to the capital; he could only be brought, at last, to take a copy of one which had been prepared, and which he promised to transmit, along with a report of his visit, to the Governor of the Province.

So far, then, beyond accepting from the Japanese a treaty on a Western model, the Coreans could hardly be said to have derogated greatly from their traditional policy. But events were tending to bring about a greater change, and to induce them to plunge boldly into the stream on whose brink they were shivering. We have seen that the father of the reigning monarch represented the ancient Toryism of the country in its most intense form; but it seems to be a curious fact that Corea, like England, has its Liberal as well as its Conservative party; and the king himself—mainly, it is said, through the influence of his wife, who comes of a Liberal stock and is said to have tampered, even, with Christian teaching—inclines to the Liberal side. His coming of age and personal assumption of power were, therefore, the signal for a change of policy. Liberals were installed in places of power, while the regent and his allies retired in dudgeon to their estates. So that, when circumstances brought the Foreign question once more to the front, political conditions were favourable to its solution. It was reserved for the great Chinese Minister, Li Hung-chang, to bring it to an issue.

With what exact degree of truth it is difficult to say, Russia has been credited with a yearning to possess, on the Asiatic coast, a harbour more fitted for winter quarters than her Amoor territory can boast; and the so-called Port Lazaref, in Corea, has been indicated as a special object of her ambition. This inlet, which is known in local parlance as Yung-hing, and is situated between 39·10° and 39·20° N., and 125·10° and 125·20° E., constitutes a splendid harbour which is not frozen in winter, and would have been in every way a desirable acquisition. The project is said to have been put forward during the dispute with China anent the ownership of Kuldja which threatened, at one time, to eventuate in hostilities that would have rendered such a harbour of first-class value; and it is said that China advised the Corean Government, as the best means of protecting itself against such a contingency, to accept the friendly intercourse which foreigners were pressing upon it. However that may be, and whatsoever the motive may have been, Li certainly advised the king to accept foreign intercourse, and his counsel was accepted. Treaties were negotiated, through his instrumentality, with the United States, Great Britain, and Germany; and were formally signed, when all had been cut, dried, and prepared, at the village of Jenchuan, in the neighbourhood of the capital.

It was not likely that such a complete subversion of the national policy would pass unchallenged. There is always, in every State, a party opposed to change because it is change; and we have seen that this party lacked neither representatives nor leaders in Corea. The Chinese Government passed through a severe ordeal after we had compelled it, in 1858, to abrogate pretensions that were a very article of faith with the ruling classes. The foreign wars and internal convulsions which followed the acceptance of European intercourse in Japan attracted, for a time, an interest scarcely less than had been excited by the romantic descriptions of its first visitors. Corea, a country broadly divided by faction, could not hope to pass unscathed through a similar change; and the ex-Regent and his allies were, as a matter of fact, hatching a plot which should everthrow their opponents and replace themselves in power. Already, in the spring, there had been rumours of political dissension, and of hostile demonstrations against Japanese settlers; and on July 23rd, 1882, the storm burst. In the afternoon of that day, the Japanese Ambassador received a note from the Governor of Söul, saying the mob had risen, that he was endeavouring to put them down but feared his ability to do so, and that the members had better keep inside the Embassy and prepare for contingencies. The Legation did, in effect, become the object of attack, and was gallantly defended by the inmates till fire was applied to the neighbouring houses. Mr. Hanabusa and his countrymen, some thirty in number, then determined to cut their way out; and, after a futile attempt to obtain shelter at the palace, made their way to the seacoast, where they seized a boat and were fortunate in finding the British gunboat *Flying Fish*, which took them on board and conveyed them to Nagasaki. They had, however, lost eight of their number during the retreat, besides others who had been killed in Söul. Later reports were received, to the effect that the rioters had subsequently proceeded to the palace and had either murdered, or intimidated into committing suicide, the Queen, the Crown Prince and several of the highest officials, while the ex-Regent had grasped the reality of power.

Intense excitement was naturally caused by the receipt of this intelligence in Japan, and steps were at once taken to exact reparation. Mr. Hanabusa was sent back to Söul on board an ironclad, with a fitting escort, and preparations were made for war if the employment of force became necessary. China acted, however, in this emergency with a promptitude little to be expected from her usual dilatory habits. Directly the news arrived, Ma Kien-chung, an active and intelligent official who had just returned from a mission to India, was despatched with an ironclad squadron and several thousand soldiers, to the scene of action; and grave fears were entertained lest war between China and Japan should arise out of the imbroglio. Such a contingency was, however, fortunately averted by the good sense of the respective Governments. Japan recognized that redress for the outrage was her ultimate object, while China made use of her influence and preponderating force, to overawe the reactionary party and restore the king and his ministers to power. Terms of settlement, under these conditions, were speedily arranged. The Corean Government, which made no attempt to palliate the wrong done in defiance of its authority, and could only endeavour to mitigate the Japanese demands, agreed to pay $500,000 to defray the cost of Japanese military preparations, and $50,000 as compensation to the families of those who had been killed during the riot. The maintenance of a Japanese guard at the Legation for a year, the execution of certain ringleaders, the opening of an additional port, and the despatch of a mission of apology to Kioto, were other conditions with which Japanese *amour-propre* appears to have been amply satisfied; while the Chinese envoy, to put an end once for all to the ex-Regent's machinations, carried him off to China, where an Imperial edict subsequently ordered him to be interned. The temptation is great to reproduce a full translation of this characteristic document, which gives a concise summary of the course of events and recapitulates the Regent's political crimes, but we must confine ourselves to the concluding terms:—

> Considering [runs the Imperial utterance] the constant arrogance with which he has intimidated his sovereign, and his plot that endangered the State, he should be punished with all the rigour of the law. But we bethink ourselves of the ties of kindred that render him an object of reverence to the prince, and that if heavy sentence be meted out to him the latter will be involved in a state of helpless misery. For these reasons we, of our special favour, most leniently lighten his sentence. Let Lo Cheng-ying escape the punishment due to his crimes, and live at peace at Paoting-foo in Chihli, nor ever return to his country.

Successful treachery is no disgrace to an Oriental,

and many a mandarin head will have wagged with delight when the story was told, in China, of the arrest of the Corean rebel. Ma paid a visit to Söul, accompanied as was natural by a strong escort, invited the object of his attention to dinner, carried him off in a sedan-chair from the heart of the capital, and placed him on board a Chinese ironclad, almost before his partisans could hear the news or gather breath to interfere if they had been disposed to incur such a risk. There is a dash of the ludicrous in this closing incident; so effectual is the extinction of the rebel leader, and so complete the answer afforded to the questions which had been raised, as to the reality of Chinese suzerainty over the country.

Before these vigorous measures, the Conservative opposition seems to have collapsed. The king resumed the reins of power, and showed a disposition to act loyally on the new lines. Even the queen came back to life, the fate destined for her having been averted by putting forward one of her maids to receive the fatal cup, while her Majesty escaped to a neighbouring village where she remained in hiding till the storm was past.

It remained for the Governments with which Corea had been persuaded to conclude treaties, to ratify these engagements and clench the new policy. Some hesitation appears to have been felt, for a moment, on account of the ill-defined nature of Corean relations to Peking. These were quite well understood, no doubt, by the parties concerned; but Western Powers might be pardoned for desiring to know more precisely whether they were dealing with an independent kingdom or with a vassal state. They had seen China disclaiming responsibility when appealed to by M. de Bellonet and M. Low; yet interposing, with sovereign authority, in the difficulty with Japan. The United States appear to have decided on ignoring the complication, and looking directly to Söul. As nearly as possible twelve months after Admiral Schufeldt's first visit, General Foote arrived off the mouth of Han river; and ratified copies of the American treaty were exchanged at Söul, on May 19th, 1883, with a degree of pomp and circumstance that would have well become a more pretentious State. The ceremony—marking as it did, for Corea, a final severance with the past—has many points of interest; and a sketch of the proceedings, condensed from the narrative of an eye-witness, may be worth preservation.

The Council of Ministers were present in full Court dress of dark green satin, while the American Minister was accompanied by nine officers of the *Monocacy*, besides his personal suite. . . . The rich robes of the Corean noblemen, the plain black of the American Legation, the glittering epaulettes and lace of the naval officers, combined to make a scene both novel and striking, the more so when it is considered that the object of the assembly was to complete the destruction of a nation's political traditions. On the following day, General Foote and his suite were received in audience by the King, who wore a round-topped hat, with fan-shaped wings sticking out behind; his dress consisting of a single garment of bright red silk with long flowing sleeves, secured at the waist by a belt of crimson and gold; while on each shoulder and on the breast were large dragons in heavy gold embroidery. Altogether, his Majesty appears to have very favourably impressed his visitors, and the usual expressions of satisfaction at the establishment of friendly relations were appropriately formulated.

A most successful banquet was given at the Foreign Office in the evening, when the building was brilliantly illuminated; and two days later the Americans returned to their vessel well pleased with their visit, and not a little surprised at the magnificence of a reception which appears to have far exceeded their most sanguine expectations.

As already stated, the Cabinets of London and Berlin were in less haste to accept the situation. The prompt and decisive intervention of China, at the time of the anti-Japanese outbreak, had so clearly marked the vassalage of Corea that any engagement entered into with her assumed a fresh significance; and doubts were felt as to the wisdom of concluding, with her, a treaty less liberal in many respects than that governing our relations with China. Mr. Aston, of H.M.'s Consular Service in Japan, was sent accordingly to Corea to collect information regarding the country and its resources, and to prepare the way, if possible, for the desired modifications. It will be sufficient to add that the Corean Government was persuaded to yield the points at issue, and that Sir Harry Parkes succeeded, during a subsequent visit to Söul, in obtaining a revised treaty—more likely in every respect to promote commercial intercourse. It would be tedious to enter on an analysis of its provisions; but two marked variations from the Chinese exemplar claim a word of comment. Opium is expressly excluded; and, as opium seems happily to be neither grown nor used in Corea, this provision will have the sympathy even of those who deprecate the sacrifice of the Indian trade for the benefit of the native cultivator in China, where the product and the habit are alike ineradicable. A second remarkable variation from the prevalent type of our treaties with the Far East, is the absence of a clause stipulating for freedom of missionary enterprise; and this leads us to remark on the absence of France from the list of nations that joined in the new departure. The precise circumstances under which the clause in question was excluded were not explained; but it is not difficult to conceive that the internal and external troubles to which the advent of Roman missions had given rise, indisposed the Corean Government to grant them a firmer foothold. Neither America, England, nor Germany would be disposed to enforce such a concession; though France, virtually uninterested in commerce, and concerned chiefly to assert political influence and advance the cause of Oriental missions, might decline a convention from which her favourite clause was absent.[1] Germany soon after concluded a treaty nearly identical with the British. Russia was in no haste to join a rush which she can hardly have regarded with favour; but she could not afford to hold aloof, and soon followed the general example.

As a necessary consequence of the seclusion in

[1] A treaty was subsequently negotiated (4th June, 1886), containing a clause designed, apparently, to admit missionaries by a side-wind as teachers. French residents may (Art. ix.) engage Coreans as literati, interpreters, etc.; and, reciprocally, Frenchmen may be similarly engaged by Coreans.

which the Coreans had hitherto dwelt, few foreigners had had an opportunity of becoming intimately acquainted with them or their country. Hamel gave, as we have seen, an excellent idea of the nature of the Government and the state of civilization prevailing in his day; but his narrative has long passed into the domain of archæology. British Consular officers, who pushed quickly through the half-opened barriers, are already giving valuable information regarding the commercial resources and general aspect of the country. But it is to the missionaries of Rome that we have still to look for an exhaustive picture of Corean life; and the curious reader will find, in the introductory chapters of M. Dallet's characteristic work,[1] a succinct account of the language, institutions, manners, and customs of the people, as well as of the topography and products of the soil.

The people seem to be Mongolian in type, though there are local traces of Japanese admixture. They are said to be superior, physically, to both Chinese and Japanese, though their standard of education and civilization is lower, and they are less polished in manner. They are frank-mannered towards foreigners, and in the last degree curious as to the strange countries and people from whom they have been cut off. Mr. Oppert, on the occasion of his remarkable voyages, Mr. Spence, in describing the visit of the Duke of Genoa, Mr. Aston, in relating

[1] "L'histoire de l'Eglise de Corée," etc. Par. Ch. Dallet, Miss. Apostolique. Paris, 1874.

his experiences, and Mr. Carles, during a more recent tour, all bear testimony to these features in their character; and, if their curiosity impels them to a somewhat disagreeable familiarity, this will probably resolve itself into a willingness for friendly intercourse, as the novelty wears off. Even M. Dallet, who can certainly not be accused of sparing their defects, pays a high tribute to their hospitality and their generous readiness to help each other. His description of the state of morality is singular, but it seems on the whole to be low. Despite certain superficial marks of respect, women are alleged to be singularly liable to outrage, and to enjoy immunity from legal responsibility for the simple but uncomplimentary reason that they are not supposed to be responsible for their acts: so remarkable, in fact, is the state of affairs depicted, that we cannot help fancying the writer has been inspired to lay on the colour with a somewhat heavy brush. The testimony of recent foreign visitors goes chiefly to emphasize their extreme timidity. Mr. Carles, who has made an extensive tour through the two central provinces, says:—

> The seclusion in which they [the women] and even girls live is marvellous. No matter how poor the hovel in which we were stopping, it was rare that we got even a glimpse of a woman in the house; and when met on the road they either struck off at right angles or, turning their backs on us, stood still until we had passed.

Some of this may of course be due to fear of strangers; and it is curious to note that, according to M. Dallet, if they have grave disabilities they have also some quaint privileges, not the least remarkable of which is the right to circulate freely at all hours, even at night, in the streets of the capital; whereas no man can go out between 9 p.m. and 2 a.m., except in case of absolute necessity, without exposing himself to a heavy fine.

The government is founded on the Chinese model, with national variations; and, as in China, Confucianism tempered by Buddhism is the prevailing religion. But the Buddhistic element is said to command little affection; the temples are few and poor, and the priests rank low in the social scale. As in China, the so-called worship of ancestors is the one cult which touches the heart of the people; and the uncompromising war which Christian missionaries have declared against this practice is a chief cause of the difficulties and hostility they encounter, in both countries. What seems a curious survival of Fire Worship deserves a passing notice :—

> La plupart des familles [writes M. Dallet] conservent précieusement le feu dans la maison, et font en sorte de ne jamais le laisser éteindre. Si un pareil malheur arrivait, ce serait pour la famille le pronostic et la cause des plus grandes infortunes.

It is related, for instance, of a nobleman who was told by a slave that there was no fire in the house, that, quitting his guests, he rushed to the different braziers and examined the ashes with feverish anxiety. At last he perceived a spark; and, though we may suspect the verbal accuracy of the comprehensive speech with which he is credited, we may note with interest the implied significance of the cult.

Victoire, s'ecrie-t-il, en rentrant dans le salon ; les destins de ma race ne sont pas encore terminés. J'ai recouvré ce feu que mes ancêtres se sont fidèlement transmis depuis dix generations, et je pourrai à mon tour le léguer à mes descendants.

In its physical aspect, the peninsula of Corea presents a remarkable likeness to the peninsula of Italy. An axial range of mountains, similar in trend and appearance to the Apennines, runs along its whole length, close to, and parallel with, the eastern coast. Consequently, the streams running into the Pacific are but short mountain torrents, tumbling in a few miles from source to sea ; while those running into the China Sea are rivers of a certain magnitude, flowing through cultivated or cultivable plains. These physical peculiarities mark the distribution of the population and the present productive area of the country. Roughly speaking, the portions of the peninsula which lie to the west of the watershed are the most populous and fertile.

The valleys are fertile and fairly cultivated, though there does not seem to be, among their products, very much available for exportation to Europe. Cotton, hemp, flax, tobacco, indigo, hides and furs have been among the articles exported through the Japanese ; and these with, possibly, some silk, appear to indicate the principal elements of foreign commerce. "Of silk culture" Mr. Spence saw none in the country ; but, he adds, "they spin the cocoons of the wild ailanthus, and I procured hanks of their silk which to my inexperienced eye seemed closely to resemble Shantung silk." The tea shrub grows wild, but is also neglected. Hempen clothes are universally worn by the labouring classes, and the thread is spun much finer than would be possible with European hemp. "It must," Mr. Spence thinks, "be the same as the Chinese flax which grows in the neighbourhood of Newchwang; and, as the importation of that fibre into England has long been desired by our flax-spinners, and is only restricted on account of its high price, attention will probably be drawn to the Corean hemp as an article of commerce." The cotton shrub thrives, and white cotton cloth is largely manufactured. Tobacco and indigo are also grown; and, most valuable of all, the ginseng root which plays so important a part as a tonic and restorative in the Chinese pharmacopœia. Some idea of the value of this product may be formed from the fact that the duty paid on it in one year, at the Chinese frontier station, is said to have exceeded 100,000*l*. One of the chief curiosities is a remarkably small race of ponies, which are smaller and more shapely than our own Shetland breed. Another source of wealth which has been much neglected, is timber. The nature and capabilities of the country at the point where the peninsula merges into the continent are little known, further than that it is said to be richly wooded and that it is traversed by the greatest of the Corean rivers. But, even if this source failed, the grandly wooded range which we have seen on the eastern coast is covered with seemingly illimitable supplies.

The population, which is estimated at from eight to ten millions, is sparse except at a few principal centres, and generally poor; and the standards of comfort and industry are low. "Of ornamental art work," writes Mr. Spence, "such as porcelain, bronze, etc., they have none. . . . . The ceramic art is quite rudimentary, and they attach an excessive value to the commonest Japanese ware." Their greatest excellence seems to be attained in the manufacture of paper made from hemp, which is so strong that it is difficult to tear, and, as in Japan, is oiled and made into excellent waterproofs. The cabinet-makers also, according to Mr. Carles, show a certain amount of skill in their manufactures, and the brass and wicker work are not without finish.

The crudity of the financial arrangements is sufficient to indicate a very primitive state of trade. It required two ponies, each bearing a load of 280 lbs., to carry currency to the value of 30*l*., for which Mr. Carles' party had occasion. Almost the same difficulty might be predicated of the copper *cash* which form the prevailing medium of exchange in China; but the Chinese have invented an elaborate system of banking whereas, in Corea, though "merchants are said occasionally to give bills on each other," the arrangements are of a very restricted character. The Chinese have also a sufficiency of silver, which they cast into shoes of *sycee* of standard purity; whereas, in Corea, "failing paper and copper *cash*, silver ingots and gold-dust are to be bought sometimes, but not in large quantities, nor of a fixed standard." Obviously, if the people have made so little progress in finance, it is because they have not trade of sufficient volume to require a more elaborate system. The state of things indicated is, in fact, not far removed from barter.

It is time, with these few prosaic facts, to close our sketch of the so long Forbidden Land. A curious change has come over the scene since Father Frois described to wondering ears the great invasion of Fidejosi, and Henry Hamel narrated his strange experiences among a stranger people. As yet, the romance partly holds. A recent letter in the *North-China Herald*, describing a sacrificial visit by the king to the temple of Confucius, deals with a barbaric pomp of procession, a quaintness of costume, an idiosyncrasy of ceremonial as striking as any of the pictures which have been drawn for us, of Eastern life.

Mounted warriors resplendent in robes of various colours . . . then more flags, and a row of trumpeters, behind whom walked an officer bearing a red silk banner on which was embroidered a disk in the most brilliant gold thread. After the banners came a bevy of officers surrounding a man (the king) on horseback, dressed in a scarlet robe with gold embroidery on the chest and back, a lacquer belt studded with amber medallions, etc., etc. Before and behind the king open sedan-chairs were carried, and after these came a large covered litter, borne on the backs of ponies, which was draped inside and out with leopard skins. More mounted warriors and soldiers . . . were succeeded by a fresh batch of trumpeters, who marched in advance of a second banner similar to the one carried before the king, except that it was blue instead of red. Then came a second litter, in which was seated a diminutive boy dressed like the king, who, I was informed, was the Crown Prince. After the litter came more trumpeters, warriors, and foot-soldiers, and the procession had gone by.

We have here doubtless, as the writer suggests, an exact reproduction of a solemnity that has been observed for centuries but which will probably soon, now, become a thing of the past. Cavalry officers who are obliged "to maintain their balance by clutching hold of a handle fastened to the peak of the saddle for that purpose," and who have "one servant to lead the pony and another to hold them on," are an anachronism in these days of Uhlans and utilitarianism. But while they last—both processions and warriors—they will secure for the descriptive letters of first visitors some of the quaint interest which clings to the experiences of Hamel and Wettevree. "It is altogether," writes the same correspondent, "a strange country, this hermit kingdom. The pale, monotonous colours affected by the common people in their dress; the noiseless way in which they move about; the total lack of wheeled vehicles; the absence of street cries, or indeed of shouting of any sort, have a most weird effect; and as one passes through the silent, white-clad multitude, one almost finds oneself wondering whether it is all real, or whether one has not been suddenly transported to dreamland."

A similar interest attached to Japan, when that country first opened its doors to foreign visitors;

and there seems a remarkable similarity to Japan, in the thoroughness with which both Government and people are accepting the intercourse they had so long been at pains to repel. Let us hope that there will be no cause for reaction from all this *empressement*, but that it will settle down into steady working without the collisions, friction, and other unpleasant experiences that have characterized our early relations with other Oriental peoples.

It may be interesting to append an extract from the last report by H.M. Consul-General, on the trade of Corea (for 1892), to illustrate how far experience has modified the impressions of earlier visitors, and what has been the effect so far, upon the little kingdom, of the strange influences with which it has been brought in contact. Two great drawbacks to the development of trade are, still, want of proper currency arrangements and want of roads. Various minting experiments have been made, but without apparently much success. After describing them, Mr. Hillier goes on to say:

> While it must be admitted that, under present circumstances, the outlook is not encouraging, it would, I think, be premature to say that reform is impossible. It must be remembered that it is only a decade since Corea emerged from a condition of complete isolation, before which time all communication with the outside world, except under strict limitations, was absolutely prohibited. With the opening of the country to foreign commerce a new state of things commenced, and the history of the past few years has afforded undeniable evidence of the desire of the ruler of the

kingdom to do everything in his power to develop the resources of his domain, and to follow the example set by the neighbouring empire of Japan. Amongst the enterprises which owe their initiation to his personal energy, and have been supported entirely by his private funds, the following is by no means an exhaustive list: a paper manufactory, a match factory, gardens for the cultivation of the mulberry and the breeding of silkworms, looms for weaving silk and satin fabrics, a model farm conducted on Western principles for the growth of foreign cereals and the breeding of foreign stock, a powder manufactory and arsenal, a steamer company for developing trade with non-treaty ports, foreign schools, a foreign hospital for the treatment of indigent sick, a Government mint, an army drilled in the foreign fashion, a postal system, etc.

The melancholy fact has to be admitted that not one of these undertakings has been carried to a successful issue, with the exception, perhaps, of the foreign school, which still continues to exist, and would certainly flourish if encouragement were given to the pupils it turns out. The money absorbed in these enterprises forms a formidable total, and it is hardly to be wondered at that the King begins to weary of experiments that have cost him a fortune, and for which there is nothing to show but deserted buildings and rotting machinery. The fault lies in the system that has been adopted. There is no reason why, under proper conditions, success should not have attended almost all of them.

The error that has hitherto been committed is to carry on these undertakings as Government concerns with capital supplied by the Sovereign and filtering through native hands. The system must be changed if success is to be attained. What is wanted is to interest foreigners themselves, and to embark foreign capital in these schemes. The responsible authorities have hitherto been deluded into the belief that this country is a second El Dorado, and they consequently meet any overtures for the working of mines, etc., with exorbitant demands for the sale of concessions, followed by royalties which are practically prohibitive. The capabilities of the country in the matter of mineral wealth have never been properly tested, but it has certainly been proved that gold and other minerals do exist in sufficient quantities to be worked at a profit if the taxes upon the output are not exorbitant. It would be perfectly possible to secure the right of taking over such mines when the Government was ready to work them with any degree of success, and meanwhile a steady revenue could be obtained with no pecuniary risk whatever. As regards the actual debts of Corea, they are, comparatively speaking, trifling, and it would be a simple matter to pay them off in a year or two if the attempt were seriously made, and no more money was sunk in futile efforts to recover past losses by new undertakings under Corean management. Local taxation, as at present levied, would yield a fair revenue under honest management; but it must be years before a change can be expected in this quarter.

The agricultural capabilities of the country can be testified to with confidence. Not more, possibly, than half the available land is at present under cultivation, and the export of grain could easily be increased tenfold, and would be increased if facilities were given for bringing it to the sea coast. But roads must be made, and it is the business of no one to make them. Until this fact is recognized there is no likelihood of any great increase in the export trade of this country, upon the extent of which the import trade must depend. A bad agricultural year like the past season makes an immediate impression, but none the less there is a steady if gradual improvement, which will, I venture to predict, continue to go on in spite of the great drawbacks to its development which I have endeavoured to indicate.

The total export trade of Corea in 1892 amounted to $3,296,490, of which $852,721 was rough gold; and the imports to $4,598,485, of which rather less than half seems to have been represented by English cotton goods. The total foreign trade of Corea, as exhibited in the Customs Returns, thus amounts to about 1,000,000*l*. But Mr. Hillier suggests that these figures do not by any means represent the total trade of the country.

It has been estimated, indeed, that it would be safe to double them. However that may be, it is certain that foreign goods in no inconsiderable quantities are landed at places and ports along the coast which are not open to foreigners. At Pingyang, on the west coast, there is constant communication by junk with the Chinese mainland, and on the south and east coast there is not a bay or inlet in which Japanese fishing boats are not to be found. These vessels are constantly going and coming from Japan, and it is more than probable that they bring over with them small parcels of goods for sale at the various places which they frequent. There are no custom-houses to take cognizance of their proceedings, and no preventive service of any kind exists except at the treaty ports. Lastly, allowance must be made for the trade on the Russian and Chinese frontiers. No returns of this trade are procurable, but there is every reason to believe that the value is appreciably increasing.

CHAPTER X.

PORT HAMILTON.[1]

THE diffuseness of Blue-Books has been a standard subject of criticism since Blue-Books began, and is one cause, without doubt, that so very few of her Majesty's lieges peruse these records of their country's current history. Life is not long enough to disentangle the thread of a story from the jumble of despatches and telegrams, departmental correspondence and ambassadorial reports which go to make up these official records of a political episode. Yet the story is usually interesting when we do make up our minds to unravel it, and lets light into many dark corners which Press telegrams and even correspondents' letters had failed to illumine during the course of the episode.

Such a story has been given us in a Blue-Book about Port Hamilton. Here is no striking description of newly discovered lands. The Namhow islands themselves are unproductive and uninteresting, and the proceedings of the occupying force seem to have been of the most prosaic description. The

[1] Written in August, 1887.

interest lies in the side-light thrown on current history, in the glimpses we obtain of national sympathies and antipathies, and of political leanings and counteracting influences, which go to make up the sum of high policy in the East as well as in the West.

Few more curious cases of political evolution have occurred, of late, than the sudden rise into notoriety of the little kingdom of Corea, of which the Namhow group (constituting Port Hamilton) is an appanage. A few years ago, Corea was still outside the pale of European politics. It would hardly be an exaggeration to say it has now become, in one sense, the Belgium of Eastern Asia—a spot on which Chinese, Japanese, and Russian jealousies tend to converge, and in whose future England also takes a lively interest. The story of its darker days and of the experiences which heralded its entry into international life has been briefly told in the preceding chapter. There was room, at the time the king and his advisers were persuaded by China to enter into relations with Western Powers, for much speculation as to its social and commercial future; but there seemed no special reason to anticipate the development of Russo-Chinese antagonism which has brought it into strategical importance, or the access of Anglo-Russian hostility which has given notoriety to its outlying possession. All this, however, happened, and Corea soon found itself mixed up in a political turmoil that might well make it look back, yearningly, to the days of its isolation. For if the acceptance of European intercourse has marked a subversion of past conditions, it has energized latent forces. The story of Japanese invasions and Chinese interventions, of foreign intrusion and angry isolation, of Oriental intrigue and Western adventure—all this passed suddenly, as it were, into ancient history; but fresh jealousies and antagonisms came to supplement, and in a measure to supplant the old. Chinese and Japanese interests remained, though undergoing rapid transformation; while England and Russia found one more point of contact and antagonism. A likeness to Belgium has been suggested, but it is in point of political situation and not of commercial or national importance. The opening of Corea has, in fact, been rather disappointing from a commercial point of view. It yields gold, which might be extracted in greater quantity by more scientific methods; it has products which might be increased in value under better government and more enlightened auspices. But it is not its mineral or agricultural resources that have lifted it into sudden importance. It is the fact of its situation at a point where great national interests and rivalries tend to converge. Corea is an old battle-ground of China and Japan; and though the latter may have no thought, now, of realizing the dream of conquest which dictated the invasion of Tycosama, there may linger a flavour of jealousy in her attitude towards the protectorate which, after much vacillation, China is at length decidedly asserting. That feeling, which springs more from political tradition than from present aspirations, may be trusted to yield before greater and more urgent interests. The crucial feature of the situation is dread of Russian encroachment. China, which has already had practical experience of this proclivity, on the Amoor, seems determined to maintain Corea as a buffer between herself and her northern neighbour: determined, knowing that acquiescence would entail war sooner or later, to risk it sooner rather than later, in order to prevent Russia pressing down on the Yaloo river and weighing, from a Corean harbour, on the entrance to the Yellow Sea and the approaches to Peking. Japan, which has already had to exchange Saghalien for the rocky chain of the Kurile Islands, is scarcely less anxious than China to avert the presence of Russia on the opposite side of the Japanese Sea and of the Corean Strait. England's interest is less vital, but not less real. That interest is to fend off Russia from the China Sea. The most southerly harbour Russia at present possesses on the Pacific coast is Vladivostock,[1] in 43·7 N.; and Vladivostock is frozen up four months of the year. England is anxious she should not establish herself farther south, in a harbour open at all seasons, from whence her ships

[1] The position which Russia has obtained on the Tumen river (during negotiations for the delimitation of the Russo-Chinese frontier in that region) is about 1° farther south than Vladivostock, and may possibly come to supersede it, as the latter has superseded Nicolaefsk; but the change would scarcely be material to England from the point of view we are indicating, though it might have the inconvenience for China of raising up an important Russian station at the portals of Manchuria.

might issue in case of war to harass English commerce on the China coast or, still farther afield, in the Pacific Ocean. And so it happens that England, China, and Japan are impelled, by mutual interests, to resist Russian encroachment on Corea.

These, then, were the political conditions when the British Government resolved, in April, 1885, to occupy the three little islands situated in the mouth of the Corean Strait, which our sailors had christened Port Hamilton. The great object of Russian ambition on the Corean coast was well known to be an inlet at the head of Yung-hing (or Broughton) bay, lying between 39·10 and 39·20 N., which she has named Port Lazareff; and more than one scare had been occasioned, at Peking, by rumours that she was about settling herself in possession. As a point well suited to countervail the advantages of such a position, English officials had kept an eye on Port Hamilton; and a glance at the map seems to justify the selection. Though not actually land-locked—for there are outlets between Yesso and Niphon and between Niphon and Kiushiu, to say nothing of the northerly route through La Peyrouse Strait—the Sea of Japan is so far enclosed that the Corean Strait forms the easiest and most natural outlet into the China Sea; and Port Hamilton, lying in the centre of the Strait, practically commands that outlet, besides being in convenient proximity to the channel between Niphon and Kiushiu. Port Hamilton, therefore, in the hands of Russia—and there was reason to apprehend that, if we did not occupy it, Russia would

—meant a convenient naval station from whence to harass English commerce on the China coast; while Port Hamilton in the hands of England meant a station where our ships could rendezvous and re-coal, and around which they could cruise to prevent such raids—a station directly in the path of Russian ships descending from Vladivostock or Port Lazareff, a depôt some 1500 miles nearer than Hongkong, if it became necessary to attack the chief Russian station on the Pacific coast. Such, were, without doubt, the considerations which induced the British Government, during the height of the Pendjeh scare, to order the Admiral commanding our fleet on the China station to occupy Port Hamilton.

There never has been, however, and probably never will be, a topic on which opinions do not differ, and Port Hamilton is no exception to the rule. Sir Harry Parkes, our late representative at Peking, never ceased to insist on its importance. Admirals Ryder and Shadwell, former commanders-in-chief on the China station, were equally impressed with its value. But Admirals Willes and Dowell, who immediately succeeded those officers, and Admiral Hamilton who came after them, are of a different opinion. The convenience of the place seems beyond dispute; the situation is, in fact, ideal; it is the possibility and cost of fortifying and defending it that are called in question. A large initial outlay and a considerable garrison would, it is contended, be necessary to make it self-dependent; and its protection, without these precautions, would hamper much more than its possession would aid the movements of our fleet. These considerations, however, only assumed prominence at a later date. The question of the moment was not whether we could make the place a northern Hongkong, but whether it was likely to be useful as it stood, and especially whether we could afford to let it pass into other hands. The Government of the day decided that we could not, and telegraphed to Sir W. Dowell, on April 14th, 1885, the laconic order :

> "Occupy Port Hamilton, and report proceedings."

To which the Admiral replied, on the following day :

> "*Agamemnon*, *Pegasus* and *Firebrand* leave immediately for Port Hamilton to occupy harbour. Not to hoist flag until further orders, unless Russian men-of-war come in."

And a further telegram, dated May 12th, reports that the incident in question had taken place :

> "Russian volunteer ship *Vladivostock* visited Port Hamilton 10th May, remaining twenty-four hours. Union Jack hoisted on the island. Formation of harbour mines and other defences being proceeded with."

So, simply and briefly, was effected the British occupation of Port Hamilton. Twenty-four hours previously, it may be safely affirmed, hardly one European in a million had known that the islands exist; nor was the proportion much greater of Englishmen who knew where they are situated, when news came of their occupation. The incident, however, raised them at once into notoriety. They became a subject of comment in nearly every European capital, of question after question in Parliament, of frequent comment in the Press, and of diplomatic attention from all the four Powers whose interests have been shown to cluster in their neighbourhood.

The Admiralty orders given and executed, the Foreign Office accordingly took up the running. The islands are Corean territory; Corea is a tributary of China; and Japan could not be indifferent to the occupation, by England, of a position immediately opposite her coast. It is more than probable that diplomatic soundings had been taken, both at Peking and Tokio, if not in Söul itself, before the order for occupation was issued; and we shall risk little in assuming that the two former, at least, were tacitly content with a measure designed to exclude Russia. They would have preferred, no doubt, that the islands should remain in their previous insignificance; but they were willing to have them occupied by England, to avert a worse fate. So much would seem probable, and such is the inference that may be fairly drawn from the tenor of the replies to the communication which it behoved us to make to the respective Cabinets.

Japan acknowledged the intimation in a few well-chosen words, and then apparently held her hand. The following, at any rate, is the only despatch from our representative at Tokio which bears upon the subject:—

"While acknowledging the courtesy of Her Majesty's Government, the Foreign Minister replies that Japan cannot view without concern the occupation of a place so adjacent, even by a Power with whom her relations are so cordial. He wishes to learn, when proper, what arrangement has been made with Corea. His Excellency reserves further remarks."

China and Corea were more awkwardly situated. However well disposed they might be to see the islands under a safe ægis, they were likely to be vexed by the representations of a Power which was less willing to see Port Hamilton become a British station; and the existence and effect of these representations became soon apparent. Nothing could be more courteous or more cordial than the Marquis Tsêng's reply to the communication which Lord Granville made to him on April 27th.

". . . As these islands [wrote the Chinese Minister] belong to the kingdom of Corea, a country which is not only conterminous with China but which is a vassal of the Chinese Empire, the reported occupation of them by a foreign Power naturally could not be viewed without concern at Peking. This feeling, however, I am happy to be able to inform your lordship, has in some measure been allayed by the assurance contained in the communication under reply, that the occupation would only be of a temporary nature, and that Her Majesty's Government, being desirous of not doing anything which would be injurious to the prestige of China, would be prepared to come to such an agreement with the Chinese Government as would not be hurtful to Chinese rights and interests in those parts. The Imperial Government, after having taken due note of this assurance, and of the statement that, but for the exigency of circumstances, Her Majesty's Government would, before authorizing the occupation of the islands, have sought to come to an understanding with the Chinese Government on the subject, have instructed me to request your lordship to inform me of the kind of agreement which Her Majesty's Government would propose, in order to secure these objects."

The assent of China was affirmed, denied, and re-affirmed, during the discussions to which the occupation gave rise. It is at any rate clear, from this language, that the Imperial Government was willing to recognize the accomplished fact; and a strong inference as to previous understanding may be drawn from the following draft agreement, which Lord Granville was able to submit (within twenty-four hours) in immediate response to the Chinese Minister's request:—

"Earl Granville, K.G., Her Majesty's Principal Secretary of State for Foreign Affairs, and the Marquis Tsêng, Envoy Extraordinary and Minister Plenipotentiary from His Imperial Majesty the Emperor of China, having met this day at the Foreign Office, an exchange of views took place with regard to the possible occupation of Port Hamilton by Great Britain.

"The Marquis Tsêng stated, in answer to Lord Granville's inquiry, that he was authorized by his Government to declare that, in the event of the British Government desiring, at any time, to occupy the islands lying off the south Coast of Corea, known by the name of 'Port Hamilton,' His Imperial Majesty the Emperor of China would offer no objection to such occupation; and Earl Granville having taken due notice of this declaration, it was mutually agreed that from the day on which Her Britannic Majesty should deem it advisable to occupy those islands they should be acknowledged by His Imperial Majesty the Emperor of China as lawfully occupied and administered by England.

"It is understood between the two High Contracting Parties that Her Britannic Majesty's Government shall, at the expiration of twelve months from the date of occupation, pay to the Corean Government the whole of the revenue that may have been received by them from the islands, and a similar sum at the expiration of every twelve months during the continuance of the occupation of the islands by Great Britain, deducting therefrom and paying to China any portion of that revenue which has hitherto been paid to China by Corea as tribute in regard to these islands.

"It is also understood that the British occupation is not to prejudice either the rights or the privileges of the subjects of Corea inhabiting the islands."

If the second paragraph did not speak for itself, a strong conclusion might be drawn from the very promptitude of the reply: diplomatists do not formulate such documents off-hand, nor utter them officially without previous consultation. Everything, in fact, seemed settled, and all susceptibilities conciliated. Nine days later, however, a disturbing influence had clearly been at work; and the Marquis Tsêng was obliged, on May 6th, to communicate the following polite refusal, by his Government, of the proposed arrangement:

"The Chinese Government would have been much gratified had circumstances permitted their meeting the views of Her Majesty's Government in the matter of the proposed occupation; but in view of the Russian Minister at Peking having given the Yamên to understand that, should the Chinese Government consent to a British occupation of the islands forming Port Hamilton, the Russian Government would feel it necessary to occupy some other island or portion of the kingdom of Corea; also in view of the possibility of Japan following in the same course, the Chinese Government regret that, in order to avoid these inconveniences and the possible complications which might result from them, they cannot authorize their Minister to sign the arrangement proposed by Her Majesty's Government, and instruct him to express the hope that Her Majesty's Government will not find it necessary to occupy the islands."

It is rather amusing to note that all this passed in full view of the fact that the occupation had been effected; and it is significant that, even on May 18th, the Chinese Government acquiesced in the laying of a cable between Port Hamilton and the mouth of the Yangtze. Nor is it till six months later, when the Afghan difficulty had subsided, and Russian protests had evidently become urgent, that we find any serious remonstrance against the continued presence of our ships.

Before passing, however, to these subsequent negotiations, we may take the opportunity of seeing how Corea treated the occupation of what was really her territory, however outlying and slightly held. Her assent also has been affirmed, but it is fair to say that no such inference can be drawn from the published despatches. These express, rather, surprise, objection, and nervous fear of ulterior complications. The King's first step was to send two high officials to ask explanations, and to lodge a protest with the English Admiral; and his next to address (May 20) to our representative, at his capital, the following emphatic protest :—

"A rumour has lately reached me from the 'inner seas' that Her Britannic Majesty's Government has designs upon the island of Chü Wên, otherwise called Port Hamilton.

"This island is a possession of my Government which no other country has the right to trespass upon, such an act being justified by no principle of international law. The intelligence caused me alarm and suspicion, which it is inexpedient that I should give clear expression to, and some days ago officers were sent to the island in question to ascertain whether the rumour was true or not. Although they have not yet returned, I have received an official communication from you, which is a note sent from the Legation at Peking, upon careful perusal of which I learn from its purport that I must now give credence to the correctness of the earlier report. It is inconceivable that a Government like that of Great Britain, which attaches importance to the obligations of comity, and has a clear perception of the requirements of international law, should act in a manner so unexpected, and I am inexpressibly astonished at the disappointment of the hopes which I had formed.

"If Her Majesty's Government does attach importance to the obligations of comity, she will reverse her aims and at once withdraw from this island, to the great good fortune of my country, while she will also secure the respectful admiration of all. Should she fail to do so, the moral obligations of my Government will not allow them to remain silent spectators of this proceeding, which they will, moreover, make known to all countries with whom they have Treaty relations, and submit the proceeding to the test of public opinion.

"This matter admits of no delay, and I therefore send you this preliminary letter, giving an explicit expression of my views, to which I earnestly beg the favour of an immediate reply."

No time was lost in assuring the President of the Corean Foreign Office, in reply, that "the occupation had been brought about by force of circumstances; that it was in no way intended to prejudice the veritable interests of Corea, and that there was no desire whatever to menace her integrity." A willingness was further expressed to come to any satisfactory arrangement, and a rent of 5000*l.* was subsequently offered. Tempting, however, as this price must have been to a poor Government, the King evidently dared not accept it; and we need probably go no farther than a letter from Mr. Consul-General Baber, dated October 23rd, 1885, to find an explanation of the refusal. The President of the Corean Foreign Office had, Mr. Baber reports, called on the previous evening,

"to inquire whether any communication had been received from Her Majesty's Government in reply to his letter of the 7th July, remonstrating against our occupation of Port Hamilton. M.

Waeber (the representative of Russia) had, on the previous day, been pressing him somewhat closely on the matter, asserting that he had learnt that a project was on foot by which Corea was to sell Port Hamilton to Great Britain. The President further requested Mr. Aston to repeat to the British Government the representation of the difficulty in which our occupation of the islands had placed Corea with regard to other Powers."

It is clear indeed that, at Söul as well as at Peking, the motive of our occupation was perfectly understood, and that the wish to be rid of us was dictated much more by fear of Russia than by irritation at our presence. The very protest we have quoted—formal and almost indignant though it sounds—was withdrawn shortly after, at the instance of our Consul-General, supported probably by the Chinese Government; and even the Nanhow islanders seemed to comprehend that our presence implied no shadow of hostility to their Government. It is likely, in fact, that the language of the official utterances lost nothing in vigour from the presence in the Foreign Office of a gentleman named von Mollendorff, who had been delegated by the Grand Secretary, Li Hung-chang, to assist Corea in her foreign relations, but who took up an attitude hostile to his patron, and so favourable to Russian influence, that he was displaced and recalled during the course of the episode.

Once more, in the summer of 1886, we find the Corean Government urging the embarrassing position in which it was placed by our continued presence; but the project of safeguarding the islands in some other way had already come to supersede, in the mind of Her Majesty's Government, any question of ulterior occupation, and the King and his Ministers were destined to be very soon relieved of their anxiety.

We return, now, to the negotiations with China which constitute the important feature of the episode. Reference has been made to a despatch from Peking of October 14th, 1885, mentioning that Li Hung-chang had raised seriously the question of our prolonged occupation:

"The Russian question had [said the Grand Secretary] now been settled, and it was time that the British Government did something to put an end to the present unsatisfactory state of things, which placed the Chinese Government in a very unpleasant position *vis-à-vis* to other Powers, and, if continued, was even calculated to mar the friendship between England and China. The question was a very grave one, and ought not to be allowed to drag on in this unsatisfactory way. Corea had declined, and he now thought rightly so, to part with any of her territory, and he could assure me, as a fact within his own positive knowledge, that if the Corean Government accepted to rent the island, a demand would be presented from another quarter, within ten days, for the cession of other territory on the same terms."

This position was still more clearly formulated in a communication made to the Foreign Office by Sir Halliday Macartney, on March 11th, 1886, by direction of the Marquis Tsêng:

"He [Sir Halliday] stated that 'the Russian Minister at Peking has on several occasions urged the Chinese Government to obtain the withdrawal of the British force from the islands forming Port Hamilton, and has stated that, in the event of the British occupation being continued, Russia would feel obliged to occupy some place in Corea.' Under these circumstances, Sir H. Macartney was instructed to ask what were the intentions of Her

Majesty's Government with regard to the prolongation of the occupation of Port Hamilton, which it was understood, at the time it was made, was to be only of a temporary nature."

Lord Salisbury had, however, already intimated, in reply to the observations of the Grand Secretary, that England would be ready to withdraw if the Chinese Government would undertake that the islands should not be occupied by any other foreign country. And Lord Rosebery, who had in the meantime taken up the seals, now (April 14th) elaborated that suggestion into a formal proposal:

"Her Majesty's Government have no desire to prolong the occupation of Port Hamilton in opposition to the wishes of the Chinese Government, but it appears to them that it would be against the interests both of China and England if it were to be occupied by another European Power. If the Chinese Government are prepared to guarantee that no such occupation shall take place, one of the chief objects which Her Majesty's Government had in view in taking possession of Port Hamilton would be accomplished.

"Should the Chinese Government be unwilling to undertake such a responsibility, Her Majesty's Government would suggest that China should propose to Russia and to the other Powers interested, to enter into an international arrangement guaranteeing the integrity of Corea. If this proposal is accepted, Her Majesty's Government would be ready to become parties to the arrangement, and to retire at once from Port Hamilton on the understanding that it should be recognized as forming part of the guaranteed territory of Corea."

It was, as is well known, on these lines that a solution was eventually reached; and we may perhaps pause here, while the Chinese Government is considering and working out the suggestion, to review the opinions of Her Majesty's naval officers as to the value of Port Hamilton as a possession. The geographical position of the islands had, as we have seen, strongly commended them to Admirals Ryder and Shadwell, as a naval station, and a glance at the map must certainly sustain that impression. But their successors in command looked at the matter from another standpoint. So early as May 20th, 1885, within five weeks of the occupation, Admiral Dowell telegraphed:

"As long as we have command of the sea, Hongkong sufficient base. Port Hamilton can be shelled from without unless fortified; consequently must have squadron for its protection. It could be used as an anchorage whenever necessary, without occupation. Any Power holding it permanently must make a second Malta of it. I have taken captains' opinion; they quite agree with me."

And again, on July 15th:

"I think it my duty to again point out that, unless Port Hamilton is adequately fortified and garrisoned, it must be a source of weakness to the navy rather than strength. I am glad to observe that Sir Cooper Key when suggesting, in 1882, the occupation of Port Hamilton, recommended that it should be made 'a first-class fortress'; if this were done I should certainly advocate its retention."

These two paragraphs appear to contain the kernel of the question. Made a first-class fortress, Port Hamilton would be a valuable possession; but its openness to attack from three separate entrances would make it "a source of weakness to the navy rather than of strength," unless this were done; instead of being a safe coaling station and place of resort for our ships in emergency, it would require the constant presence of an efficient squadron to protect it; and it would be wiser to rely for supplies, in case of war, on a steam flotilla to accompany the fleet. Admiral Willes, who appears to have been consulted during the occupation, clearly expresses this view in a letter dated January 7th, 1886:

"I went to Port Hamilton several times during my command, and I still hold the opinion which I then formed, that Port Hamilton is useless and expensive in ordinary peace times, and in war or during one of the 'periodical scares' would be a source of weakness, as the Admiral in command would have to detach some of his ships to defend the islands (forming the harbour) instead of employing them in the protection of our commerce.

"It was said, last spring, that if England did not take possession of Port Hamilton some other nation would. A short study of the chart and a few minutes' reflection will show that this is absurd. Only the nation which 'commands the sea' can hold our new acquisition, for the islands are practically barren.

"It is supposed that, in war, a coaling-station in the northern part of the command is necessary. I am not of that opinion. Steam colliers properly fitted must be filled with Welsh coal at Hongkong, and follow our ships."

Captain Long, of the *Agamemnon*, writes:

"If the place is to be a base for, and not to be a tax upon, the navy, it will require a garrison and fortifications. At present it requires the constant presence of a large proportion of the naval force on the station, to preserve the flag from insult in the event of war."

Admiral Hamilton, finally, writing in December, 1885, says:

"Considering that military defence is still a work of time, it cannot be expected Port Hamilton can become, as Sir Cooper Key considered necessary, a first-class fortress for many years. Its defence must therefore, till then, devolve on the navy. Until it is properly fortified I look on its occupation 'as a source of weakness in war time to the cruising power of the squadron in the China command.' . . . I quite concur in the views of my predecessor, as expressed in his letter of the 28th of May last, as to our true base for naval work being a steam flotilla, which can always be obtained here, to accompany the fleet with the necessary coal, provisions, stores, &c., and a temporary base established at the most suitable port on the enemy's coast, near the port to be attacked."

And the Lords of the Admiralty, summing up the case in March, 1886, opine that,

"unless it be the intention of Her Majesty's Government to fortify and garrison the island, so as to place it in a proper condition of defence to resist the attack of iron-clads, their Lordships are decidedly of opinion that it is not advisable to retain possession of Port Hamilton.

"It is impossible, however, to overlook the fact that, if Her Majesty's Government is prepared to incur the expense of placing the island in an efficient state of defence, its possession might prove valuable to the squadron in the China Seas."

The nation has not, assuredly, shown any unwillingness to spend money on the defence of coaling stations; but political motives no doubt combined with these qualified opinions as to the value of Port Hamilton to dissuade the Government from putting forward any proposal for its permanent retention. It would have been clearly impolitic to prolong an occupation, begun with China's goodwill, in defiance of China's opposition. The solution suggested in Lord Rosebery's despatch of April 14th met all difficulties; and Sir John Walsham was able, on November 5th, 1886, to inform Lord Iddesleigh that China had obtained the requisite assurances from Russia, and was able therefore to give the required guarantee to Great Britain. The following extract from the Chinese despatch will explain the present situation:

"A long time has now elapsed, and British vessels of war continue to hold these islands, thus giving rise to embarrassing questions from without. For instance, rumours have recently been disseminated from Corea that Russia was interfering with China's feudatory. The Chinese Government accordingly demanded an explanation from Russia as to the existence or otherwise of this fact, and in due course the Russian Foreign Office gave the Chinese Minister Liu the most frank assurances that the Russian Government had absolutely no such intentions. M. Ladygensky, the Russian Chargé-d'Affaires at Peking, further went to Tien-tsin at the orders of the Russian Foreign Office, and had several personal conversations with the Grand Secretary Li, to whom he repeated and enlarged upon the answer earlier given to the Minister Liu. He also stated that the Russian Government gave a sincere promise that, if the British would evacuate Port Hamilton, the Russian Government would not occupy Corean territory under any circumstances whatsoever.

"The Grand Secretary Li then told M. Ladygensky that what was feared was that after the British vessels of war had retired from these islands they would be again taken possession of by some other Power. Russia, therefore, must guarantee that she would not hereafter seize these islands, and on the faith of this guarantee China could officially address the British Government, and urge their speedy evacuation.

"In course of time, M. Ladygensky, in obedience to instructions from the Russian Government, gave a most explicit guarantee, distinctly declaring that in the future Russia would not take Corean territory.

"The Chinese Government is therefore naturally in a position, on the faith of the guarantee of the Russian Government, to give a guarantee to the British Government; and in making this communication as is their bounden duty, to Her Britannic Majesty's Minister, they would express a hope that he will lose no time in communicating the above particulars to Her Majesty's Government, with a view to the issue of orders for the evacuation of Port Hamilton by their vessels of war, so that friendly relations may thereby be consolidated."

The object of later negotiations having been thus obtained, Her Majesty's Government at once intimated to the Chinese and Corean Governments their readiness to terminate the occupation. Despatches from those Governments, expressing satisfaction at the decision and appreciation of the loyalty with which Her Majesty's Government had acted, terminate the series; and a telegram from Admiral Hamilton, dated February 28th, 1887,

"Flag hauled down at Port Hamilton on 27th,"

closes the episode as laconically as it was opened.

The British occupation of Port Hamilton is then at an end. It remains only to sum up the results of the adventure, and to examine the conditions which the settlement has brought about; for the incident involves a political departure more pregnant than might be apparent at a surface glance. Port Hamilton belongs, as we have seen, to Corea; and the first reply (in January, 1886) of the Chinese Government, to our suggestion that they should occupy it themselves or give us a guarantee that it would not be occupied by any other European Power, was that "the territory was Corean, and that it was not the practice of China to occupy her vassals' territory; that they did not see how they could undertake that the islands would not be occupied by any other European Power; and that such an undertaking was not a matter of immediate concern." We are not concerned, here, with the nature of the relations between China and her tributaries in the past. Suffice it to say that, although perfectly understood between the Middle Kingdom and its neighbours, those relations have proved apparently less intelligible to Western Powers—insufficiently definite, at any rate, to withstand the influence of changing conditions; and China, as explained of late by the Marquis Tsêng,[1] seems determined to place them on a less equivocal footing for the future.

> "The arrangements [writes the Marquis] for the government of her vassal States which, until the steamer and the telegraph brought the East and the West so near, had been found sufficient, having on different occasions of late led to misunderstandings between China and foreign Powers, and to the loss of some of the more important of her possessions, China, to save the rest, has decided on exercising a more effective supervision over the acts of her vassal princes, and on accepting a larger responsibility for them than heretofore. The Warden of the Marches is now abroad and looking to the security of China's outlying provinces of Corea, Thibet, and Chinese Turkestan. Henceforth, any hostile movements against these countries, or any interference with their affairs, will be viewed at Peking as a declaration on the part of the Power committing it of a desire to discontinue its friendly relations with the Chinese Government."

Her Imperial Crown having, in short, lost some of its brightest jewels,[2] she is determined to protect the remainder. The Marquis guards himself, it is true, by a protest that he is writing irresponsibly; but neither can we forget that he took, immediately on

[1] "China: The Sleep and the Awakening." By the Marquis Tsêng. *Asiatic Quarterly Review*, January 1887.

[2] Annam and Tongking, Burmah, Siam, and the Liuchiu Islands—all once more or less tributary—have all passed away, more or less, from allegiance; while Russia has absorbed a large slice of the old Manchu country, the cradle of the reigning dynasty.

his arrival, a prominent position on the Foreign Board at Peking. We may, therefore, fairly look on the Chinese guarantee in the case of Port Hamilton as one feature only in a larger scheme of policy. Port Hamilton will be protected, not only because it has strategical importance, but because it is Corean territory and Corea is a vassal State; and the declaration which China has obtained from Russia applies not only to Port Hamilton, but to all Corea.

The English occupation has, therefore, been fruitful at least to this extent: it has strengthened the Chinese position in Corea, and it has been the means of eliciting from Russia a declaration not only that she will not touch Port Hamilton, but (indirectly) that she will refrain also from occupying Port Lazareff, inasmuch as she promises to respect completely the integrity of Corea. The declaration might not stand the test of exigency in time of war, but it has at least the advantage of removing apprehension of suprise in time of peace.

That Port Hamilton will be guarded as safely under the Chinese ægis as by British artillerymen and marines, even the Chinese would hardly venture to affirm. There is always a prospect, when the pendulum has swung too far one way, that it will swing too far the other; and there is a tendency, in Europe, to pass from the *quantité négligeable* theory which prevailed before the Franco-Chinese war, to an over-estimate of China as a military power. Huc has very reasonably urged that the ease of our success in the war of 1841-2 was due more, even, to the superiority of our arms than to that of our men; and that what was condemned as cowardice on the part of the Chinese was really, in part at least, an intelligent recognition of the utter hopelessness of the conflict. The better success of their recent stand in Tongking and Formosa was due no doubt, in great measure, to the better weapons they have tardily obtained. These at least gave confidence to the soldier, though they did not magically inspire brigades with discipline, nor officers with dash and tactical skill. That the Chinese should themselves be elated at the successful resistance offered by their troops in the highlands of Tongking is, perhaps, natural. Their pride and courage had been depressed by the issue of former conflicts with Europe, and both revived with the first shadow of encouragement. But though her almost limitless numbers will always make China a formidable antagonist, it will be long before the looseness of Chinese discipline and the incapacity of Chinese officers will be so far amended as to make a Chinese army a fair match for that of any Western Power, in pitched battle; while the incapacity of her fleet was the chief reason she had eventually to surrender Tongking. The fact has been recognized at Peking, and great efforts are being made to increase the strength and efficiency of her armament afloat. The English officers who had been helping to organize her navy withdrew at the outbreak of hostilities with France; but it is possible that a war involving the safety of Port Hamilton might be fought under different conditions; and the presence, on board, of a few foreigners might not impossibly energize the capabilities of a nominally powerful iron-clad fleet.

Port Hamilton, therefore, declared to be so implicitly under Chinese protection that any attempt to occupy it would entail war with China, will be in a very different position from a mere outlying possession of a kingdom powerless in itself and hardly protected by its ill-understood relations with the Chinese Empire—a group of islands lying half-derelict in mid-channel, a sort of No Man's Land, at the mercy of the first comer. It was one thing to steam in and "squat" on this neglected spot; it will be quite another, now it is distinctly understood that China would resent the intrusion. We may rely, therefore, that no foreign Power will venture on such a step, unless war with China has been either decided on or declared; and it is not unlikely that, in such case, others than China might avow an interest in the event. There seems no room, therefore, for criticizing the decision of the British Government to yield up Port Hamilton to Corean and Chinese hands. We may regret losing hold of a place so conveniently situated as a coaling station for our ships in these northern seas—a station that would become, too, of increasing value as our interests in the Pacific grow and develop with the establishment of communication between Canada and our Eastern settlements. But it would have been bad policy to sacrifice China's confidence and friendship, over a wider field, for the sake of a possession whose value would be measurably lessened by the mere fact of her disapproval; to say nothing of the fact, which has been sufficiently emphasized, that its retention would almost certainly have involved a counterbalancing annexation by Russia. Our occupation has served at least one-half its purpose, in evoking a guarantee that neither it nor any other Corean port shall be used against us. To have retained it would have been to jeopardize these results, and to invite at least one of the dangers which its occupation was designed to counterpoise.

We have seen, then, that the story of Port Hamilton involves political considerations of wider scope than the mere incident of its occupation, for strategical purposes, at a moment of quarrel. That occupation has disclosed political leanings, and hastened the development of political groupings, that may exert a powerful influence on future history in the East. It is reported that China has begun to fortify the islands over which she has extended her ægis. The natives will, in that case, probably regret the change; and those who have been prone, of late, to criticize the British soldier, might learn a useful lesson in questioning the Nanhow fishermen as to their relative experience of the respective garrisons.[1] However that may be, the change will, we may rest assured, be cordially welcomed by those

[1] It is a remarkable fact that, although we had at times over 2000 men in the place, no single case of interference with the women occurred. It may be inferred from this how excellent was the discipline, and how sincere were the thanks expressed by the native headmen, on the departure of the Marines, for the respect paid to their customs.

upon whom the task of occupation devolved; for it is no exaggeration to say that Port Hamilton is, to naval men, an object of cordial detestation. If it represent to them, in future, a memory of skilful enterprise, it will also be a tradition of wearisome, dreary stay. If they sometimes look in at their temporary anchorage, they will recall the day when the Union Jack floated over Observatory Island with far less regret than they regard, from time to time, the painted fragments of ancient storehouses which recall our former occupations of Chusan.[1]

[1] This island which was occupied by us in 1840-6, and again in 1860, was also protected, on our withdrawal, by a guarantee against occupation by any other foreign Power.

CHAPTER XI.

RUSSIA AND CHINA.

WRITING after a recent visit to Manchuria, with the fate of Burmah and Tongking fresh in his recollection, the present Minister of the United States at Peking hazarded a conjecture that "the vast outlying territories on the north and west of the Chinese Empire . . . will some time be subjected to a similar experience;" and Sir Thomas Wade, late H.M.'s representative in China, has expressed even graver apprehensions in speaking of the ignorance and apathy of the Chinese. He disclaims, it is true, any purpose of "pointing particularly either to Russia, or France, or ourselves, or anybody else, as directly menacing the independence of China"; but he goes even beyond Colonel Denby in the "dread with which he looks forward to the possibility of her succumbing to a foreign power, out of sheer backwardness and inertia."

The words are pregnant with suggestion regarding the possibilities of the future in Eastern Asia. They echo, too, an anxiety which finds expression in high places in China itself; for, though the charge of ignorance is true as regards the mass of the people, there are enlightened statesmen who can perceive the danger. Nor do they, less guarded than

Sir Thomas Wade, make any secret of the quarter towards which their apprehensions are directed. It is the Power whose frontiers march with their own from the Pamirs to the Pacific whose restlessness excites their alarm, and with which events seem tending to bring them into ever closer contact.

Fifty years ago, the Chinese Emperor claimed to rule as a sovereign or suzerain over the whole enormous stretch of territory from the 73rd parallel of west longitude to the Pacific coast, and from about 50° north to the China Sea and the Indian Ocean. Chrysé has since been reft from his grasp: Siam has thrown off allegiance, Annam and Tongking have passed under the protectorate of France, Burmah has been drawn under the ægis of the Kaiser-i-Hind. But, though curtailed on the south, the Chinese Empire still extends over the whole great mass of highlands known to us as Thibet, Turkestan, Mongolia, and Manchuria: and along 3200 miles of northern frontier it is conterminous with Russia. More than once during the last two thousand years, this great territory has been subdued, lost and brought again under the Chinese yoke. The early emperors of the reigning dynasty had, last, to reconstruct the empire their fathers had shattered. Mongolia was again subjected; Chinese rights were successfully asserted against Russia on the Amoor; and Kien-lung (1735-96)—in defiance, it is said, of the advice of his councillors, who opposed the annexation as a probable source of weakness rather than of strength—forced his authority on Thibet, and reduced Sungaria and Eastern Turkestan. For nearly a hundred and fifty years the fruits of these victories were preserved; but then the long peace was broken up. The great Mahomedan insurrection which gave excuse for the Russian occupation of Kuldja reft away, for a time, the whole region along the Central Asian trade route, from Shense to Kashgar, and seemed likely, for a moment, to result in a fresh dismemberment of the empire. Dynastic and national pride, however, were engaged; and by a mixture of arms, intrigue and diplomacy; by the perseverance, victories, massacres, and bribery of Tso Tsung-tang, and by the skilful diplomacy of the Marquis Tsêng and his foreign colleagues, these provinces have been again recovered.

It has been otherwise in Manchuria; and nothing is more significant of the change that has taken place in European appreciation of events in the Far East, than the contrast between the interest shown in the Chinese recovery of Kuldja and the inattention amid which Russia was able, thirty years ago, to effect a vastly more important annexation on the Pacific coast. It is, indeed, only lately that the real value of this great territory seems to have dawned on Chinese statesmen, their perception having been sharpened by a keen appreciation of threatened loss.

The Russians made their first appearance in Manchuria about the time of the Manchu conquest of China. Certain Cossacks sent out from Tomsk to collect tribute had continued advancing till they stood (in 1637) on the shores of the Sea of Okhotsk;

and the news they brought back led to the despatch of others, who established themselves on both banks and erected fortresses at Albazin and Kamarskoi before China was ready to cope with the emergency. It would be superfluous to dwell on the exploits of the adventurers during the next nine years; Mr. Ravenstein,[1] to whom we are indebted for an admirably succinct narrative of the invasion, thus summarizes the results:

"The natives appear to have been exposed to all manner of extortion. Tribute was levied to an unlimited extent without any commensurate good being conferred. No settlements of tillers of the soil were founded. The resources of the country were soon exhausted by perpetual foraging expeditions of Russian adventurers. When they (the Russians) first arrived on the Amoor the natives cultivated fields and kept cattle. Ten years afterwards those fields had become deserts, and a country which formerly exported grain could not even support its own reduced population."

The reports that reached Moscow had begun, however, to inspire a more definite purpose of annexation, and one Stepanoff was sent with a force of 3000 men to effect that object. But the Chinese, who had been preoccupied, and comparativelv indifferent to the earlier raids, began to turn serious attention to this invasion. An army of 10,000 men was despatched to the scene; and Stepanoff, after repulsing with much valour an attack on Kamarskoi, was slain with 270 of his men in attempting to re-descend the river. Several years seem to have elapsed, after this disaster, before the Russians again entered the Amoor basin; but the project was too tempting to

[1] "The Russians on the Amoor."

be relinquished, and a renewed occupation of Albazin led to renewed hostilities in which the Chinese were again successful. They threw a strong garrison into Aigun, on the right bank of the Amoor, and from thence advanced westward, driving the Russians before them till all the settlements on the lower Amoor and its tributaries had been captured or destroyed. Intermittent hostilities continued during three following years; but negotiations were opened in 1686 with the object of preventing, in future, these perpetual collisions; and a frontier was eventually settled that left Nerchinsk and the Upper Shilka to the Russians, but excluded them from the Amoor basin, which was affirmed to belong entirely to China.

The treaty of Nerchinsk held good for a hundred and sixty years. There were encroachments by hunters, and troubles arising from ill-defined tribal boundaries; a fresh convention was even negotiated, for the mutual surrender of deserters, in 1768. But the frontier remained unaltered; nor was it till the middle of the present century that Russia resumed her movement of aggression. Full of fish; running through broad tracts of pasture and cultivable land; having forests of valuable timber and gold-fields on its banks; navigable for nearly two thousand miles, up to the point of junction of its parent rivers; and receiving four great tributaries, the Dzeya and Bureyn on the north, and the Sungari and Usuri on the south, besides minor affluents—the Amoor might well excite the cupidity of the Governors of Irkutsk.

But it was the means it afforded of access to Kamtschatka and the Pacific coast, that led to its final appropriation. Already, in 1854, Lieutenant Orloff had entered it from the Pacific, and founded Nikolaefsk and Marinsk as trading stations—on land, be it noted, belonging to China. When, during the Crimean War, the superiority of the English fleet rendered these places inaccessible by sea, the idea occurred to Mouravieff, who was then Governor of Eastern Siberia, of reaching them by means of the Amoor. The Chinese protested, but did not venture to oppose: the journey was accomplished; and Mouravieff went to St. Petersburg to advise the acquisition of a region and a waterway of such evident value. His project was approved. Times had changed since Kanghi had imposed terms at Nerchinsk: the Taeping rebellion was convulsing China Proper; the Anglo-French armies were threatening Peking; and he was able to exact a treaty containing the following vital clause:

> "The left bank of the river Amoor, from the river Argoun to its mouth, shall belong to the Empire of Russia, and its right bank down to the river Usuri, to China. The territories situated between the river Usuri and the sea, as up to the present, shall be possessed in common by the Empires of China and Russia until the frontier between the two states shall be defined. . . ."

Regaining confidence with the repulse of the Allies at Taku, the Chinese showed a disposition to repudiate this concession; but the capture of Peking brought them again to their knees: General Ignatieff succeeded, in 1860, in imposing a fresh treaty confirming the first and ceding, besides, the whole coastline between the Usuri and the sea as far south as the Tumen river which constitutes the boundary of Corea.

Russia has since been frequently accused of a desire to overleap the Tumen and add Corea to her Pacific seaboard: Vladivostock, her most southern port, is ice-bound during a portion of the year, whereas the harbours of Corea are free from that inconvenience. She repudiates, of course, any such conception, and placed her disclaimer on record during the negotiations that attended our withdrawal from Port Hamilton. China seems hardly yet convinced; having observed perhaps, like ourselves, that circumstances are occasionally too strong for the good intentions of the Czar. She may find, however, in the conflicting interests of others, a safety greater than even treaties could ensure; for other great Powers have been showing, lately, an interest in the once Hermit Kingdom that may prove its best safeguard against annexation to Primorsk.

The next negotiation carries us to the opposite end of the long frontier, and marks a change in the tone of Chinese diplomacy. The Anglo-French war is at an end; rebellion has been put down, and the Imperial Government no longer feels helpless amid a chaos of disaster. The Amoor is ceded and gone; but the Ili, at least, may be reclaimed. Chunghow's famous treaty, which so nearly cost him his head, has never been made public; but the surrender of the Tekkes Valley is known to have been one of its most objectionable features, and it is further understood to have rectified frontiers and conceded privileges with somewhat reckless freedom. It is to the credit of the Marquis Tsêng that he was able to recover the lost ground, and to procure the surrender of Kuldja without more serious concessions than the right to appoint Russian consuls at various points in Mongolia and Turkestan and facilities for commercial intercourse.

One important reason for China's anxiety to recover Kuldja was that it constituted, in Russian hands, an open door into Sungaria; and it is mainly because they command passes into Kashgaria that she is disturbed by Colonel Yanoff's occupation of the Pamirs. For it would be the very madness of land-hunger to covet them for the sake of territorial possession, and the idea of the Chinese ever crossing them to attack Ferghana may be simply dismissed with a smile. Captain Younghusband's excellent map [1] enables us to appreciate the situation, by following the Russian movements and noting wherein they clash with Chinese interests and claims. A line drawn diagonally from N.W. to S.E. will guide us from the Russian base at Khokand past Karakul (which is admittedly Russian), past the Rangkul (which Russia claims, but which China asserts to be within her sphere), to Aktash, on the River Aksu (in about 37·35 N. and 74·55 E.), where a Russian post has now been established. A little to the N.N.E. of

[1] "The Pamirs and Adjacent Regions." *Proceedings of R.G.S.* April, 1892.)

Aktash is Tagharma, where there is said to be also a Russian outpost; a little to the S.W. is Boshai Gumbaz, where Captain Younghusband came in contact with Colonel Yanoff in 1891; and N.W. from Boshai we find the Alichur, where a brush between Afghans and Cossacks is reported to have lately occurred. So that the Russians would seem to have encircled the Great and Little Pamirs, and taken up positions not only on the frontiers of Wakhan and Shighnan but within the province of Sarakul, which is an admitted appanage of Chinese Turkestan.

It has been a leading principle of China's policy to surround herself with "buffer" States, and Turkestan itself is probably valued less as a dependency than as an outwork masking the approach to her north-west provinces. When the tribes were independent they were prone to invade China—the blaze lighted by Yakoob Khan spread to the frontiers of Pechili—and so the policy was adopted of trying to hold them subject at home, instead of having to repel them from her threshold. Kashgaria, has, however, been a traditional worry, and is likely to become a still graver source of anxiety under the changed conditions that result from Russia's occupation of Khokand. Colonel Mark Bell,[1] who traversed, in 1887, the great Central Asian trade route from China to Kashgar, opines frankly—and it will be noted that he is in accord with the advisers of Kien-

[1] "From Peking to Kashgaria." *Proceedings of the R.G.S.* (February, 1890.)

lung—"that it must be considered an unnatural dependency of China, impossible to defend against Russia so long as the Chinese troops are not trained and led by European officers, and without communication by rail between it and Shense." The immense distances, the badness of the roads, and the intervening desert are important elements in this assumption; but the incapacity of the Chinese garrisons to oppose an European force is equally essential. "They are," he says, "either Chinese braves practically uninstructed, under totally uninstructed officers, of no value against a trained European force; or local militia, a force of negative value."[1] It is 3400 miles from Peking to Kashgar by the route which Colonel Bell followed, and 2500 by a straighter route across Mongolia which was traversed by Captain Younghusband about the same time. The mere mention of these distances is sufficient to affirm the urgency for railway communication, if the territory is to be made defensible. Yet these very distances—and it is the longer route, across Shense and Kansuh, which a railway must admittedly follow—make the undertaking only less gigantic than the Siberian railway itself, and assuredly beyond reach of the Chinese Government under its present organization. A section might be within their means: say from Singan, the capital of Shense, to the border

[1] [The upcome of the Pamir question has induced the Chinese to meet this defect. We have heard, lately, of the despatch of troops, guns and drill instructors, from Peking to Turkestan; and a considerable Chinese force is said to be now massed on the frontier.]

of the Gobi Desert; but even that involves 1000 miles; and the whole Dominion is on the other side of this desert, which Colonel Bell declares to be practically impassable for an army if its only outlet, Hami, is held by a hostile force.

We are concerned in these remote regions, on account of their proximity to India, as much as in the growth of Russian power on the Pacific. Yet we seem to have done but little to arrest Russian progress towards our frontier. The Government of India—reflecting it is to be feared, in this respect, the alternations of impulse at home—seems to have had no continuous policy: at one time doing the wrong thing with surprising energy, at another neglecting to avail itself of opportunities made to its hand. During the meteoric career of Yakoob Khan—at the risk, nay, with the certainty, of offending China, it did not hesitate to accredit an envoy to the usurper, in the hope of strengthening Kashgaria as a buffer between ourselves and Russian territory. But since he has passed away and Chinese rule has been re-affirmed, we have done little to promote a more efficient alliance. Englishmen have, it is true, paid frequent visits to the region. From Sir Douglas Forsyth to Captain Younghusband there has been a going to and fro of travellers, with more or less of official cognizance and approval; but ought we to have depended on transitory visits? The political relations of Turkestan now centre in Peking, and it should not have been difficult to obtain Chinese sanction to the appointment of a permanent representative. Even as a question of commerce this might be worth while, for much of the fine wool which goes to make the shawls of Kashmere is said to come from Turfan in Chinese Turkestan. But that is not all. A British consul at Kashgar would be a means of letting light into the darkness that now shadows Central Asian politics. The local Chinese officials are incapable of comprehending the scope and purport of Russian proceedings; and the statesmen of Peking would be benefited, even more than ourselves, by intelligent reports. For the Russians are always busy. Russian explorers have been hovering for years round the confines of Thibet, while others wander in Mongolia and Turkestan. Colonel Yanoff began by exploring the Pamirs; and it is much to be feared that, if China does not awake in time, she will find the "exploration" carried on past Aktash into the region between Kashgaria and Thibet, with the result of enclosing the former in a semicircle whose arms will tend ever to approach.

But Turkestan offers only one point of contact with Russian territory. North of Turkestan lies Sungaria; north again of Sungaria, and north of the Altai mountains, Uliasutai; and east of Uliasutai, conterminous throughout its whole length with Siberia, Mongolia stretches up to the Khingan mountains which divide it from Manchuria. In the principal cities throughout this vast region, Art. X. of the St. Petersburg treaty permits Russian consuls to be stationed, while Art. XII. stipulates that "Russian trade shall be free, at present, in all the region, as far as the Great Wall; [though] this immunity shall be abrogated when development of trade necessitates a customs tariff." And Russian traders appear, in effect, to be everywhere making way. At Hami they have been established several years. There are Russian shops at Uliasutai and at Kobdo. There is a Russian consul at Kashgar with an escort of fifty Cossacks; and Colonel Bell found a Russian merchant at Suchau, even within the Great Wall, within the frontier of Kansuh.

Turkestan and Mongolia are, however, regions of great distances; and it has been plausibly contended that China's best way of defending them would be by attacking Eastern Siberia in case the emergency arose. It is, indeed, mainly towards Manchuria that Russia professes to be looking with apprehension when she speaks of China's aggressive designs; and it may not be uninteresting to examine a little closely the actual position of affairs in a region which the Chinese, on the other hand, are trying to fortify against Russia.

Before the Emperor Kwangsü took over the reins of power, the clever woman who had been governing the Empire as Regent had pronounced in favour of railways; but had postponed their introduction till the Emperor should be old enough to throw his personal weight into the scale. His accession proved the signal for a storm of opposition which threw the whole question again into the crucible, whereupon he appealed to the great provincial satraps for their opinion; and it may not be out of place to glance, here, at certain of the replies which bear upon the Russian question. Liu Ming-chüan, who conducted the defence of Formosa against the French, and who is designated for command in the North in case of disagreement with Russia about the Pamirs, has, he says, "read in the papers" that—

"the Russian Czar had ordered a railway 3000 miles long, from Tomsk to Sta (? Vladivostock) within 200 miles of the Chinese province of Hei Lung Kiang . . . . This shows that the mouths of the Russians water for our Manchurian provinces. Let us then make ourselves strong while we have yet time. And we cannot take a better means to that end than the extension of railways."

Hwang Pen-nien, then Governor of Kiangsu, is equally emphatic in his allusions:

"China now finds herself in a different position *vis-a-vis* the world from any which she has occupied during the last four thousand years. Europe and Asia are now united in a way that they have never been before, and this union has been effected by no sudden exertion of force, but by a natural and gradual development of events. To return to her old isolation would be now a hopeless task for China, and while preserving those great principles which have given her pre-eminence in the past, she must now assimilate to herself, circumspectly and discriminately, so much of the spirit of the age as will prevent her from being outwitted and exploited by her astute Western competitors. The first railways that China should build, therefore, should be one from Tientsin to Shan Hai Kuan, thence on to Hei Lung Kiang, another to Ninguta in Kirin [all in Manchuria], a third north-west from Shensi and Kansu to Ili, and a fourth to Kashgar. We shall then be able to send troops, money, &c., anywhere in our empire within ten days, and besides that, we shall be able to found prosperous colonies in these outlying regions, of people who in China proper are only a starving proletariat and a source of trouble to the Government, but who, once

transplanted thither, will be able to find a fruitful field for their now unemployed labour, and will turn the desert into a garden."

It would be wearisome to review the causes which hindered the inception, even, of these great projects ; personal jealousies, timid counsels, national exclusiveness all had their share. Suffice it to say that the construction of a line northward from Tientsin towards Manchuria was eventually sanctioned, and that the work has so far advanced that the despatch of troops during the late disturbances in that region was materially facilitated. This line will be gradually extended to Moukden, the capital of Manchuria, and onward to Kirin, the strategic centre of the dependency. In the first thrill of the alarm which the great Siberian project excited, extensions to Port Arthur and to the Amoor were earnestly discussed. Engineers were even commissioned to make a preliminary survey of the route, and it seemed likely that both schemes would be pushed forward with the promptitude their importance demands. But it is the misfortune of China that even her best statesmen seem to lack energy or influence to carry out the reforms whose wisdom they can discern, and the project has temporarily shrunk from those comprehensive schemes to a slower process of construction.

The delay is to be regretted, for Kirin is, without doubt, an important terminus. Situated in about 43½ N. and 127 E., on the upper waters of the Sungari, it is in communication, by means of that river and its affluents, with Tsitsihar, Sansien, and other principal places in northern Manchuria. Its importance has been recognized by the construction, there, of an arsenal which astonished Mr. James[1] by its completeness and efficiency—"a large establishment filled with foreign machinery, with boilers and engines, and steam-hammers, such as one might see at Woolwich or at Elswick, all erected and managed by Chinese [trained, of course, under foreigners in China] without foreign assistance of any kind," and turning out apparently excellent weapons, from repeating rifles to machine guns. Kirin is, in fact, the centre upon which all traffic between China Proper and Northern Manchuria seems to converge. Yet it is nearly four hundred miles from Newchwang, the nearest port, and the intervening roads have been described as the worst in the world and practically impassable except in winter when hard frozen. So that a railway would have commercial as well as strategic value. If, indeed, the Chinese had the energy of the Canadians, they would push on the line past Kirin into the vast unoccupied regions of the north and east. Seventy years ago Chinese emigration into Manchuria was forbidden; and though the prohibition was removed in 1820, the absence of organization and uncertainty of life and property prevented, at first, any considerable movement. Gradually, however, the tide has gathered strength: millions of Chinese are said to

[1] "A Journey in Manchuria," by H. E. M. James, H.M. Bombay C.S.

have crossed the frontier during the last twenty years, and there is now little unoccupied land in the southern province. The emigrants are stretching, therefore, ever farther north, overflowing even into Mongolia and spreading out like a fan over Kirin and Tsitsihar. Tens of thousands migrated thither during a late famine in the north; myriads more have since followed in their wake; and China's wisest policy would be to encourage the movement by every means in her power, for not only is it a relief to her own congested districts but the barrier of population is one of the best she can raise against foreign intrusion. Russia understands this well, and is said to entertain a lively fear of the progressive increase of Chinese colonization in the Usuri region, where the few Russian settlers command but indifferent success.

But if her construction of strategic railways is likely to be slow, China is pushing forward military preparations more consistent with her instincts and traditions. It is almost impossible to ascertain, even approximately, the strength of her garrisons in these outlying portions of her empire. The true relation between the actual and paper strength of a Chinese regiment is, in fact, so indeterminate that it would be difficult to form a reliable estimate, even with the returns of the Chinese War Office before one. Colonel Bell accounts for a considerable number, scattered in this city and in that, in Sungaria and Turkestan; he heard, for instance, of 20,000 men around Hami, though he only verified the presence of 2000 as an actual garrison in the city. But whatever may be the case in the north-west,[1] Manchuria is, without doubt, much more strongly held. There are, that is to say, many thousand soldiers with many Winchester rifles and many Krupp guns. Mr. James found "throngs of young Manchu recruits who were, in fact, members of the militia being turned into regulars;" and the work has since gone steadily on. Some 30,000 fairly drilled men are said to be now concentrated in Kirin, besides a still larger number at Sansien; and it is proposed, I believe, to create fortified camps at Tsitsihar in the north-west, and at Ninguta, which lies nearly on the same parallel as Kirin, near the Usuri frontier. These four places would thus form a strong quadrilateral, obstructing any advance up the valley of the Sungari, which seems to be considered the only practicable line of approach for a northern invader. There are other military stations at Hulan Pei'rh and Aigun (opposite the Russian town of Blagoveschensk), on the northern (Amoor) frontier; at Hunchun near the frontier of Corea; and at Boduna, or Petuna, on the west, near the junction of the Nonni and Sungari rivers. But it is at Sansien, which would incur the first brunt of attack by an enemy advancing up the Sungari, that the Chinese have concentrated their chief strength.

[1] A recent *Peking Gazette* mentions that during the year 1888 various provinces of China proper were required to furnish the Governor-General of Kansuh with subsidies amounting to Tls. 4,800,000, in order to support the army maintained in Kansuh and Turkestan for the defence of the north-west.

Distances are great in this region; and though it is the first important obstacle a Russian force would encounter, Sansien lies one hundred and eighty miles south of the Amoor, and three hundred miles from Khabarofka, the chief military station as well as the capital of the new Russian province of Primorsk. It is surrounded on three sides by rivers, and is said to be of great natural strength. It has, however, one element of weakness. Failing communication with the sea—of which more anon—it depends for supplies upon the provincial city of Kirin, from which it is distant about two hundred and fifty miles by land and water; and a like difficulty seems to affect every station that has been named.

From every point of view, then, railways across Manchuria would be an inestimable advantage. But what is almost more surprising than the slowness to improve communications by land, is that the Chinese should neglect the means of access by water which have been expressly secured by the very treaties that register the Russian depredation. It has been mentioned that Sansien depends for its supplies upon Kirin, which has to draw them in turn from the port of Newchwang. But Sansien is on the Sungari, and Art. I. of the treaty of Aigun (1858), while preparing the way by its vague allusions for the eventual cession of the great territory lying between the Usuri and the sea, contains the following important clause:—

"The navigation of the Amoor, the Sungari, and the Usuri is

only permitted to vessels of the Chinese and Russian Empires; the navigation of these rivers is forbidden to vessels of every other State."

The stipulation was omitted from the treaty negotiated two years later, by General Ignatieff, at Peking; but it was expressly revived by the Marquis Tsêng, in the treaty of St. Petersburg, in 1881.[1] Yet it may, I think, be safely affirmed that the Dragon flag has never yet been shown on these rivers. It may well seem inconceivable, in face of the efforts China has made to create a navy of modern ships, that such an obvious method of employing them with effect should have been neglected. If she can send a squadron of ironclads to Singapore and Japan, she can surely send gunboats on to the Amoor. The right of navigation is a valuable one, both commercially and strategically. But it is necessary, for either purpose, to assert and preserve the right, and to ascertain the channel by practical experience in time of peace. There is, at present, a commercial steamer company trading on the Amoor, founded, I believe, somewhat like the Delagoa Bay Railway Company, with English money but under a Russian organization; and rumour has it that so jealously does Russia guard the rights secured by her by the quoted treaties, that not an Englishman or even a Chinaman is allowed among

[1] Art. XVIII. "The stipulations of the treaty concluded at Aigoun . . . concerning the rights of the subjects of the two empires to navigate the Amoor, the Sungari, and the Usuri, and to carry on trade with the populations of the riverine localities, are and remain confirmed."

the crews of these boats. By all means let the railway be hastened on: a railway to Kirin would not only facilitate the despatch of troops and stores, but would have the ulterior advantage of opening up a fertile country which is now hidebound for want of communication with the coast. But it surpasses one's conception even of Chinese "backwardness and inertia," that the assistance which Chinese warships on the Amoor and light draught gunboats on the Sungari and Usuri rivers might afford, in case of war, should be ignored.

It would seem to the Chinese like leaving out the part of Hamlet to omit mention, in a review of the military strength of Manchuria, of the naval station which has been especially designed as a fortified port, arsenal, and dockyard for their fleet and a basis of defence for their capital. But Russia might overrun the whole country, or China might recover Primorsk, without Port Arthur having a word to say, unless a naval policy varying widely from that hitherto in vogue be adopted as an integral portion of the military scheme.

The military strength of China has been the subject, by turns, of extreme depreciation and of wild exaltation. M. Challemel-Lacour spoke of her as a *quantité négligeable* before the outbreak of the war which cost M. Ferry his career. Then, after her soldiers had made a stand amid the highlands of Tongking, and had repulsed an ill-planned attack on Kelung, opinion veered round and people saw visions of Chinamen overrunning the world. It is hardly necessary to say that, in this as in most other cases, the middle is the safer course. Immense numbers of men with arms of precision in their hands can never be safely despised; especially when those men are frugal, hardy, and enduring. But there is a general failure among Chinese statesmen to realize that educated, skilled, and daring leaders are as essential to success as repeating rifles. To go back to the Franco-Chinese war for an illustration—without referring to the eccentricities of the southern squadron, which cut a worse than ridiculous figure off the Yangtze Cape, the Chinese had, in the north, two swift and heavily armed Armstrong cruisers that could have sunk any vessel in the French fleet except the ironclads, and of those they had easily the heels. In the hands of dashing officers these two ships alone could have rendered the blockade of Formosa impossible, by attacking the French at long bowls while themselves out of range, and steaming off at will if an ironclad came to the fore. Yet they never left the shelter of Port Arthur! And as with the navy so with the army. It is open to question whether a certain tendency to slovenliness[1] and looseness of habit would not prevent the Chinaman from being ever drilled up to the standard of the Sepoy; and it may be contended, further, that something more than endurance, docility, or even a

[1] The Peking correspondent of the *Times* lately affirmed that the Russian military attaché in that capital had ascertained that all the Krupp guns and rifles in Manchuria are being ruined by neglect.

readiness to accept death, is required to make a fighting man. There is a want of discipline in that higher sense which implies absolute certainty that commands will be obeyed and duty done. If there could be added the spirit of the Russian soldier who, at a time of such cold that it was necessary to change the sentry every two hours, was overlooked for four and found dead at his post, a higher tribute might be passed; but it is just this indefinable something which marks the contrast and the defect.

It is not, however, the capacity of the Chinese soldier so much as the incapacity of his officers which is our present object of concern. China needs to educate a whole series of officers, from general downwards, who would recognize that war is a science, and that an officer's duty is to lead as well as to direct. The considerable force organized by Li Hung-chang in the environs of Tientsin is well armed and (for Chinese) well drilled. The few European instructors have doubtless succeeded, too, in the course of years, in creating a very considerable and excellent leaven of non-commissioned officers. But it is commissioned officers, officers with the skill to plan and the daring to lead, in which the Chinese army is so lamentably deficient; and various circumstances combine to neutralize the best source whence these defects could be supplied. China could probably attract, into her service, English and other half-pay officers who would serve her faithfully and well. But she is too vain and jealous to give them full power, even if she were not deterred by the reflection that her army would be disorganized by their withdrawal at the first breath of war, as the English officers were withdrawn from the Chinese fleet at the outbreak of hostilities with France. Otherwise, the prospect of an English alliance in the future, with English disciplining help in the present, might convert China into a valuable ally against the day of struggle on the Indian frontier. It may be doubted whether she could be relied on to observe the conditions of a strict alliance, binding her beforehand to take action in a given emergency. But it is far from impossible that such an alliance might come to pass, by sheer force of gravitation, when the emergency arose. It will, however, be by so much the less efficient if it is not provided for by careful defensive provision. A Chinese army and Chinese fleet, with English stiffening and help, might be able to recover their own lost ground, and effect an important diversion in Eastern Siberia while we were engaged in Candahar. The Russians themselves have recognized the possibility of such an event: Turkey, it has been remarked, is no longer to be reckoned on, and Persia is too weak; but Chinese, instructed by British officers and supported by British money and arms, might render excellent service.

But why, it may be asked, so much stress on all these things? Russia professes to be strengthening her garrison from pure precaution, and China is in the last degree unlikely to cross the Usuri with deliberate purpose of reconquest. Where is the risk, if Russia so emphatically repudiates aggressive designs, and China so certainly excludes them? The answer is that there is always the risk of chances. Nothing could have been more emphatic than Russia's repudiation of an intention to annex Merv and other territory up to the frontier of Afghanistan; yet the annexation occurred. Russia scouts the idea of invading India, yet we fortify the north-west frontier against her by every means that science can supply. And Manchuria is far more open to attack than Candahar; and China is a country even better worth possessing than Hindustan. Officials act irresponsibly, and the Russian Government sustains instead of reprehending and disavowing them; and this may happen, any day, at any point along the vast contiguous frontiers of Tartary and Siberia. Take the Pamir question, for instance. The Russian Foreign Office never put forward any claim to the Pamirs when negotiating the treaty of St. Petersburg with the Marquis Tsêng; merely asking him, as his predecessor was asked at Livadia, to recognize Mount Maltabar (39·30 N. and 74 E.) as the extreme limit of their common frontier. Yet Russian *éclaireurs* have expelled Chinese soldiers from the neighbourhood of Yesh-el-kul, which is far away south, in the district of Alichur, and are taking up positions in a region which Prince Gortschakoff actually recognized, in 1873, as belonging to Yakoob Khan. There is always risk of disturbance in territory loosely held and imperfectly settled. There may be difficulties with the tribes, difficulties with robbers, difficulties about cattle-lifting, difficulties about gold-fields, or a collision between soldiers. There may be troubles, again, in Turkestan that may give excuse for another occupation of Kuldja. There may occur difficulties, any day, about the gold-fields on the banks of the Amoor. The *Isibir*, a Siberian semi-official paper, gave quite a romantic description, not long ago, of a community of gold diggers in a corner of Chinese Manchuria, on the bank of the Tumen River. The spot was said to be in a wild country, difficult of access; and it had been some time before the Chinese even knew that the diggers were there. When they did, they sent troops to assert their rights, and some alarm was excited by reports of a collision between them and the Russian forces. The whole thing was greatly exaggerated; and the effervescence, whatever it was, promptly calmed down. But the incident may be noted as an example of what might occur if ever an aggressive frontier officer should be in command near a similar region, on a similar emergency, with an aggressive governor-general enthroned at Irkutsk. And the gold-fields on the Amoor are more extensive, more approachable, and more wealthy than this placer on the Tumen.

There is danger too, from the very proximity of Russian and Chinese camps: for Russian and Chinese soldiers in Manchuria are, it may be feared, less well in hand than Russian and Austrian soldiers on the frontiers of Galicia. The Governor-General of Eastern Siberia is constantly urging, now, that his military position should be strengthened in view of Chinese preparations. There may, some day, arise a case of the wolf and the lamb ; and he may then find himself sufficiently strong to take the water, once for all, under his protection. That will not, probably, happen yet—not till the Siberian railway is more advanced, and till there are greater facilities for the transport of reinforcements in case the emergency should arise. But the Russians are not likely to dally with their work, like the Chinese. A few versts of the section up the Usuri valley, from Vladivostock towards the Amoor, were completed in time for the Czarewitsch to open them, as he passed through, in 1891 ; and the fortifications of Vladivostock have been rendered, it is considered, impregnable against any attack they might conceivably incur. The pace, on the other hand, at which China is travelling seems almost a satire on Russian exclamations. If her decision to make a railway across Manchuria had really the aggressive purpose St. Petersburg professes to detect, she would surely try to anticipate the completion of the rival route. Yet Prince Mestchersky, in the *Grashdanin*, lately accused the *Novoe Vremya* of attempting to create popular ill-feeling against the Chinese, "which would be a terrible danger for Russia," by its comments on the situation. He is so far right that the Chinese could, at the present moment, sweep the Russians out of the Usuri province. Whether they could keep them out is another question, and they show little disposition to attempt its solution.

Their anxiety takes, in fact, an opposite direction—an anxiety stimulated, no doubt, by previous experience and hardly likely to be lessened by the present incident in the Pamirs.

It is always rash to prophesy, and especially so in dealing with a people of whom Sherard Osborn pithily remarked that the best way to judge them is to decide what an Englishman would probably do, and to conclude that they will do the opposite. It is certain, however, that China resents and has protested against the Russian advance; and the reported despatch of an expeditionary force to the Rangkul would appear to be evidence of a purpose to stand by the objections he has raised. But we are concerned, for the moment, with the situation as it is at present. And enough has probably been said to show why it is that, at Peking no less than at Constantinople and Calcutta, the bugbear of Russian aggression is ever present; and why Chinese mandarins have come to admit that a railway to Kirin would be a desirable possession, in case another Mouravieff or another Ignatieff should think that the Sungari as well as the Amoor and the Usuri ought to belong to the Czar.

INDIA AND THIBET.

CHAPTER XII.

PROJECTS OF COMMERCIAL INTERCOURSE.

A HUNDRED and twenty years ago, Warren Hastings conceived the idea of opening up commercial relations between India and Thibet; and there seemed a likelihood, at first, that he would effect his object. Circumstances conspired subsequently to defeat it, and it was allowed to lapse altogether under his immediate successors; but attention has been directed towards the Himalayas, of late, with renewed interest, and the threads of Hastings' policy have been gathered up with better assurance that they will lead, this time, to a successful issue.

There may not, at a first glance, seem any necessary connection between the constitution of Thibet and the problem of commercial intercourse with its inhabitants. That constitution is, however, so peculiar that some perception of it is essential if we would realize the position. The great reform in Thibetan Buddhism out of which it has been developed is, of course, familiar to students of Eastern literature; but a few words of recapitulation will not be out of place, to clear the ground for the general reader.

Not only had the Buddhism practised in Thibet become strongly tainted, in the fourteenth century, with the heresies which had corrupted its purity in India; but "both the people and their native sovereigns were dominated by an hereditary priesthood, who had engrafted on the Buddhist doctrine of monasticism and celibacy a supplementary religious code in which Brahminical ideas were distinctly apparent."[1] To rectify these abuses, and advocate a return to the earlier and purer doctrines of the faith, there arose, about the beginning of the fifteenth century, a young priest named Tsung Kaba who, issuing from an obscure monastery on the confines of China and Thibet, witnessed during his lifetime the complete overthrow of the influence of the Ssakia priesthood, and the substitution of his own doctrines for those hitherto in vogue. So great, indeed, was his success that he was able, at his death, to bequeath his influence to his two principal disciples—called respectively the Dalai Lama and Panshen Lama—whose successors have come to be hierarchs of Thibet; and not only so, but the belief has come to prevail that the soul of Tsung Kaba himself passed into the former, "and that the imperishable spirits of both are born and reborn again into the world in

[1] *Illustrations of the Lamaist System in Thibet*. By W. F. Mayers.

perpetual succession."[1] Hence the well-known fact that, as soon as either dies, search is made to discover the child into whose body the spirit has passed; and that child becomes Dalai or Panshen Lama, keeping up the continuity of the succession. It is necessary to keep in mind these well-known features of the Thibetan creed, in order to explain the origin of the dual hierarchy which has been evolved out of the religious conception.

The revolution out of which the present system was elaborated, occurred in 1746. Native sovereigns, owing fealty to China, had still held a more or less nominal sway over Thibet up to that time; but a revolt which broke out in the middle of the eighteenth century led to their complete abolition, and to the placing of the chief authority in the hands of the Dalai Lama, under the supreme control of two Chinese Residents (called Amban) who became, in reality, Regents of Thibet. It was, perhaps, natural that to the senior of the two hierarchs should fall the greater share of influence under the new arrangement: but neither was the other ignored;

[1] I have relied on Mr. Mayers' interesting paper in sketching this account of the curious dual papacy which prevails in Thibet. A highly-wrought description of Tsung Kaba's birth and noviciate, and of the tree which grew from his hair, will be found in the Abbé Huc's sparkling pages—he and M. Gabet having stayed some months at the monastery founded on the spot. Huc seems rather to confuse the attributes of the Panshen Lama with those of an official called Nomen Khan, whom he speaks of as "Spiritual Emperor." But this is one of the mistakes he makes when trying to define a system of polity he failed to clearly fathom during his short stay in the country.

for, while to the Dalai Lama was allotted the temporal power, to the Panshen Lama was confided the maintenance of the purity of religion. And so, while the former resides in the capital, Lhassa, in the province of U, the latter dwells at the monastery of Teshu Lumbo, near Shigatze, in the province of Tsang.

These, then, were the conditions which Warren Hastings found existing when he first endeavoured, in 1774, to open up intercourse with Thibet; and we may go on, now, to review the story of that pioneer mission, as Mr. Markham[1] has told it in his introduction to the journal of its enterprising chief.

The Himalayan States, in the last century, were far from being so peaceful as at the present day. About the year 1770, especially, they seem to have been in a general turmoil. The Goorkhas, under Prithi Narayan, had just conquered Nepaul; while the little State of Sikhim, crushed between that country and Bhootan, was worried alternately by both. The immediate origin of the episode with which we are now concerned was an invasion of Kooch Behar, in 1772, by a Bhootanese chief named Deb Judhur. The Rajah appealed to Calcutta for help, and Hastings despatched a small force under Captain Jones, which drove the Bhootanese back to their hills and forced them to sue for peace. The Teshu Lama thereupon wrote a letter of intercession, on their behalf, which gave an opening for further

[1] *Narrative of the Mission of Bogle to Thibet, &c.*, with Introduction by Clements R. Markham. London, 1876.

negotiations. The misconduct of the Deb was admitted; "but I now," wrote the Lama, "take upon myself to be his mediator, and to represent to you that he is dependent on the Dalai Lama who rules this country," and who would be annoyed if the campaign against him were pressed. With far-sighted statesmanship, Hastings at once acquiesced; and, having thus gratified the Lama, proceeded to follow up the step he had gained. He came to terms with the Deb, and despatched a young civil servant named Bogle, accompanied only by Dr. Hamilton and one Purungir Gosain, to visit the Teshu Lama and open up commercial relations, if possible, with Thibet. Bogle set out in 1774, travelling by way of Kooch Behar to Tassisudon, the capital of Bhootan; concluded a satisfactory agreement with the Deb; and pursued his journey into Thibet, by way of Parijong, in the autumn of the same year. It was, as we have seen, to the Teshu Lama that he was accredited; but news of his approach was, of course, communicated by the latter to Lhassa.

The Dalai Lama was at the time a child, and the Regent seems to have assumed an attitude unfriendly to the mission—so much so that the Teshu Lama wrote, in deference to his wish, desiring that Bogle would return to India. But neither Hastings nor Bogle were men easily rebuffed. They persuaded the Teshu Lama to write again to Lhassa, representing that the English had stayed hostilities against Bhootan at his request; and the Regent then consented to his reception. He refused, however, to allow him to come to Lhassa and neglected to answer his letters, though he received his servants and accepted some trifling presents. The Teshu Lama, however, who was staying at the time at Desheripgay, on the north of the Tsanpo, received him in a most friendly manner, and took him back to Teshu Lumbo, where quarters were given him in the monastery and every consideration was shown him. A very cordial personal friendship sprang up, in fact, between Bogle and his host; so much so that something nearer akin to grief than to regret seems to have been felt at parting;[1] we shall see, in the course of the narrative, that the Thibetan belief in re-incarnation has lent to this friendship a curious significance and continuity. Still, no great political progress was made, owing to the jealousy of the Regent, whom Bogle seems to have thought under the influence of the Chinese, but the Teshu Lama said more could probably be done when the Dalai Lama assumed the reins of power. "You know," he

[1] "Teshu Lama repeated his concern at my departure, the satisfaction he had received in being informed of the customs of Europe, and concluded with many wishes for my prosperity, and that he would not fail to pray to heaven on my behalf. He spoke all this in a manner and with a look very different from the studied and formal compliments of Hindustan. I never could resign myself to taking a last leave of anybody; and what from the Lama's pleasant and amiable character, what from the many favours and civilities he had shown me, I could not help being particularly affected. He observed it and, in order to cheer me, mentioned his hope of seeing me again. He threw a handkerchief about my neck, put his hand upon my head, and I retired." —*Bogle's Journal.*

said, in bidding Bogle good-bye, "what difficulty I had about your coming into the country, and how I had to struggle with the jealousy of Gesub Rimboché and the people at Lhassa. Even now, they are uneasy at my having kept you so long. I am in hopes my letter to the Lama will have a good effect in removing this jealousy; and I expect that in a year or two the government of the country will be in the Dalai Lama's hands, when I will inform the Governor, and he may then send an Englishman to me and to the Dalai Lama." But communications had, he added, better pass through native hands in the meantime.

Bogle returned to India in 1775, and was about to set out on a fresh mission to Thibet in 1777, when news came that the Teshu Lama had been summoned to Peking. It was hoped that even this diversion might turn out advantageously, as it was arranged that Bogle should meet his friend at the Chinese capital, and return with him possibly to Lhassa; but a double calamity came to defeat that purpose. The Lama died at Peking[1] in November, 1780, and Bogle died at Calcutta in April, 1781.

The check was regrettable, but Hastings was not easily discouraged. News reached Calcutta, in 1782, that the infant re-embodiment of the Teshu Lama had been discovered; and he thereon despatched Captain

[1] The Lama seems to have been accompanied to Peking by Purungir Gosain, who stayed for a time afterwards at Teshu Lumbo with the Regent, and was eventually dismissed with most friendly messages.

Turner to congratulate the new Lama, and renew the previous friendly intercourse. Following Bogle's route across Bhootan, Turner reached Teshu Lumbo in September, 1783. He found the late Lama's brother acting as regent, and experienced a very friendly reception at his hands. He was allowed an interview with the infant Lama, who impressed him by an intelligence and dignity of bearing "which almost seem to confirm the assurance of the Thibetans that he could understand everything, though he could not yet speak"![1] and returned to India at the end of the year.

This was, however, destined to be the last chapter of the volume which Hastings had so cleverly opened. His career as Governor of India closed in 1785, and the whole scheme of border policy which he had inaugurated collapsed with his departure. Boiling over still with the turbulence which had impelled them to effect the conquest of Nepaul, the Goorkhas determined, in 1792, to proceed to an invasion of Thibet. The excuse was some question of debased currency; the real motive, apparently, a desire to possess themselves of riches stored in Teshu Lumbo, about which their imagination had been fired by the tales of a refugee monk. The Goorkha army, 18,000 strong, marched from Khatmandu to Teshu Lumbo with extraordinary rapidity, and took and sacked the palace without meeting any resistance. The Regent fled to Lhassa with the young Lama, and despatched urgent entreaties for help to Peking. The

[1] *An Account of an Embassy to the Court of the Teshu Lama in Thibet.* By Captain Samuel Turner. London, 1806.

Chinese sent an envoy to demand restitution and, on receipt of a defiant reply, despatched an army of 70,000 men under General Sun Fo to punish the invaders. The General seems to have acted with remarkable energy. He defeated the Goorkha army in a pitched battle, overtook and defeated them again at the entrance to the passes, and followed them into Nepaul. The fugitives rallied twenty miles from their capital, but Sun Fo gained another decisive victory, which closed the campaign, in September of the same year.[1] The Nepaulese had to restore their plunder, and to promise to send an embassy with tribute to Peking every five years.

British policy, throughout the entire episode, seems to have been pitiably weak. We might, as Mr. Markham suggests, have endeavoured to control the Goorkhas at the outset, thus earning the gratitude of Thibet and obviating the Chinese expedition which entailed the subsequent isolation. But Lord Cornwallis did nothing. To an appeal from the Nepaulese for help, he replied that we were too much interested in commerce with the Chinese to oppose them; but offered mediation, and made a similar proposal in reply to a letter from the Dalai Lama acquainting him with the Chinese victory. He did actually send

[1] It is curious to note that the Chinese general had with him leathern artillery, which, although it only stood some half-dozen rounds and then burst, served him admirably in the mountains from its portability. During this last battle it is reported that he fired his guns into his own army from the rear, to drive them against the Nepaulese! His losses, both on this occasion and throughout the whole march through the snowy range, were fearful, but his numbers carried him through.

Colonel Kirkpatrick to Khatmandu with that object, but the Chinese general had already settled matters his own way; he had closed the passes into Thibet against natives of India, and closed they have remained to the present day. The opportunity was missed. "We had lost all the fruits of Hastings' policy, together with the friendship of the Lamas; we had excited the jealous suspicion of the Chinese, and the scorn of the Nepaulese."

Here the matter practically rested till the occurrence, in 1884, of a fresh quarrel between Nepaul and Thibet called fresh attention to the subject. For nearly a century the prohibition imposed by the Chinese general had been maintained; and the Himalayas continued to be a social as well as a geographical barrier between India and Thibet. Intercourse of some sort was kept up, through the medium of the Himalayan States. Some Indian goods found their way into Thibet, and some Thibetan products filtered through into India; but the difficulties of transport and the weight of transit charges prevented any considerable trade, while the prejudices of the Lamas combined to direct what actually existed through Nepaul, instead of allowing it to pass along the shorter route through Sikhim. So rigidly was the exclusion enforced that it was thought a triumph of enterprise when certain Pundits,[1] trained by the

[1] General Walker, late Surveyor-General of India, has done justice to the achievements of these gentlemen, in a paper entitled 'Four Years' Journeyings through Great Thibet, &c.," read before the R.G.S. in December, 1884.

Indian Geographical Department, succeeded in crossing the frontier under the guise of merchants, and obtaining some knowledge of the country. Cooper's plucky attempts[1] to make his way across the Thibetan frontier, both from China and Assam, and Prejevalsky's later experiments from the north, are familiar reminiscences. But to all these attempts the Yellow-robed followers of Tsung Kaba, who appear to have inherited the full influence of their Red-capped predecessors,[2] opposed a successful resistance. And the Chinese, holding Thibet by a loose tie, and caring chiefly for peace, have acquiesced in (if they did not inspire) a policy that was far from shocking their own instincts.

The time was, however, at hand when the selfishness and greed of these sectarians were to furnish a weapon against their own ascendency. There is held

[1] *Travels of a Pioneer of Commerce in Pigtail and Petticoats.* By T. T. Cooper. 1871.

[2] The temptation is irresistible to quote, here, the exquisite bit of irony in which Bogle summarizes the great Tsong-kaban reformation:—"It may be necessary to state that there are two sects of clergy in Thibet distinguished by, and classed under, the names of Yellow Caps and Red Caps. . . . In times of old there were violent disputes between them, in which the Yellow Caps got the victory, as well by the assistance of the Tartars as by their superior sanctity. But as I adhere to the tenets of this sect, and have acquired my knowledge of religion from its votaries, I will not here say much upon the subject lest it should be thought spiteful. I may be allowed, however, just to mention two things which must convince every unprejudiced person of the wicked lives and false doctrines of the Red Caps. In the first place many of the clergy marry; and in the next they persist, in opposition to religion and common sense, in wearing red caps."

every New Year, in Lhassa, a kind of carnival, during which the Ministers of State practically resign their duties into the hands of the great Lamaseries.[1] In 1884, the monks of the Debang Monastery, which seems one of the largest in the capital, took advantage of the opportunity to plunder certain Nepaulese traders to the extent, it was said, of half a million rupees. The Nepaulese Government demanded full restitution, which the Thibetans refused. Nepaul prepared for war; and the mediation of the Chinese Residents barely succeeded in effecting a compromise. About the same time, and with the idea possibly of closing the whole southern frontier under stress of Nepaulese threats, the Thibetans also blocked the trade route to Darjeeling; and the Government of Bengal thereupon deputed Mr. Colman Macaulay to visit the frontier and ascertain the real position of affairs.

There appear to be three principal passes into the section of Thibet which, driven down like a wedge between Sikhim and Bhootan, offers the readiest access from India to the interior. The southernmost

[1] Huc confirms this abdication of the Executive Power. On the third day (he says) of the New Year, innumerable bands of Lamas from all the neighbouring monasteries rush into Lhassa, where they stay six days, the ostensible object being to visit the celebrated Morou Monastery. "Pendant ce temps les tribunaux sont fermés, le cours ordinaire de la justice est suspendu, les ministres et les fonctionaires publics perdent en quelque sorte leur autorité, et toute la puissance du Gouvernement est abandonnée à cette armée formidable de religieux bouddhistes." The result is great disorder, and occasional rioting and fighting.—*Souvenirs d'un Voyage dans le Thibet et la Tartarie*, vol. ii. cap. viii.

(the Jeylep) lies nearest to Darjeeling; the Parijong, on the east, was traversed by Bogle on his way from Bhootan. It was part of Mr. Macaulay's mission to ascertain the possibility of making a road up the Lachen Valley to a third pass, called Kongralama, on the west; and it was here, seemingly, that he met the Governor of Kombajong, into whose district this third route gives outlet. It may be added that all three roads appear to concentrate on Gyantze, whence they again diverge—north-westward to Shigatze, the city of the Teshu Lama, and north-eastward to Lhassa, the chief city of Thibet.

Wedged in between Nepaul on the one side and Bhootan on the other, Sikhim sits astride the best road and the most natural line of communication between Darjeeling and Lhassa. Like its neighbours, its policy has always been closely dependent on that of Thibet. The Rajah resides, indeed, during six months of the year in Thibetan territory, passing only the remaining six in his own capital, Tumloong. Like its neighbours, also, Sikhim claimed authority, in days gone by, over a considerable tract of the fertile Himalayan slopes; but, like them, it has been pushed back and punished by successive confiscations for the raids which its subjects were wont to perpetrate on adjacent British territory. Darjeeling itself, with all the (then jungle-covered) hills now occupied by the great tea-gardens which contribute yearly increasing subsidies to the Indian crop, was once Sikhimese territory; though it had long passed under British administration when the ill-advised arrest, in 1850, of two Englishmen (Drs. Campbell and Hooker) who had ventured on an expedition into the mountains, led to the confiscation of the rental that had been so far paid. Even that lesson, however, and the withholding of 28,000 rupees which had been paid in annual compensation for some previously annexed territory, failed to restrain the marauding habits of the people; and a fresh expedition became necessary, eleven years later, which placed our relations with Sikhim on the present footing. That expedition, commanded by Colonel Gawler, and accompanied by Mr. Ashley Eden as special envoy, occupied Tumloong, and imposed a treaty whose most important provisions were permission to English subjects to circulate freely through Sikhim, the encouragement of trade with India, reduction of the exorbitant transit dues which had been previously exacted on merchandise passing between India and Thibet, and the construction, to facilitate that trade, of the very road whose obstruction at the Jeylep Pass gave occasion for Mr. Macaulay's visit.

Once only, it would seem, since Hastings' day, had any meeting occurred between British and Thibetan officials; and that only incidentally, on the threshold of Thibet. The Rajah of Sikhim having taken occasion, in 1873, to visit the Lieutenant-Governor of Bengal, at Darjeeling, Mr. Edgar was deputed in the autumn to return the visit. The Rajah was then staying in Thibet, and Mr. Edgar offered to follow him thither; but the Governor of Parijong, who met him on the frontier, pleaded the Chinese interdict against intercourse. The impression left on Mr. Edgar's mind, however,—as with those who preceded and followed him—seems to have been that the Thibetans themselves were far from being indisposed to friendly intercourse; though the Governor, of course, was bound by his instructions. The Rajah, who came into Sikhim to meet Mr. Edgar, concurred with his ministers in saying that the key of the situation was at Peking: let a declaration be obtained from Peking that the obstacles now put in the way of intercourse were unauthorized, and the hands of our well-wishers would be strengthened to break down the barrier.

Like his predecessor, Mr. Macaulay experienced a friendly greeting; but he, equally with Mr. Edgar, encountered the *non-possumus* of political tradition. The Teshu Lama had died just before his visit, and nothing seemed more natural to the Thibetans than that Bogle's successor should ask about the re-embodiment of Bogle's friend; but not even these amenities could lessen the force of the interdict. The Regent sent a cordial reply to the letter which Mr. Macaulay despatched to him, and wrote to the Viceroy in equally friendly terms: but the solution of the frontier question was alleged to lie, now as formerly, at Peking; and to Peking, accordingly, it was resolved to turn. An effort should be made to take up the threads again where Warren Hastings had dropped them, and Mr. Macaulay was entrusted with the conduct of the negotiations.

Fortunately for his chances of success, the ground was somewhat prepared on the Chinese as well as on the Thibetan side. The growing desire to penetrate Thibet and open up intercourse with its people had found an echo in the British Legation at Peking; and Sir Thomas Wade had taken the precaution, in negotiating the Chefoo Convention of 1876, to append the following clause:—

> Her Majesty's Government, having it in contemplation to send a mission of exploration next year by way of Peking through Kansuh and Kokonor, or by way of Szechuen, to Thibet, and thence to India, the Tsungli Yamen, having due regard to the circumstances, will, when the time arrives, issue the necessary passports, and will address letters to the High Provincial Authorities and to the Residents in Thibet. If the Mission should not be sent by these routes, but should be proceeding across the Indian frontier to Thibet, the Tsungli Yamen, on receipt of a communication to that effect from the British minister, will write to the Chinese Resident in Thibet; and the Resident, with due regard to the circumstances, will send officers to take due care of the mission, and passports for the mission will be issued by the Tsungli Yamen, that its passage be not obstructed.

No step having yet been taken to make this clause available, it might perhaps have been held, in literal strictness, to have lapsed; but the delay in ratifying the Convention, caused by difficulties about the opium agreement, had no doubt something to do with the neglect; besides, we were on excellent terms with China, and had every reason to anticipate that our overtures would be well received. The ratification of the Convention in the summer of 1885 having removed, therefore, the last hitch in its validity, and it having no doubt been ascertained by private inquiry that the way before him was fairly clear, Mr. Macaulay was sent to Peking in the autumn of that year, to obtain the sanction of the Chinese Government to the prosecution of the enterprise. An inkling of his purpose had already filtered through the Passes, and there had been time for the voice of Lhassa conservatism to make itself heard at the imperial capital. Mr. Macaulay found the Grand Secretary, Li Hung-chang, who had acted as plenipotentiary in negotiating the Convention, well disposed to forward his views; but the ministers of the Tsung-li Yamen were inclined to raise difficulties. A report had, they said, been received from the Chinese Resident at Lhassa, alleging that the Thibetan people were hostile to the project and begging that the exclusion might be maintained: of what use would it be to issue passports, in face of such opposition? The excuse is such a stereotyped one, where Chinese officials wish "not to do it," that a suspicion might have been justified as to the precise origin of the demurrer. The truth seems to have been, however, that the Senior Chinese Resident had been persuaded to play this card in the interest of the Lama faction; and Mr. Macaulay was able, from his own experience, to throw some light upon the case; for, while representations were being made from Lhassa, to Peking, that the Thibetans were hostile, the Thibetans had declared to him that it was China which was obstructive and had shown him, at the frontier, a Chinese placard prohibiting intercourse! The

Ministers at once denied responsibility for this device, and vindicated their own good faith by promising to give the passports sought, and to write to Lhassa that "the Mission was sent to establish relations of amity, to promote commercial intercourse between India and Thibet, and to be the bearer of messages of friendship and respect to the Dalai Lama, in all of which objects it had the concurrence and support of the Imperial Government."[1] The Resident was also instructed to issue proclamations at the frontier and elsewhere, to remove any suspicion that the Emperor was unfavourable to the entry of British subjects into Thibet. Everything appeared satisfactorily settled. It was resolved to defer the Mission till May, in order to allow ample time for communication with Lhassa; but preparations were made to start at the time named.

The Lamas were not yet, however, at the end of their resources, and we were to have one more lesson in the frequency of slips between the cup and the lip. The *personnel* of the Embassy had assembled at Darjeeling, and the intended presents been collected; everything was in readiness for a start, but there was unaccountable delay. Favourable reports were telegraphed from Darjeeling, about its probable reception, but still it did not move; and then, simultaneously from Calcutta and from Peking, came rumours of a hitch. The Chinese, while expressing all good wishes for success, feared lest the constitution of the Mission should excite opposition; while from

[1] Correspondence of the *Standard*, February, 1886.

India came reports of terror among the Thibetans, and of contemplated hostility.

Subsequent information, which has filtered through from both ends of the long line, across the Himalayas on the one side and through China on the other, enables us to form a tolerably just estimate of what actually occurred. The report that negotiations for the purpose of opening up relations between India and Thibet were being seriously revived gave rise, naturally, to much discussion in a city where questions of foreign intercourse were usually narrowed to relations with the Suzerain Power or squabbles with Nepaul. It appears, so far as can be gathered, that the bulk of the laity and a considerable number even of the Lamas were in favour of the project; but a powerful section of the latter class—a section largely interested in trade, from which they succeed, at present, in extracting a maximum of profit[1]—were opposed to a change which threatened their monopoly; and the influence of the Lamas in the ecclesiastical centre of Buddhism is, it may be conceived, predominant. They resorted, as we have seen, to the stereotyped plan of causing it to be represented at Peking that the general feeling in Thibet was hostile to the project. That report seems to have been so contrary to fact, that the Junior

[1] Huc confirms the recent testimony from Darjeeling, as to the avarice and usury of the Lamas. "Les Lamas, mis d'abord en possession de la majeure partie du numéraire par les dons volontaires des fidèles, centuplent ensuite leur fortune par des procédés usuraires dont la friponnerie Chinoise est elle même scandalisée." —*Souvenirs*, etc.

Resident is said to have resigned rather than endorse it; but it had influence at Peking, while uncontradicted, and genuine apprehension was felt there lest trouble should arise.

Nor were we, ourselves, without blame. The organization of the projected Mission was too pretentious. It was to comprise, besides Mr. Macaulay, who held the position of Chief Envoy, Mr. Paul (who had accompanied him to the frontier in the beginning of 1885) as secretary; Colonel Tanner, surveyor; Dr. Oldham, geologist; Dr. Cunningham, naturalist; Dr. Leahy, medical officer; Mr. Warry, of the Chinese Consular Service, as interpreter; Baboo Srutt Chundra Dass, who had already distinguished himself in Thibetan exploration; Captain Elwes, and Captain Gwatkin commanding the escort which was to consist of some three hundred persons. And the climax was assuredly reached when the Under-Secretary for India, while admitting that the object of the Mission was "to confer with the Chinese Commissioners and the Lhassa Government as to the resumption of commercial relations between India and Thibet," could add in Parliament, that, "looking to the delicate nature of the Mission, it had not been thought advisable to appoint a special commercial representative." Here was a Mission, having an avowedly commercial object, about to start with every other but a commercial representative—a mission to an ignorant and superstitious people, to whom the aspect of a theodolite would be more terrifying than a mountain howitzer, composed entirely of scientific men, and accompanied by an escort whose numbers would give it the appearance of an armed reconnaissance rather than a peaceful embassy. It was not so that Bogle opened his approaches; nor can we be surprised if the actual size of the party were exaggerated, and its purpose distorted, in Thibet.

Still, the Lamas seem, as a matter of fact, to have had so little confidence in the success of their machinations, that they sent an emissary to meet Mr. Macaulay at the frontier, to try and effect a compromise by inducing him to halt at Gyantze—an important trade centre half-way to Lhassa—and enter, there, upon the negotiations contemplated; so that, faultily constituted as it was, the Mission had apparently a fair chance of succeeding if it had persevered. But it never got so far. It never even started. In face of rumours from Lhassa and warnings from Peking, the Chinese and English Governments seem to have both taken alarm. News came, suddenly, that it was countermanded. The escort was recalled, the *personnel* dispersed, the presents were scattered, and the Lamas left masters of the situation. And not only so, but the withdrawal was consecrated in a convention [1] signed at Peking, in the following terms:—

Inasmuch as inquiry into the circumstances, by the Chinese Government, has shown the existence of many obstacles to the

[1] Art. IV. of Convention relating to Burmah and Thibet, July 24th, 1886.

Mission to Thibet provided for in the separate article of the Chefoo Agreement, England consents to countermand the Mission forthwith. With regard to the desire of the British Government to consider arrangements for frontier trade between India and Thibet, it will be the duty of the Chinese Government, after careful inquiry into the circumstances, to adopt measures to exhort and encourage the people with a view to the promotion and development of trade. Should it be practicable, the Chinese Government shall then proceed carefully to consider trade regulations; but if insuperable obstacles should be found to exist, the British Government will not press the matter unduly.

This clause has been criticized as an unnecessary abandonment of the vantage ground provided by the Chefoo Agreement. Even admitting, it was urged, that there was good reason for not pressing the Mission, an explanatory despatch would have sufficed, without this formal renunciation. It must be remembered, however, that the main purpose of the Convention was to settle the question of British supremacy in Burmah, and we were doubtless unwilling to insist on any matter of secondary importance. It must be remembered, too, that there is here recognized, for the first time, a formal purpose of opening up relations between India and Thibet, and that we had reason to believe the Chinese Government sincere in their avowed purpose to forward that design. So that, even if there be room to question the formula employed, the gains were unquestionably material.

But if this apparent concession was really a diplomatic victory, at Peking, the case was quite otherwise on the Thibetan frontier; for the Lamas, encouraged by their success, ventured to enter

British Sikhim and erect forts across the very road we had so anxiously fostered. The Rajah was, of course, powerless to expel the intruders, and the duty devolved upon us of accomplishing that task. It would not probably involve any great effort; but a military expedition was the last thing to which the Indian Government desired to have recourse. One cause of trouble was that the Thibetans were already unnecessarily alarmed, and forceful measures would be likely to make matters worse. Yet, there the matter stood. The vantage ground of the Chefoo Convention had been exchanged for the somewhat curiously worded agreement signed, in 1886, at Peking; the Thibetan passes had been closed rather more tightly than before, and the work must be commenced afresh. Fortunately for the prospect of doing this successfully, China was animated by the best disposition towards us, and was herself willing that more light should be let into the dark corners of Central Asia, where her own statesmen even see imperfectly, and where she is every year finding herself in closer contact with the aggressive power of Russia. Whether enlightened by surer private intelligence of her own, or convinced by what we have been able to communicate, she seemed to understand that she had been deceived as to the feeling of the Thibetan people, and to be willing to support a fresh endeavour to reknit the broken skein.

Of the commercial results which may be anticipated from open intercourse, we have fair data on which to prophesy; for a certain amount of trade has, despite all hindrance, been steadily kept up. The route favoured by the Lamas is, as we have seen, through Nepaul[1]; but a small and growing trade has been fostered since the Treaty of 1861 opened a road through Sikhim. The Darjeeling correspondent of the *Times*, whose telegrams so well describe the movements and motives of the Mission, waxes enthusiastic when this portion of the subject is approached. "Everywhere," he exclaims,

> we hear complaints of the stagnation of trade. Here is a large market waiting, if we only insist on admission. The Thibetans prize broadcloth above all things; they have begun to learn the use of piece goods, and a demand to which there is hardly any limit is springing up for them. Knives and hardware of all kinds are eagerly sought; they are large consumers of tobacco and indigo; and even with the existing restrictions on trade, the staples are gradually increasing. As regards tea, the question is not clear; but it is an instructive fact that within 100 miles of Darjeeling is a people which drinks tea morning, noon, and night, which uses practically no other beverage, and yet obtains its supply from districts of China 1200 miles away.
>
> With respect to the return trade, the chief articles would be gold, musk, live stock, and, above all, wool and woollen goods. The quantity of sheep's wool and of the fine wool of the shawl-goat available is prodigious; and it is now almost worthless from the absence of demand. Doubtless other articles of trade would appear as commerce developed. The richest part of Thibet is practically within a stone's throw, and the inhabitants, who are from the highest to the lowest keen traders, are debarred from intercourse with India through sheer ignorance and the tenacity of tradition.

---

[1] A great trade between India and Thibet is said to have been carried on by this route, before the Goorkha conquest of Nepaul, in 1769; but was almost annihilated by the heavy exactions then imposed, and by the subsequent untoward events.

Mr. Macaulay was able, even in the present condition of the roads, to march with a large suite from Kongralama. On the other hand, Shigats is fully thirty days' journey from Khatmandoo, in Nepaul. Yet it will hardly be believed that the greater part of the trade between India and Thibet goes through Nepaul. It is a tedious journey, and duties are levied on goods both on entering and leaving Nepaul. No trade thus handicapped could flourish. We have a railway to Darjeeling. There is then a fortnight's journey at the outside, and no duties are levied in Sikhim. Yet we can do nothing, while the sturdy little Nepaulese and Cashmerees have traders all over Thibet. Even Russian products and fabrics are working into the market, for Russia has a Consul at Urga; but no British subject is allowed to cross the frontier.

As a matter of fact, however, Tea seems to be at the root of the commercial difficulty, and the following extract from a subsequent article in the same paper may serve to explain this crucial cause of Lama hostility:—

"There is, it must be admitted, one great obstacle in the way of a compromise with China which shall open Thibet to the British trader, and that is the 'brick-tea' monopoly. This strange monopoly is at the bottom of Chinese prejudice and Thibetan hostility, and, when understood, goes far to account for both. The Thibetan has one passion in life—tea. To obtain a sufficiency of this is the great end and aim of his existence. The tea he consumes is not the familiar leaf with which the European markets are supplied; it is a peculiar fermented preparation, highly exhilarating and slightly intoxicating, and is only made in the western part of the province of Sz-chuan. The plant which furnishes it grows on the banks of the Ya-ho. The leaves are gathered when they are about an inch long, moistened with spittle, and rolled into little balls the size of a tea-cup, and then allowed to ferment. As soon as fermentation has set in they are firmly pressed into moulds shaped like a brick and dried over a charcoal fire. Thus prepared, the commodity is ready for the Thibetan market. In China the sale of this brick-tea is a strict Government monopoly;

and as the quantity exported every year is something like eight million pounds, an enormous revenue is derived from Yat-tsow merchants to whom it is farmed. In Thibet, again, the retail trade is, by law, in the hands of the Lamas, or priests; the Thibetan is, therefore, entirely at their mercy, and is made to pay through the nose for his favourite beverage. When ready for market the tea is packed in small boxes containing about twenty pounds, and carried on men's backs two hundred miles to Ta-tsian-loo. Thence, again, it has to go to Bathang, a sixty days' journey, on yaks, and is finally sold in Thibet at prices ranging from 4*s.* per pound for the best quality to 1*s.* 6*d.* English money for inferior varieties. As matters are now, and with the existing restrictions on trade along the Thibetan frontier, there is no competition, and no possibility of competition. The Chinese Government, the Yat-tsow merchants, and the Lamas share between them a very profitable monopoly. But the Assam tea-planters calculate that, were they allowed facilities for trading such as are now sought, they could lay down the brick-tea at Sudiya, on the Brahmapootra River, at four to six annas per pound, with a good profit to themselves; and as the journey to Bathang, if a fairly good road were made, would only occupy twenty days—as against sixty the other way—they would knock the Chinese out of the market altogether. This is perfectly well understood both at Peking and in Lhassa; and under the circumstances the objection entertained in both quarters to English traders and travellers is quite intelligible."

It is a little remarkable that a great power like British India should have consented to sit, for so many years, under the sentence of exclusion. It may be, however, that we waited instinctively until the pear was thoroughly ripe. Darjeeling, which is the natural *entrepôt* for Indo-Thibetan trade, has been annexed; Sikhim has been brought under British influence, and thrown open to transit; a railway from Calcutta enables goods to be laid down at the entrance to the Himalayas. Only political barriers prevent intercourse which the

Thibetan people appear ready to welcome. The maintenance of the obstruction has been attributed to China, and it is too consistent with the former attitude of Chinese statesmen to leave room for doubt that the hostility of the Lamas was in sympathy, formerly, with the prejudices of the Suzerain Power. A change has, however, come over the councils of Peking; and it is clear, as we have already seen, that we do not, even in Thibet, lack powerful friends, for we have encountered nothing but friendliness and goodwill at Teshu Lumbo, while the hostility seems to emanate from Lhassa, the centre of monasticism of a more worldly order.

It is, of course, difficult to gauge the precise feeling of the Thibetan people, but what we hear from Darjeeling agrees fairly with what we glean from other sources. Huc declares that they are free from the exclusive notions which have characterized Chinese policy,[1] and that his own expulsion was the work of the Chinese Resident, in opposition to the will of the Thibetan Regent; and, though Huc's opinions may not always be accepted without reserve, it is inconceivable that he can have lied so outrageously as must be the case if his elaborate

[1] "Les Thibetains ne professent pas à l'égard des autres peuples, ces principes d'exclusion qui font le caractère distinctif de la nation chinoise; tout le monde est admis à Lha-sa; chacun peut aller et venir, se livrer au commerce et à l'industrie, sans que personne s'avise d'apporter la moindre entrave à sa liberté . . . Il est probable que les Anglais ne seraient pas plus repoussés que les autres des frontières du Thibet, si leur marche envahissante dans l'Indoustan n'avait inspiré une légitime terreur au Talé Lama."—*Souvenirs, &c.*, Huc, vol. ii. cap. vi.

account of the Regent's personal bearing, and of the circumstances attending his departure, be discredited. The chances are that there are differences of opinion in Thibet, as well as elsewhere, and it would be little surprising if there were two parties where power is so curiously divided.

A curious side-light is thrown upon the situation by a Memorial which found publicity, in China, just after the incidents we have been relating. Bhootan, as we have seen, is tributary to Thibet, and indirectly, therefore, to Peking. The Chinese Amban at Lhassa are, therefore, charged also with the control of affairs in Bhootan; and the Memorial in question describes a Bhootanese embroglio in which the Resident had found himself called upon to intervene. Some time, apparently, in 1885 two Bhootanese Penlos or district governors rebelled against the Rajah, with the alleged purpose of offering the country to the English; and got so far the upper hand that they beleaguered the Prince and drove certain of his partisans to take refuge in Thibet. He (the Resident) sent Chinese and Thibetan officials and troops to restore order, and the rebels melted away at their approach. One of the Penlos committed suicide, and the other submitted. The notable features of the case are that the Penlos are stated to have relied on English help: that one of the strategic movements of the Chinese commander was to cut off their retreat into India: and that, after general harmony had been restored, "the ruler, head-men and others . . . declared with one voice that, from that time forward, they were all ready to lay aside their previous enmities, and to join heart and strength with Thibet in resisting the English." The Resident obviously thinks he has attained a political triumph.

The occurrence of an avowedly pro-English movement in Bhootan, at the time the question of intercourse was being revived in Thibet, is remarkable. It looks very much as though the Penlos represented a pro-intercourse party which had the upper hand in Bhootan, but was incontinently extinguished by the Chinese Resident at Lhassa and the Lama faction. It is never safe to fancy that one has fathomed the intricacies of Chinese diplomacy. But we probably catch, here, a tardy note of the old exclusiveness that had so long inspired the policy of the Suzerain State. There is reason, as we have seen, to suppose that, whatever may have been the attitude of Chinese statesmen in the past, they are willing to concur in our design of opening up intercourse with Thibet at the present. But it seems clear that no great pains had been taken to prepare the Resident for the change of purpose, or, at any rate, that that purpose does not extend to Bhootan.

It is interesting, in the meantime, to trace back the story to Bogle's early mission, and to realize the curious isolation of the country we desire to approach. Three Europeans only—Huc, Gabet, and Manning—have succeeded in reaching Lhassa during the present century. Natives of India have succeeded from time to time in crossing the frontier; notably the Pundit Nain Singh, who is now living in retirement on lands granted to him by the Government in reward for his services, and Baboo Srutt Chundra Dass, who succeeded in penetrating Lhassa itself and who was to have been associated with the abandoned mission. But against Europeans—with the exception of the three just named—whether approaching from the Indian or the Chinese side, the frontiers have remained sealed. Blakiston tried to reverse the Abbé Huc's route, after the last China War; but failed to reach even the frontier. Cooper, also, tried to make his way through Szechuen, but was turned back by the Lamas from Bathang, and found it equally impossible to effect an entrance from Assam. Everything had, seemingly, been made smooth for Mr. Macaulay's recent attempt; but the moral resistance of Lamadom defeated him on the south, as more practical measures had, six months earlier, closed the Keria mountains against Prejevalsky on the north. There is, however, an ominous tottering of old walls among the hitherto exclusive nations of the East. The hermit kingdom of Korea has opened its doors; and Thibet cannot expect much longer to escape its fate.

CHAPTER XIII.

THE POSITION IN 1888.

THE spring of 1888 found matters very much in the position in which they had been left in the autumn of the previous year. Thibetan troops were still blocking the road through Sikhim, and the Lamas seemed as far as ever from relaxing their opposition. China had been promised that ample time should be allowed for the exertion of her influence to procure their withdrawal; but it was also made clear that we could not tolerate the rebuff implied by their presence on the Indian side of the Himalayan crest; and that, failing their retreat, we should be compelled to drive them from the position they had taken up. We waited eighteen months while China did its best, or professed to be doing its best, by pacific means, to procure this result; and only after that long interval was notice sent to the intruders that they would be turned out by force if they had not voluntarily withdrawn.

The 15th March was the date fixed. Our troops then advanced slowly, in order to give them time to run away; and, after a show of resistance, they availed themselves of the privilege. They were attacked five days after the date named, and driven out of an advanced work; but promptly vacated their camp itself, before the advance of the British, two days later. The physical difficulties of the expedition were, indeed, greater than the military; for the position to be attacked was 13,000 feet above the sea-level, and the roads were deep in snow. What was almost worse was that we gained little by our action, beyond the satisfaction of expelling the intruders from British soil; for they only retired to the Jeylep Pass, and there fortified themselves afresh, while Col. Graham established himself at Gnatong, within the Indian frontier. Both parties seem, then, to have referred matters afresh to Peking.

There was, it must be confessed, a dash of absurdity in the situation. Here, nearly on the roof of the world, were British and Thibetans encamped over against each other, waiting for a *deus ex machinâ* in the shape of a Chinese mandarin to release them from their difficulty. Nothing could be farther from our wish than to annoy China, or to anger the Thibetans, by invading Thibet; nor anything, we imagine, much farther from the wish of China than such a development of the quarrel. Yet neither British threats nor Chinese pressure appeared able to modify the situation. So far from giving in, the Lamas appealed to China for assistance, while England was expecting her to persuade them to relax their opposition. The appeal was additionally awkward because one secret of China's hold on Thibet is, undoubtedly, the protection she has always been ready to afford. But her statesmen are said to have been equal to the occasion: "If the Thibetans had, as they affirmed, already defeated their opponents, Chinese help was [they replied] manifestly unnecessary!" The story comes from Calcutta, and may not be literally above suspicion; but we can scarcely refuse it entire credit, for it has a flavour so intensely Chinese that we can almost see the mandarins laughing in their sleeves while formulating the answer.

But though we can imagine that Peking statesmen were not above a quiet chuckle, we may do them the justice to believe that they were really anxious their intervention should prevail. Their interests were, in fact, doubly at state; for they had to prove to England that they could control their vassal, as well as to sustain their *rôle* of Protectors in Thibet; and it may not be inopportune, while the opposing forces are, like difficulty itself, almost literally in the air, to examine a little more closely the factors of the problem.

Let us turn for a moment to Lhassa; using the word advisedly, in preference to "Thibet," because one of the errors we have to unlearn is a conception of the great region, so designated on our maps, as an integral State governed from, and having, Lhassa as a political capital. "A supposition (writes Mr. Colborne Baber[1]) seems to prevail among Europeans that the region which geographers have included

[1] "A Journey of Exploration in Western Szu-chuan." By E. Colborne Baber. Royal Geographical Society Supplementary Papers. 1882.

under the general name of Thibet is an integral State sub-divided for administrative purposes into separate provinces. Although this assumption is quite erroneous, some palliation of it may be found in the general use by Tibetans of the term Peu (pronounced as in French), which is written Bod. . . . A Tibetan arriving at Ta-chien-lu (in China) from Lhassa, on being asked from what country he has come, will often reply from Teu Peu, meaning High or Upper Tibet. Perhaps Teu Peu is the source of our 'Tibet,' and if so it is equally correct to write Tibet or Thibet, since the word Teu is pronounced indifferently with or without an aspirate. A native employs the expression Peu Lumbo (Tibet country) to designate *en bloc* all Tibetan-speaking nationalities, without intending to convey the least insinuation that they are subject to Lhassa. The state of which that city is the capital is called Lhassa Dé (territory of Lhassa) . . . and is merely one, though admittedly the most prominent of a large number of states governed by kings very little disposed to imagine themselves subordinate to the King or Regent of Lhassa." The error is evidently as great as it would have been to speak of Italy, before its unification, as a homogeneous state governed from Rome. There is, in Central Thibet, a state called Lhassa Dé, of which Lhassa is the capital, and which the Dalai Lama—or his Government, however constituted—does really rule; and it is without question the most important in Thibet, whereas the States of the Church were of minor proportion in the Roman hierarchy. Otherwise, for purposes of illustration, the parallel between Lhassa and Rome—between Thibet and Italy in the days of its disunion—is sufficiently instructive. Whatever may be the constitution of Lhassa Dé: whether the Dalai Lama be really a political as well as a spiritual chief; or whether there be, among the four Kalons or ministers through whom he governs, one so superior as to be virtually prince or king, as Mr. Colborne Baber appears disposed to surmise, there is no doubt that the Dalai Lama is venerated throughout all Thibet as implicitly as the Pope is venerated throughout Latin Christendom. The parallel might be extended, even, to embrace people and language. There are fair-haired Venetians in the north of Italy and dark-haired Sicilians in the south; still Italy is, at the present day, a national and linguistic as well as a geographical expression; and the same thing, with the same explanations and the same reservations, may be said of Thibet. There are tall and fresh-coloured Thibetans in the east, and short and dark-haired Thibetans in the west; but all alike use the Thibetan language, and all call themselves men of Bod, though without implying subserviency to Lhassa otherwise than as a Spaniard would admit spiritual subserviency to Rome.

So much, then, seems clear. Lhassa Dé, the state bordering on Sikhim, is only one, though the most important, among a congeries of states covering the great region known to us as Thibet. And, whatever the personal share taken by the Dalai Lama in its government, the preponderance of the monastic element within its borders and in its councils is undoubtedly so great that we are justified in speaking, as we do, of "the Lamas" as a dominant influence.

A question next suggests itself, as to the source of the hostility which is shown at Lhassa to intercourse with British India; for that hostility is not believed to be instinctive in the Thibetan people. Huc declares, as we have seen, that exclusiveness is not a characteristic of the country. "Everyone (he affirms) is admitted to Lhassa; everyone can go and come, and work or trade, without anybody dreaming of interfering."[1] But he also adds—indicating, no doubt, an important element of the opposition we are now encountering—"It is probable the English would not be repelled more than other people, if their invading march in India had not inspired the Dalai Lama with legitimate fear." Bogle, as we shall presently see, found traces of the same feeling, though he was disposed to attribute his difficulties mainly to Chinese inspiration. Without labouring the point, then, we may take it for granted that we have here one cause of hostility; and to political, may very possibly be added a spice of ecclesiastical, jealousy. Buddhism is by no means an intolerant religion, but no hierarchy likes to see its position endangered; and it is quite likely that British-Indian intercourse involves danger, or at least disturbance, in the minds of the Thibetan priesthood. A third,

[1] "Souvenirs d'un Voyage dans le Thibet," vol. ii. cap. 4.

and a very important, influence is unquestionably commercial. By far the most important article of commerce between China and Thibet is tea; and the interests bound up in this trade are relatively immense. "Tea," writes Mr. Cooper,[1] "is, for the Thibetans, the prime necessary of life; to their need of it may be ascribed the final success of the Chinese conquest of Eastern Thibet. Their whole business of life seems to be to procure a sufficiency of it; and it is no cheap luxury, for the Lamas—keeping in their hands the retail, as the Chinese monopolize the wholesale, trade—by this means reduce the people to absolute dependence on them, exacting in return for the precious article labour and produce. Grain, yaks, sheep, horses, and even children, are given to the rapacious priesthood in exchange for tea." And, extravagant as the language may appear, we have high authority for believing that it is fairly in accord with facts. "To the Thibetan," writes Mr. Baber,[2] "tea is more than a luxury: it is an absolute necessary. Deprived of the costly but indispensable astringent, he suffers from headache, grows nervous, restless, out of condition, and altogether unhappy. In outlying districts mothers are careful to keep the seductive beverage from their children lest they should grow up unable, on occasion, to go without it." And information gleaned from, among others, an

[1] "Travels of a Pioneer of Commerce," *ut supra*, cap. xiv.

[2] In an instructive paper on "The Chinese Tea Trade with Thibet," published in the *Gazette of India*, Nov. 8th, 1879.

apostate Lama, convinced him that Mr. Cooper hardly exaggerates the tyranny and rapacity of the priestly vendors.

So far the demand. We come now to its influence on the question of intercourse with India. The day has passed when China possessed a monopoly of supply. Tea could, the Lamas are well aware, since the development of its cultivation on the Himalayan slopes, be imported more easily from the south than from the east, for access to Lhassa Dé is infinitely easier from Darjeeling than from Bathang; and we may conceive the alarm which such a prospect must excite among the men who now control the trade with Szechuen. Not only do the Chinese find a lucrative market in Thibet for the refuse of their plantations—"tea brushwood," Mr. Baber calls it, to which "the veriest sweepings of the Assam godowns" would be preferable; but the Lamas, who have succeeded in monopolizing the supply, are profoundly interested in maintaining the present conditions. The price of common Szechuen brick tea in Lhassa is said to be about half a rupee a pound; but the price "rises in a ratio altogether out of proportion to the distance of the market from the tea route, and very quickly reaches a figure which puts the article beyond the purchasing power of the country people." This state of things arises, however, not from the difficulties and dangers of the bye-roads so much as from the policy of the Lamas, who, being the traders and money-lenders of the country and the only capitalists, have many motives for confining the traffic in a channel which they can most easily direct to their own advantage. They make greater and steadier profits by restricting the trade to one main line, along which they can monopolize it, than they could do by opening new markets in districts at a distance from their lamaserais, where it would be liable to stray from their control. This they can the more easily effect because the supply of tea is inferior to the demand, and because it is not liable to much fluctuation. It would be easy to multiply illustrations, but sufficient has been said to show what a hold on Thibet the craving for tea has given China as the sole source of supply; what a hold their monopoly gives the Lamas over the people; and what interest they have in opposing change.

Turning, now, to the political position and influence of the Suzerain Power, we enter a much less lucid atmosphere. Still the surmise would not, probably, be far wrong that—though differing in motive—Lamas and Mandarins have sympathized, in the main, in the policy of exclusion that has prevailed. It is due to this exclusiveness that the amount of European evidence at our command is slight, but all that we have points to this conclusion. While admitting that the Thibetans—however little exclusive by disposition—viewed with apprehension the march of English conquest, Bogle and Huc concur in attributing the actual opposition they encountered, to Chinese influence. The tea question had not then arisen, to energize Lama obstruction, and fear of English aggression was rather a latent than an active force; but the opposition of China was clear and unequivocal. Already, at Tassisudon, the capital of Bhootan, Bogle was met by the objection that intercourse "might give offence to the Emperor of China." A Nepaulese official who visited him at Teshu Lumbo declared that, "although well disposed towards the Government (of India), the Regent (of Lhassa) was afraid of giving umbrage to China, and had therefore ordered him, in case he visited the Residents, not to let them know that he (Bogle) was an Englishman." Some Kashmere merchants, conversing with him about the production of gold in Thibet, objected that, "if extensive quantities of the metal were exported to Bengal, the Emperor of China would be displeased." Emissaries sent by the Regent himself to compliment Bogle replied, to his advocacy of trade, that the Regent "would do all in his power, but that he and all his countrymen were subject to the Emperor of China;" whereat Bogle exclaims, "This is a stumbling-block that crosses me in all my paths." It was, in fact, the burden of the answer to all his attempted negotiations, whether with the Teshu Lama in person or with others.

It was due also to Chinese influence that Manning, who enjoys to this day the distinction of being the only Englishman who has penetrated Lhassa, was sent back by the way he came, after his remarkable excursion, thirty-six years later. Manning, who was a medical man by profession, and had qualified himself for his project by the study of Chinese at Canton, succeeded, in 1811, in reaching Lhassa alone and unaided—mainly, it would seem, by the help of these two accomplishments, for the Chinese servant he took with him appears to have been of doubtful assistance. He doctored certain Chinese soldiers whom he found at Parijong, on the Bhootan frontier, so successfully that they prevailed on their commander to let him accompany them to Gyantze, where he received a passport allowing him to proceed to the capital. And not only did he reach Lhassa, but he had more than one interview with the very Dalai Lama, by whom he was sentimentally impressed.[1] Manning's impression of the bearing of the Chinese towards the Thibetans was unfavourable ; and the frequent practice of sending to Lhassa mandarins who had fallen into disgrace at home, did not, in his opinion, conduce to amicable relations. It is (he remarks) bad policy ; and he "cannot help thinking, from what he had seen and heard, that the Thibetans would view Chinese influence in Thibet overthrown without many emotions of regret, especially if the Ruler under the new influence were to treat the Grand Lama with respect ; for that is a point in which the haughty mandarins are somewhat deficient, to the no small dissatisfaction of the good people of Lhassa." He had not been long at Lhassa before he per-

[1] "This day saluted the Grand Lama. Face poetically affecting : Could have wept. Very happy to have seen him and his blessed smile."—"Journal of Thomas Manning," edited by Clements R. Markham.

ceived that he was himself an object of suspicion to the said mandarins, and heard that a report had been sent to the Emperor, embodying the substance of interrogatories administered to his Chinese servant. What he hoped was that he would be sent, or allowed to proceed, to Canton by way of Szechuen, as Huc was thirty years later; but what actually happened was—as we are left to gather from fragmentary notes, for his journal comes, here, to an abrupt end—that an imperial decree of some sort arrived about the new year, in consequence of which he was handed back by the way he came, while his servant was sent overland to China.

It is curious that Huc, as well as Manning, found the Chief Resident at Lhassa to be a Tartar mandarin who had been disgraced for mismanagement of matters connected with the English at Canton. The Dalai Lama was an infant at the time (1844) the French missionaries made their way to the capital; but it is noteworthy that they were impressed as favourably by the Thibetan Regent, as Bogle had been by the Teshu Lama, and that they are emphatic in ascribing their expulsion to the sole action of the Chinese Resident, Ke-Shen. They had, in fact, been so kindly received by the Thibetans, and felt their position so assured, that they began to think of opening communication with Europe; and actually obtained, according to their own account, the assent of the Regent to M. Gabet going to Calcutta, by way of Bhootan, for the purpose. But they had calculated without Ke-Shen, who was not disposed to tolerate, in Thibet, a propaganda which was at the time discountenanced in China. The Regent, according to Huc—who, though not an unbiassed, can hardly be rejected as an altogether untrustworthy witness—demurred emphatically to withdrawing from them "the protection and liberty which were accorded, in Thibet, to all strangers and especially to men of prayers." But Ke-Shen was inexorable, and insisted not only on their departure, but on their being sent by the long and difficult journey through China to Canton, instead of by the comparatively short and easy one to Calcutta. "I do not permit you to stay here," he said, "but it is the will of the great Emperor, and not mine. I do not permit you to go by way of India, because the laws of the Empire forbid it;" but everything should be, and everything was, done for their comfort. The parting from the Regent appears to have been as pathetic as Bogle's from the Teshu Lama; and the expression on both sides, of a hope to meet again, heartfelt and sincere. His Highness gave them clearly to understand that he yielded to pressure, and that he was displeased at the coercion.

Ke-Shen pleaded the Imperial will and established custom, and he was doubtless right. The closure of the Himalayan passes, after the Nepaulese war of 1792, would commend itself to the Chinese mind as so simple and effectual a way of shutting out trouble, that it was sure to be approved at Peking; though different Residents seem to have exercised a discretionary power, with the effect of additionally vexing the intruder to be ejected. Manning, who wanted to travel through China, was right-about-faced to India. Huc and Gabet, who wanted to go to India, were sent back through China. And so things went on, narrowing down from precedent to precedent, till we find Mr. Edgar—who made his way to the Jeylep Pass on a mission from Calcutta, in 1873—bluntly refused permission to cross the frontier. It was vain to quote the precedents of Bogle and Turner. "The present arrangement had," said the Governor of Parijong, "been made thirty years ago, by the Chinese Envoy, Ke-Shen, who had arranged that the direct management of frontier affairs should be committed to the Amban, or Chinese Residents, and that there should be no intercourse between Thibet and British India; all he (the Governor) had to do was to obey orders." Mr. Edgar was also told—and the incident may help to throw light on the general situation—that "much uneasiness was felt in Thibet at the threatening attitude of the Nepaulese, which obliged the Dalai Lama and his advisers to make up their differences with the Amban, in order to be secure of help from China." Tea has been indicated as one secret of the Chinese hold on Thibet; and the sense of military dependence is probably another. Everything by comparison. Europeans think poorly of Chinese organization for war, but to the Thibetans it may well seem preponderant. And China appears, to do her justice, to have fairly fulfilled her sovereign duty. Whether against the Kalmucks, against Nepaul, or against Kashmere, her help has always been forthcoming; and it is quite likely that the Thibetans, an unwarlike race, have become so accustomed to look to Peking for help that the sense of military dependence acts as a strong political retainer. They may not love China much, but they fear Nepaul more; and are convinced, probably, of the truth of the maxim that it is wiser to bear the ills they have than to fly to others that they know not of.

We are concerned, however, for the moment, with the degree rather than with the secret of Chinese influence, and with the evidence that it has been used, till quite recently, to shut out intercourse with Hindustan. Whether he dictated, or whether he merely gave expression to a policy of exclusion, the Chinese Resident at Lhassa appeared always, to foreigners, as the moving spirit of obstruction, while the Thibetan authorities were held up as models of kindly hospitality. All this was now about to be reversed—reversed, at any rate, in appearance; for I deprecate any accusation of pretending to interpret with certainty the secret workings of Chinese diplomacy. Lama hostility was about to become apparent as an active force, and the Chinese Resident as a subservient rather than a directing influence.

The first to experience the change was Mr. Cooper, who set out from Shanghai in 1868, accompanied only by a Chinese interpreter, with the purpose of making his way across the frontier of Szechuen, through Eastern Thibet, into Assam. And here, for the first time, probably, tea comes into play as a factor in the problem. Mr. Cooper's object was to open up a new mart for the produce of our Assam tea-plantations; and though his journey had the countenance of China, he was repelled from the frontier of Thibet. No attempt was made to procure for him an imperial passport, though he had, it is needless to say, the cordial sympathy and support of H.M. Legation. But Sir Walter (then Mr.) Medhurst, H.M. Consul at Hankow, procured for him from the Viceroy at Wuchang a letter which seemed likely, so far as the Chinese were concerned, to remove all difficulties; for he was able, on arriving at the capital of Szechuen, to exchange this for a passport addressed to the Chinese Resident at Lhassa, which bore on its face that the Resident should exchange it for one authorizing him to proceed to Nepaul or Darjeeling. Armed with this high permit he succeeded in reaching Bathang, but was there informed privately, by the Magistrate, that he would certainly be hindered from proceeding, the Chinese Resident at Lhassa having written to say that the Lamas had given notice he would not be allowed to cross the frontier. The magistrate—who was in a dilemma between his orders from the Viceroy and his instructions from the Resident—seems, indeed, to have become highly indiscreet in his revelations, for he affirmed that the Resident was in the habit of receiving large sums, from the Lamas, to keep out foreigners.

It was, at any rate, Mr. Cooper found, perfectly understood in the neighbourhood that orders had been sent from Lhassa to stop him at all hazards; and the accuracy of the rumour was curiously confirmed by the language of a memorial addressed from Lhassa to Peking, in anticipation of his visit, of which he afterwards procured a copy. This document, which purports to give the tenor of a petition received from "all the gentry, heads of monasteries, priests, and common people" of the country, sets out that Thibet is the country of Buddha, and "inhabitants of no other country, except the Nepaulese, with whom continual trade and intercourse are kept up, are allowed to cross the border to travel." Reference is then made to Huc and Gabet, who were at once sent back by Ke-Shen, but whose visit still so offended the tutelary deities that all sorts of miseries fell upon the country, for years afterwards. And now letters of instruction had arrived, intimating that Englishmen are desirous of travelling in Thibet.

The news of this probable arrival of foreigners has already thrown priests and people alike into a state of excessive alarm, and they have all prayed [the writer] to make the matter the subject of a memorial [to the effect that they should not come to travel]. If, in spite of our opposition, they persist in coming, your servants can only band together all the tribes professing the same religion, and, with unanimity of purpose, do our utmost to prevent them. . . . It is now reported that an English doctor named Cooper has come from Szechuen to travel in Thibet, and men's minds have been filled with alarm which it is impossible to prevent. . . . Further, in Eastern and Western Thibet, there are over 100,000 Lamas, not one of whom but is of the most obstinate and determined character; and to the commands of these Lamas alone the whole population render obedience. These men are opposed to the officers or people of other countries entering their territory, and their determination is not to be broken down. . . .

To sum up; the Thibetan Lamas will, to the death, prevent people from visiting their country; and if the Lamas have so made up their minds, the hearts of the people will be still more excited; and though I am desirous of bringing the matter to an amicable settlement, it will be impossible for me to obey [the letter of instructions]. If the people are allowed to come and travel in Thibet, it will be impossible to prevent the commission of outrages against them as soon as ever they cross the borders. . . . [The Emperor is therefore prayed to arrange with the English Government that no one shall be allowed to travel in Thibet].

I have quoted from the memorial at some length, because it so well expresses the spirit of the opposition we have encountered, and because it is instructive to note how curiously the tactics threatened coincide with what we have heard of the attitude assumed towards the Macaulay Mission. A long stride farther has been made, since Cooper's day, towards gaining Chinese support. The Chefoo Convention of 1876 and the expressed consent of the Chinese Government in 1886 legalized, for Mr. Macaulay, what was only tacitly permitted in Mr. Cooper; but each encountered determined opposition from the Lamas, who enjoyed apparently, in each case, the countenance and help of the Chinese Resident. The revolution has since been completed: it is Lhassa which now stands out as the centre of opposition; and it is to the Chinese, instead of the Thibetan, capital that we now look for goodwill and support.

It may be doubtful whether China could suddenly reverse the current of her influence. The changes of incumbency at the Lhassa Residency have been lately frequent—reflecting, probably, phases of effort to effect political change. That we have the support of the Imperial Cabinet may be reasonably assumed—a lukewarm support it may be—made up of some willingness to oblige England and a great desire to avoid complications, qualified by a wish that things could have remained as they were; for it is easy to conceive that the question is causing it both trouble and anxiety. The Imperial Government hardly possesses, even in China proper, the decided power which the Queen's Government exercises in England; and its hold over remote dependencies is proportionately less firm. It is easy to believe, therefore, that it cannot absolutely control the Lamas, if it would. It is possible that, if an imperative order were sent, it would be obeyed; but it is also probable that there might ensue disturbances which the Resident has no adequate power to control; and it would be extravagant to suppose that the Chinese would willingly incur the cost and trouble of a military expedition to coerce the Thibetans in English interests. We have heard enough of the Lamas to know that they are not, as a class, distinguished by the amiability which, in their higher representatives, fascinated Bogle and Manning. They have, on the contrary, an evident capacity for turbulence which would be certainly stimulated by abrupt interference with their interests. In the mouth of the Chinese Government, therefore, the order to "settle" means not necessarily concession, but "compromise." It may be, as Bogle judged, and as India has always affirmed, that the Thibetan people, and even the Thibetan rulers, are not averse to commercial intercourse: they have not much love for China, and would be as willing, probably, to get their tea from Darjeeling as from Tatsienlu. But rulers and people do not constitute the whole state of Lhassa: the Lamas are more numerous, more powerful, and more actively interested than either, and it looks very much as though they were controlling the situation.

Enough has now been said, if not to elucidate the question, at least to show that its solution is less easy than people in England, looking at the surface, might be inclined to fancy. Apart from the great prestige which she has enjoyed in Eastern Asia, the two main secrets of China's hold on Thibet have been the somewhat incongruous ones of tea and military prestige. China was alone able to supply the leaf for which the Thibetans crave; China has been looked to, to protect them against the Nepaulese and other warlike neighbours. If the frontiers were opened to a competing supply of tea, and aid withheld in face of what the Lamas, of course, represent as Indian aggression, dangerous questions as to the value of the Chinese connection might arise. We cannot withhold from the Imperial Government a measure of sympathy in the difficulty; but neither need we ignore that it brought on itself a large measure of the trouble. For half a generation, the question had been before it as one that must be eventually faced. Years had passed since it was formulated in the Convention of Chefoo, yet the emergency found it apparently untouched. It must, therefore, be held partly responsible for the excitement that arose on an attempt to bring the matter to an issue, and that eventuated in the military operations to which the Government of India found itself committed.

CHAPTER XIV.

SIKHIM.

WE left the British and Thibetans facing each other on the crest of the Himalayas, awaiting the action of Chinese diplomacy. The challenge of the Lamas had been most reluctantly taken up, and their troops driven out of British Sikhim; but a halt had been then called, to give further opportunity for Chinese mediation. Six months passed without a sign that progress was being made. There was going and coming of emissaries between Lhassa and Peking; one Chinese Resident was even recalled in disgrace, and replaced by Chang Keng, the Deputy-Governor of Ili, who had strict injunctions to compose the quarrel. Nothing resulting, however, from these combinations, the Indian Government decided, in 1888, to take the matter once more into its own hands. Colonel Graham was ordered to clear the road by force, since the Thibetans would not vacate it of good will; and in two sharp actions, on September 21st and 24th, their garrisons were driven out of the Jeylep and Tunko passes, and pursued headlong into Chumbi. This display of vigour seemed to have the effect of somewhat hurrying the wheels of Lhassa statesmanship, as the Rajah of Sikhim came into the British camp, and was quickly followed by a Chinese emissary who announced that the Resident was doing his utmost to control the situation and was coming in person to open negotiations.

It might have been wiser if we had stayed awhile on Thibetan soil, now that we had reluctantly entered it. Our presence might have strengthened the hands of the Chinese Resident, who had, unquestionably, a difficult task to perform. It was decided, however, to return to Gnatong, and the consequence became apparent in a further interval of delay. Nearly three months passed before Chang Keng reached the British camp; and he took up the position, then, of a champion rather than a diplomatist. However urgent his instructions might be, to prevent any further development of the quarrel, the Lamas would, of course, expect him to support their cause; and they succeeded so far as to persuade him to assert Chinese suzerainty over Sikhim. That the Rajah might be a feudatory of Lhassa *quâ* the Trans-nivean province of Chumbi was a proposition no one wanted to dispute, but that the Cis-nivean province should be recognized as Indian was an elementary feature of the situation, and the Envoy's refusal to admit this view caused an immediate deadlock. He was, in fact, about returning to Lhassa when the Imperial Government intervened. Gnatong was in telegraphic communication, fortunately, *viâ* Calcutta, with Peking, and Chang Keng's announcement of his intention to withdraw was met by a prompt order to stay where he was until a settlement could be discovered. It may not be uninteresting, while negotiations are in progress, to trace the story of the little State which has sprung into such sudden notoriety as a recent battle-ground and prospective trade route between its two greater neighbours.

"Commanding, confessedly, the grandest known landscape of snowy mountains in the Himalayas and hence in the world," the view from Darjeeling is, writes Sir Joseph Hooker,[1] unparalleled for the scenery it embraces. The snow-clad mass of Kinchinjunga, rising 21,000 feet above the level of the observer, out of a sea of intervening wooded hills, is only forty-five miles distant; "whilst, on a line with its snows, the eye descends below the horizon to a narrow gulf 7000 feet deep in the mountains where the Great Rungeet, white with foam, threads a tropical forest with a silver line. To the north-west, towards Nepaul, the snowy peaks of Kubra and Jummoo (respectively 24,005 and 25,312 feet) rise over the shoulder of Singaleelah, whilst eastward the snowy mountains appear to form an unbroken range, trending north-east to the great mass of Donkia (23,176) and thence south-east to the fingered peaks of Tunkola and the silver cone of

[1] *Himalayan Journals; or, Notes of a Naturalist.* By Joseph Dalton Hooker. London, 1854.—There are within the field of view twelve mountains over 20,000 feet. The nearest snow is thirty-two miles, and the farthest seventy-three miles distant.

Chola, gradually sinking into the Bhootan Mountains at Gipmoochi (14,509)."—The view described is practically a view of Sikhim; and no one who has had the good fortune to visit Darjeeling can peruse without a sense of vivid pleasure the exquisite description in which Hooker recalls the surpassing splendour of the scene. A tumbled mountain mass, made up of great heights and deep-cut ravines, of heavy forest and foaming torrent, in which rises and descents of six thousand feet and more are common in passing from valley to valley, sometimes in a single day's march—Sikhim fulfils the wildest conception of mountain grandeur. Kinchinjunga itself is within its borders: over Chola and Tunkola are the passes into Chumbi which our soldiers have lately traversed. The Snowy Range marks, in fact, roughly, the frontier of Thibet.

Hidden thus in the recesses of the Himalayas, screened from the lowland by our hill-station of Darjeeling, shrouded as it were in virgin forest, Sikhim is too small a political unit to have attracted notice outside af Hindostan. As a region possessing scenery of surpassing beauty and flora of luxuriant wealth, it has been explored by travellers like Sir Joseph Hooker and Sir Richard Temple, who have given us fascinating descriptions of its natural beauty: as a troublesome neighbour, it has had to be coerced by soldiers like Colonel Gawler, who has left a humorous picture of its physical difficulties: as a vassal State and a possible hyphen between India and Thibet, it has been visited by political officers like Mr. Edgar. But of history, in the literary sense, it has practically none; for what there was of local record—a remarkable and beautiful manuscript kept in the monastery of Pemyongchi—was destroyed by the Nepaulese in 1814. What little is known of its earlier story has been summarized by Captain Temple in the Introduction to his father's diaries.[1] Practically, however, as he remarks, no European has even seriously inquired into it, nor is there much promise of valuable result if the task were undertaken. It is sufficient for us to know that the Rajah's family came originally from Thibet, and attained to princely rank, about three hundred years ago, in the person of one Penccho Namagé, who was then settled at Gantok. There had occurred in Thibet, not long previously, the great Tsong-Kaban reformation which divided the Thibetan world as effectually as Luther divided European Christendom; and many lamas of the older but defeated sect had migrated to Sikhim. Penccho seems to have taken these under his protection and, by their help, to have raised himself to the throne. The event has interest as illustrating the connection with Thibet which has been a dominant factor in Sikhimese polity, and deserves note for that reason; but it is not till towards the close of the eighteenth century that Sikhim looms upon the Indian horizon—or

[1] *Journals kept in Hyderabad, Kashmir, Sikhim, &c.* By Sir R. Temple. Edited by Captain R. C. Temple.

that it begins, at any rate, to figure as an element in Anglo-Indian politics.

Sikhim is referred to as "Bramascjon" by Van de Putte, who gathered his information from a son of the Rajah then visiting the Court of Lhassa, and as "Demo-jong" by Bogle half a century later; but neither of them crossed the frontier, nor does this nomenclature do much more than signalize its existence. Bogle learned, certainly, that there was a path across it between India and Thibet,[1] but no thought of utilizing it occurred, evidently, either to him or to Hastings. It was, in fact, closed at the moment by the same cause which was impelling them to seek a way through Bhootan. The Goorkhas, who had throttled the traditional highway through Nepaul by their exactions, had extended their conquest over the Sikhimese lowland and interfered, in this direction also, between India and Thibet. Bogle's references to Sikhim are, in fact, made only with regard to the anxiety caused by Goorkha turbulence. "There was," exclaimed the Teshu Lama—and the sentence is worth quoting as a declaration of suzerainty—"no trusting them; for though their Rajah had promised, over and over again, that he would never encroach a finger's breadth on

[1] "The commodities of Bengal used to be conveyed into Thibet through the Murung (Sikhimese lowland) and a province adjoining to it which is subject to Lhassa and governed by a chief styled Demo-jong. The fakirs, when expelled from Nepaul, generally frequented this road; but, being esteemed unhealthy, it was not adopted by any creditable merchants."—*Narrative of the Mission of George Bogle to Thibet.*

Thibetan territory, he had now attacked Demojong's country which was subject to Lhassa."

Sikhim comprised at that period what may, for convenience of illustration, be described as three sections: (1) the Trans-nivean province of Chumbi, bounded on the north and east by Lhassa-Dé and Bhootan; (2) the region known as the Cis-nivean Sikhim, bounded on the north and west by Lhassa-Dé and Nepaul; (3) the district of Darjeeling, including a tract at the foot of the Himalayas then known as the Murung. The first was, and is, admittedly Thibetan soil: the second has passed under the influence, and the third into the actual possession, of British India. Sikhim is, in fact, literally astride a dividing range of the Himalayas, with one leg on the Thibetan and one on the Indian slope. It is from Cis-nivean Sikhim that we were lately obliged to expel the Thibetan troops; and it is the passes leading from the Cis-nivean to the Trans-nivean province that we are anxious to open.

It would be worse than wearisome to follow, here, the tangled skein of local quarrel that began with the rise of Goorkha power and terminated only, in 1817, with our own appearance on the scene. We are concerned with the incident which entailed the barring of the Thibetan frontier; and the fewest possible words will suffice to maintain the connection of the story.—Having subjugated Nepaul, the Goorkhas were, as we have seen, at the time of Bogle's mission, threatening to extend their conquest over Sikhim. They had overrun the Murung, and were invading the hill region, when a Thibetan army was sent to oppose them. The incident closed with their retreat from Sikhim proper, on certain terms which are irrelevant to our purpose, but in their retaining possession of the Murung which figures thenceforth, as a sort of counter in the game of Himalayan politics. They were, however, quieted only for the moment; they invaded, sixteen years later, the very territory of the Dalai Lama, and advanced as far as Shigatze which they took and sacked; whereupon the Chinese came to the assistance of their feudatories and wound up a victorious campaign by closing the southern frontier against natives of Hindostan. "So careful were they," says Turner, whose narrative [1] forms the staple record of the event, "to avail themselves of every possible advantage within their reach, that they even occupied an intermediate country between Bhootan and Nepaul, the territory of a petty chief denominated Rajah of Segwin, or Seccum [Sikhim] . . . . and from this period, unhappily, is to be dated the interruption which has taken place in the regular intercourse between the Company's possessions and the territory of the Lama."

The "intermediate country" in question was the province of Chumbi, of which we have heard so much in connection with recent operations, and which is destined to so much prominence as a highway and

[1] *An Account of an Embassy to the Court of the Teshoo Lama in Thibet, &c., ut supra.*

possible *entrepôt* of Indo-Thibetan trade, that it may be worth while quoting Hooker's description of its characteristics :—

"Choombi is the general name given to a large Thibetan province that embraces the head of the Machoo river, and includes Phari, Eusa, Choombi, and about thirteen other villages, corresponding to as many districts that contain from under a dozen to three hundred houses each, varying with the season and state of trade. The latter is considerable, Phari being, next to Darjeeling, the greatest Thibetan, Bhotan, Sikhim, and Indian *entrepôt* along the whole Himalaya east of Nepaul. The general form of Choombi valley is triangular, the broader end northwards; it is bounded by the Chola range on the west, from Donkia to Gipmoochi, and by the Kamphee or Chakoong range to the east. These meridional ranges approximate to the southward, so as to form a natural boundary to Choombi. The Machoo River, rising from Chumulari, flows through Choombi and enters Bhotan at a large mart called Rinchingoong, whence it flows to the plains of India. . . . The Choombi district is elevated, for the only cultivation is a summer or Alpine one, neither maize, rice, nor millet being grown there: it is also dry, for the great height of the Bhotan Mountains and the form of the Machoo valley cut off the rains, and there is no dense forest: it is very mountainous, all carriage being on men's and yaks' backs; and is populous for this part of the country, the inhabitants being estimated at 3000 in the trading season. . . . From Choombi to Lhassa is fifteen long days' journey for a man mounted on a stout mule."

It is essential to the comprehension of recent events, that the political and geographical distinction between the Cis-nivean and Trans-nivean provinces be clearly realized; and it may even be worth mentioning that, when Hooker succeeded in making a detour through Chumbi from the Kongralama to the Donkia pass, "nothing would induce the Thibetan guard who accompanied him to cross into Cis-nivean Sikhim, which they regarded as Company's territory."

It was the British war with Nepaul, in 1814, that led to the attraction of Sikhim within the sphere of Indian politics. The Rajah required little persuasion to array himself on our side, against his predatory neighbours; but he suffered badly, at the outset, for his temerity. His troops were driven across the Teesta; the country was overrun, the monasteries were plundered, and that act of vandalism was committed which deprived the world for ever of a section of Himalayan history! However, we were, of course, victorious on the west; and the Rajah—partly as a reward, but mainly with a view of setting up Sikhim as a buffer between Nepaul and Bhootan—was taken (in 1817) under Indian protection, and replaced in possession of the vexed Murung region.

Fourteen years of tranquillity followed, but at the end of that period a fresh process of disintegration began. There broke out, in 1828, a frontier dispute between Sikhim and Nepaul which occasioned a visit to Darjeeling, by Mr. J. W. Grant, that resulted in its acquisition by the British. What is now a flourishing town was then a paltry village; what is now an important centre of tea and cinchona cultivation was then impenetrable jungle. But Mr. Grant was so impressed with its potential value as a sanatorium, a commercial depôt, and a military station if need be, that he induced Lord William Bentinck to negotiate for its cession. There was a little delay in realizing the project, but the Rajah was eventually persuaded (in 1835) to yield the territory in exchange for a pension of 300*l*. For some years all went smoothly between the new settlement and the parent State; but a change for the worse ensued with the advent, into Sikhim, of a new Minister who is described as a Thibetan of the worst Lama type. The institution of slavery, which seems common along the Thibetan border,[1] and the propensity for kidnapping British subjects from the plains, were at the root of the new trouble. But a crisis was caused by the seizure and imprisonment of Dr. Campbell, then Superintendent of Darjeeling, in the preposterous hope of obtaining, among other things, the rendition of certain runaways who had found refuge on British territory. The incident occurred while he was travelling with Dr. Hooker on one of those adventurous journeys to which we are indebted for the latter's graphic sketches.

Hooker was the first European to thoroughly explore and describe Sikhim. His steps have since been often trodden: Colonel Gawler has sketched for us the expedition of 1861, which occupied Tumloong and exacted the treaty designed to open up communication with Thibet; Mr. Edgar has described a visit paid by him to the Rajah in 1873; and Sir Richard Temple has given us a pleasing diary of

[1] Captain Gill, for instance, writing of Bathang, on the Chinese frontier, says: "Slavery is a great institution. There are rich families who own 500 or 600 slaves. . . . A family always counts its riches in slaves and cattle."—*River of Golden Sand*, vol. ii. ch. v.

excursions through British Sikhim in 1875; but for charm of description and comprehensive observation, the *Himalayan Journals* still hold the field. Hooker's main object was, of course, botanical research, but his narrative ranges widely beyond the flora which it was his special purpose to examine. A lover of Nature able to appreciate the magnificent scenery, and an observer capable of sketching a quaintly interesting people, he has given us a book of travel which is not only fascinating in itself but a valuable contribution to the geography of the Himalayan region.

Not the least curious feature in Sikhimese polity is the variety of races hemmed into Cis-nivean Sikhim. The most numerous as well as most attractive element is the Lepcha, which prevails south of the snowy range, and is most friendly to British rule; but there are also Limboos and Moormis on the side of Nepaul; Thibetans, *pur sang*, in the regions bordering on Thibet; Bhooteas, who have immigrated from Bhootan; Mechis, who dwell in the forest bordering on the plain; and Magras, who appear to be remnants of an aboriginal race displaced by the Lepchas, as the latter have been encroached on by the hardier races of Thibet and Bhootan. All except the Mechi, who is Indo-Chinese, are of markedly Mongolian origin, and all are impregnated, in a greater or less degree, with the religion and customs of Thibet, though all have languages and customs of their own; and it is, as Hooker remarks, not a little curious that six or seven different tribes should dwell in peace and unity, in such a confined territory, under a Sovereign whose temporal power is unsupported by even the semblance of force. It is probably the veneer of Buddhism and of Thibetan civilization which constitutes the cement; for even the Lepchas, who are the least affected by it, pay an implied reverence to the Lama creed. The Sikhimese belong to the "Red Cap" or unreformed sect, the Yellow-capped followers of Tsong Kaba, though in the ascendant in Thibet, having never made way on the southern slopes of the Himalayas. Buddhist temples are numerous, and a large number of the people seem to pass through a religious apprenticeship, spending a certain period in the monastery, and returning anon to cultivate the soil. The principal of these establishments is Pemyongchi; and the appreciation of natural beauty which has characterized the religious of all ages seems to have pre-eminently influenced the selection of its site; for the view of the Snowy Range from it is one of the finest in Sikhim, "the eye surveying at one glance the vegetation of the tropics and the poles. Deep in the valleys the river-beds are but 3000 feet above the sea, and are choked with fig-trees, plantains, and palms. To these succeed laurels and magnolias and, higher up still, oaks, birches, and chestnuts from 4000 to 10,000 feet. Pines succeed for 2000 feet higher, and give place to a skirting of rhododendrons and berbery," while high above all towers the giant height of Kinchinjunga, "the snow descending in one continuous sweep from 28,000 to a level of 15,000 feet, radiating from the summit along spur and shoulder for ten or fifteen miles towards each part of the compass." Nor does the building seem unworthy of the situation; the marvel being, indeed, how a people so poor can have managed to erect such a comparatively handsome structure. The ornamentation and characteristics are of course essentially Thibetan, "the square end of every beam being ornamented either with a lotus flower or Thibetan characters, while the walls are covered with allegorical paintings of lamas and saints expounding and in contemplation, with glories round their heads, mitred and holding the dorje and jewel."

While admitting the Thibetan religion, however, the Sikhimese appear to have excluded some objectionable features of Thibetan polity; for polyandry, among the Lepchas at any rate, is declared to be unknown and polygamy rare. Mention has been already made of the attractive qualities of this curious people, and Hooker never tires of paying tribute to their kindness and good-humour. "A gloomy-tempered or morose master they avoid, an unkind one they flee; but if they serve a good hill's-man like themselves, they will follow him with alacrity through every hardship, sleep on the cold bleak mountain exposed to the pitiless rain without a murmur, lay down their heavy burden to carry their master over a stream, or give him a helping hand up rock or precipice—do anything, in short, but encounter a foe;" for the Lepcha seems to be a veritable coward, and it is, perhaps, his peaceful disposition which has preserved him from extinction at the hands of his hardier and more warlike neighbours. Their standard of civilization may be low, and their talents few; but "they are conspicuous for their honesty, their power as carriers and mountaineers, and their skill as woodsmen; for they build a waterproof house with a thatch of banana leaves in the lower, and of bamboo in the elevated, regions, and equip it with a table and bedsteads for three persons, in an hour, using no implement but their heavy knife." Dr. Hooker seems indeed, on the whole, to have carried away a most pleasing impression of his temporary hosts. Trouble and hindrance he encountered, but they arose from the ill-will of the chief Minister or Dewan, and in no way from unkindliness in the people. There were times when he came near to starvation, but never through the indisposition of his neighbours; there were times when the locality was so poor that they had not food to give, and times when they dared not, or dared only surreptitiously, sell what they had; but hospitality and kindness seem to have been the prevailing characteristics when the neighbourhood was fertile and circumstances were propitious. Presents[1] of fruit, fowls and eggs, rice,

[1] The following, sent on one occasion by the Rajah, may serve as a typical and comprehensive catalogue :—A brick of Thibet tea; 80 lbs. of yak butter, done up in yak-hair cloth; 3 loads of rice, and 1 load of murwa for beer; rolls of Thibetan bread; fowls, eggs, dried plums, apricots, jujubes, currants, and sultana raisins (purchased at Lhassa, but imported from N.W. Thibet), and some trays of coarse white salt dug in Thibet.

butter, and beer seem to have poured in, indeed, at times with inconvenient profusion.

The *Journals* are full of characteristic touches portraying the manners and customs of the people, their dress, houses, and pursuits, as vividly as their physical surroundings. Here, for instance, is an interview with the Rajah, which gives us an estimate of Sikhimese civilization at its best:—

"A roofed shed of neat bamboo wattle, about twenty feet long. Two Bhooteas, with scarlet jackets, and with bows in their hands, stood on each side of the door, and our chairs were carried before us for our accommodation. Within was a wicker throne six feet high, covered with purple silk, brocaded with dragons in white and gold, and overhung by a canopy of tattered blue silk, with which material part of the wall was also covered. An oblong box containing papers, with golden dragons on it, was placed on the stage, or throne, and behind it was perched, cross-legged, an odd, black, insignificant-looking old man with twinkling, upturned eyes. He was swathed in yellow silk, and wore on his head a pink silk hat with a flat, broad crown, from all sides of which hung floss silk. This was the Rajah, a genuine Thibetan, about seventy years old."

And here is a village high up in the Himalayas (11,480 feet), close on the Thibetan frontier, which introduces us to the opposite extreme:—

"The village of Tallum consists of a few wretched stone huts, placed in a broad part of the valley, which is swampy and crossed by several ancient moraines. . . . The cottages are from four to six feet high, without windows, and consist of a single apartment containing neither table, chair, stool, nor bed; the inmates huddle together amid smoke, filth, and darkness, and sleep on a plank; and their only utensils are a bamboo churn, copper, bamboo, and earthenware vessels for milk, butter, etc."

Dr. Hooker's first journey occupied the winter of 1848-9, and resulted in a magnificent botanical collection, comprising, among other trophies, the Himalayan rhododendrons, which were afterwards planted at Kew. Not yet content, however, he started again in the autumn of 1849, and was joined by Dr. Campbell, who wished to see the Rajah about various causes of difference. The description of this journey introduces us to fresh delights and fresh drawbacks of Himalayan travel. The travellers see false sunsets in the eastern sky; they encounter glaciers and hot springs—in one of which a coolie, who had gone back to look for a thermometer he had dropped, elected to pass the night as a comfortable refuge! A vagrant Thibetan, who "gained a livelihood by going up and down the country blessing, cursing, and doing other such necessary business," dances for alms. They meet with scenery that defies description, and cold that is almost intolerable. Eventually, however, they reach Tumloong, the capital of Cis-nivean Sikhim, and opportunities are afforded of sharing the hospitality and observing the life of the people, by which the *Journals* largely profit. Allusion has been made to the ethnic and political kinship between Sikhim and Thibet, and the likeness extends to dress and manners. Here, for instance, is a cameo of a lady which may serve as a comparison to the picture of the Rajah on a former page. Dr. Hooker is at Tumloong, and approaches

"a concourse of women dressed in their pretty striped and crossed cloaks, who had brought tokens of good will: amongst them . . . , conspicuous from large necklaces of amber (in lumps the size of a fist), corals, and silver filagree work, with which her neck and shoulders were loaded. She wore on her head a red tiara, bedizened with seed pearls and large turquoises, and a gold fillet of filagree bosses united by a web of slender chains. Her hair (plaited in long tails) was elaborately woven with beads, and her cloak hooked in front by a chain of broad silver links studded with turquoises. White silk scarves, the emblems of peace and friendship, were thrown over our heads by each party; and rice, eggs, kids, goats, and murwa beer poured in apace, to the great delight of our servants."

Amber, pearls, coral, and turquoises seem to be the favourite ornaments in Thibet. Gill and Bogle have given us similar sketches of the women of Bathang and Lhassa-Dé; and a picture of the mother of the Teshu Lama, drawn for us by Turner, is simply an enlarged photograph of the Sikhimese lady just described. Whether, in fact, the pages before us be Gill's, Huc's, Turner's, or Hooker's; whether the locality be the Chinese frontier or the city of Lhassa, Bhootan, Teshu Lumbo, or the capital of Sikhim, we are met by the same peculiarities. An oratory at Tumloong is adorned with paintings by Lhassa artists. A colony of Thibetans, who have come to pasture their cattle near Kinchinjow, display the "butter ornaments" made familiar to us by Huc. Lamas, turquoises, coral, amber, tsanba,[1]

[1] Barley-meal mixed in tea. The Thibetans habitually put butter and salt (or soda) in their tea; adding barley-meal to make a repast. A correspondent of the *Calcutta Englishman* draws an amusingly wry face at the tea (mixed with butter and salt) offered him on the occasion of a recent visit to the Rajah of Sikhim. Huc speaks of *tea and meal* (tsanba) as the customary food of the Thibetan people. "If one will traverse the desert and reach Lhassa, one must resign oneself to eating tsanba." In every house entered by Captain Gill in the marches of Szechuen, "butter, cheese, and tsanba, were immediately forthcoming!"

khatas, and profuse hospitality meet us at every turn. The difficulty is, where customs are strange, to convey in a few words the import of the comparisons they suggest. Nothing short of parallel quotations from the several writers named would adequately meet the case, and such elaborate reproduction is evidently impossible within these limits.

Dr. Hooker's last picture, however, introduces us to a custom so peculiar and so widely prevalent that it deserves a more elaborate description. Nothing in the whole range of Thibetan etiquette is more curious than the khata, or "scarf of felicity," which flutters perpetually before our eyes. We have just seen white scarves thrown over the heads of Dr. Hooker and his party by his Sikhimese hosts. Turner exchanges khatas at every turn during his journey through Bhootan, and makes memoranda to investigate their import—which fail in their purpose, but leave him still more impressed by the custom. On the occasion of Bogle's farewell to the Teshu Lama, the latter "throws a handkerchief about his neck;" and readers may remember the meeting with the Deb Patza and his wife, when Bogle "is so taken up in getting a handkerchief ready for the former that he does not observe the lady till she is passed," notwithstanding which, the Deb "courteously declined to receive my handkerchief till he had given me his." A few dozen khatas were among the purchases Captain Gill found it necessary to make before setting out from Tatsienlu; and he mentions, among their uses, that "pious people visiting a lamaserai generally tie one on the rails in front of the image of Buddha"—a ceremony akin to that which Turner underwent on quitting Teshu Lumbo, when he "bound a white scarf round the capitals of each of the four columns that stood within the apartment he had occupied." So universal, indeed, is the custom, so all-pervading the part the khata plays in Thibetan etiquette, that we turn to Huc for a full description of its uses. The khata, or scarf of felicity, is, he tells us, "a piece of silk whose fineness approaches that of gauze. Its colour is white with an azure tint. Its length is about three times its breadth; and the two extremities end, usually, in fringe. There are khatas of all sizes and prices, for it is an object with which neither rich nor poor can dispense. No one ever sets out without carrying a provision of them. When one goes to pay a visit of etiquette, when one wishes to ask a service or express thanks for one rendered, one begins by displaying a khata. One takes it in both hands, and offers it to the person one wishes to honour. If two friends who have not seen each other for some time chance to meet, their first care is to offer each other a khata. That is done with as much warmth, and as quickly, as one shakes hands in Europe. It is customary also, in writing, to enclose a little khata in the letter. One would hardly believe the importance the Thibetans, the Si Fan, and all the peoples who live towards the west of the Blue Sea, attach to the ceremony of the khata. For them it is the purest and most sincere expression of all noble sentiments. The finest words, the most magnificent presents, are nothing without the khata. With it, on the contrary, the commonest objects acquire an immense value. To refuse a favour asked for, khata in hand, would be to express contempt for all proprieties." The custom seems as prevalent on the slopes of the Himalayas as on the borders of Szechuen, on the shores of Koko-Nor as in the capital of the Dalai Lama: and Mr. Colborne Baber even tells us that there is found, in the forest land bordering on China, a kind of moss growing pendent on the trees somewhat in the shape of a scarf, which the Thibetans call "fairy khata."

There are few regions where a sharp line can be drawn, and affirmation made that there exist, on either side, distinct races of different types, instincts, and religion; but nowhere, probably, could such a line be drawn with greater approach to accuracy. What Turner writes of Bhootan is true, approximately, of Sikhim: "So wide a difference is evident between them and their neighbours of Bengal, that, were a stranger to both desired to give an opinion of them when placed together, he would not hesitate to pronounce them natives of regions the remotest from each other, and would never suppose that they belonged to a contiguous soil."

It is time, however, to turn from these glimpses of Himalayan life, and resume our sketch of the political situation. We had declared a protectorate over Sikhim, in 1817, with a view of setting bounds to the extension of Goorkha power ; we had acquired Darjeeling in 1835, both as a sanatorium and as a *place d'armes* in case it became necessary to affirm the position taken up. The time was now approaching when the fact of British ascendency and the situation of Sikhim in a direct line between Calcutta and Lhassa, were to suggest its adaptability as a highway for trade between the two regions.

We left Dr. Campbell intent on visiting the Rajah with a view to improve, if possible, our relations with Tumloong, but under the shadow of an outrage that was to provoke a diametrically opposite result. Affairs began badly, with a misunderstanding that might have been avoided by a clearer appreciation of Thibetan etiquette. Campbell seems to have been huffed because he was not at once received in audience. As a matter of fact, however, it is the Thibetan—and, for that matter, Chinese—custom to leave the visitor a day of rest before worrying him with visits. Bogle and Turner had precisely the same experience in Bhootan and Thibet, and were impressed by the consideration that allows a guest this repose on his arrival from a journey. Dr. Campbell, however, impatient of delay, set out with his companion on an excursion to the frontier. Their purpose had been to make a detour through Chumbi, but they were stopped at Chola by the Thibetan guard, and had retired to Chumanako when, suddenly, without warning, Campbell was knocked down and pinioned by the Sikhimese escort. There seems no necessary connection between the two incidents. One was a misunderstanding; the other, apparently, an act of political pressure. For there was, Dr. Hooker was assured, no complaint or ill-feeling against himself; he was free to travel where he chose: the animus was against Campbell, who would be held in durance at Tumloong till the Governor-General confirmed certain articles which he would be required to subscribe! To seize the representative of a neighbouring State and confine him till he should become amenable seems, in fact, a recognized practice in the border region; and it is illustrative of a difficulty others than Sikhimese occasionally experience in viewing matters from other than an habitual standpoint, that Hooker descanted in vain on the immorality of the proceeding.

Still, though consonant possibly with Himalayan law, the arrest seems to have appeared, even to the Sikhimese, of questionable taste, and was attributed by the victims to the sole influence of the Dewan and his clique. The aged abbot of Pemyongchi came in person to remonstrate; a certain Cheboo Lama, who played a conspicuous part, afterwards, in Himalayan politics, was loyal in his friendship; and a vehement protest from Lord Dalhousie seems at last to have carried conviction that the arrest would not be considered, at Calcutta, the every-day incident it appeared at Tumloong. It was determined, accordingly, to restore the hostages without awaiting fulfilment of the conditions; but so obtuse did the Dewan seem, to the last, to the enormity of the wrong, that he actually set out for Darjeeling with them in custody, taking merchandise and ponies for sale at Titalyah as though nothing had happened. His courage oozed away, however, as Darjeeling was neared; and he eventually let his prisoners go, halting himself on the north of the frontier.

It is significant of the progress since made in our conception of mountain warfare, that the General commanding at Darjeeling feared to venture on a punitive expedition. Troops were collected at Darjeeling; but even Sir Charles Napier was afraid to launch them, lest a Thibetan army should be summoned and they should be overwhelmed in the mountains. Other means of coercion, fortunately, were at hand. The Rajah's pension was stopped; all Sikhim south of the Rungeet was annexed, and the dismssal of the Dewan was secured by this pressure. The punishment was, however, imperfect, and failed in ultimate effect; for the Rajah was so impoverished that we were obliged to restore his income; the Dewan regained his former influence, and renewed troubles compelled the adoption, ten years later, of the measures from which Sir Charles Napier had shrunk.

The propensity for kidnapping—that prolific source of border trouble—was at the root of the new difficulty. British subjects were periodically carried off; our demands for restitution failed of effect; and the Government of India decreed, in 1860, the seizure of Rinchipoong—a district lying between Nepaul and the great Rungeet—as a means of pressure. The occupation was effected by Captain Murray and a body of native sappers, without opposition; but they were attacked, three weeks later, by a mixed force of Thibetans and Bhooteas, and obliged to retreat in confusion. The task had been undertaken with inadequate means and, but for the warning and goodwill of the Lepchas, might have resulted in worse disaster. This repulse brought matters to a climax, and it was decided to send an expedition to convince the Court, once for all, of the necessity for submission. The command was given to Colonel Gawler, who has left us a graphic description [1] of the difficulties of the march—for it turned out to be a promenade only. There had been great preparations, but they were put to little use; there were numerous breastworks, but they were vacated on our approach; the Dewan had even tried to enlist Bhootanese help, but either his heart or his allies seem to have failed him at the pinch. Tumloong was reached practically without fighting; and a treaty was imposed which had, for one important object, the facilitation of trade between India and Thibet. The Government had been slow in concentrating its purpose, but the decision was at last taken, and found expression in the following clauses:—

"(11) On all goods passing into or out of Thibet, Bhootan, or Nepaul, the Government of Sikhim may levy a duty [not to

---

[1] "Sikhim: With Hints on Jungle and Mountain Warfare." By Colonel Gawler. London: 1873.

exceed 5 per cent. *ad valorem*], when a pass shall be given exempting such goods from any further liability.

"(13) In the event of the British Government desiring to open out a road through Sikhim, with the view of encouraging trade, the Sikhim Government will raise no objection thereto, and will afford every protection and aid to the party engaged in the work. If the road is constructed, the Government of Sikhim undertakes to keep it in repair."

Clauses 17 and 19 bind the Rajah to refrain from hostilities against neighbouring States, to submit disputes to British arbitration, and not to cede any portion of his territory without our assent; while clauses 18 and 20 provide that "the whole military force of Sikhim shall join and afford every aid and facility to British troops when engaged in the hills," and that "no armed force belonging to any other country shall pass through Sikhim without the sanction of the British Government." Suzerainty could not well be more emphatically asserted; nor could any agreement be more hopelessly and helplessly broken than these two clauses were broken during recent operations. With the ulterior stipulations—provisions against a recurrence of disorder, and affirming rights of trade and travel—we are not now concerned. It will suffice to add that, since 1861, the Sikhimese have been on their good behaviour.

Here, for thirteen years, the matter again rested. The road stipulated for in Article 13 was promptly made, from Darjeeling to the Jeylep Pass, and trade grew in response to the facilities offered; but it was carried on solely by hill-men, the frontier being closed as tightly as ever against natives of the plain.

It was not till 1873 that a willingness was shown to re-knit the threads of Hastings' policy, and recover the privilege of access to Thibet which Bogle and Turner had laboured to obtain. Early in that year, Dr. Campbell and Colonel Gawler—the two men who had had, probably, most to do with establishing British influence in Sikhim—presented to the Secretary of State a memorandum summarizing the position, and urging upon him the opportuneness of a new departure. The population was friendly: Sikhim offered the shortest and most direct route between Lhassa and British territory; the Chola Pass was open nearly all the year round; and Chumbi, a large market town, whence there is a good road to Lhassa, is only three hours' journey from the frontier. By a branch extension of the East Indian Railway to the foot of the Darjeeling hills, the transport of Indian and English goods intended for Thibet, as well as our Darjeeling tea trade, would be greatly facilitated. The head of the Sikhimese religion, moreover, was in Thibet. Many of the officials were Thibetans, and the Rajah himself received a salary from Thibet, and spent half his time at Chumbi within the Thibetan frontier. With the advantages here enumerated, there could, it was suggested, be no great difficulty in establishing a consular agency at Chumbi to begin with, and in eventually sending an envoy to Lhassa.

Whatever share it may have had in producing the result, the date of this document coincides remarkably with a movement in the direction indicated.

The old Rajah had lately died. In the summer of 1873 the new Rajah visited Sir George Campbell at Darjeeling: in the autumn of that year his pension was increased, and Mr. Edgar paid him a return visit, at which the question of opening up intercourse with Thibet was seriously discussed.[1] Refused permission to enter Chumbi, Mr. Edgar was, nevertheless, visited at Chola not only by the Rajah and his chief Minister, but by the very ex-Dewan Namgay—the hero of Dr. Campbell's arrest in 1849, and of his repulse in 1860—who now professed himself anxious to further our projects. There would, it was affirmed, with an unanimity in singular contrast to the event, be no difficulty with Thibet: it was China which had sealed the passes, and it depended upon China to reopen them: the Emperor held the key of the situation. Twelve more years were to pass before a resolution was taken to approach the Chinese Government in the sense suggested. But two important steps had been gained in the interval: the railway suggested by Messrs. Campbell and Gawler had been completed to the foot of the Himalayas, and a clause inserted by Sir Thomas Wade in the Convention of Chefoo, recognizing the purpose of Englishmen to travel between India and China, through Thibet.

The story merges, henceforth, in the larger field of Indo-Chinese policy. We have seen the little State disclosed (in 1730) by Van De Putte—the

[1] "Report on a Visit to Sikhim and the Thibetan Frontier." By J. Ware Edgar, C.S.I. Calcutta. 1874.

first European who ever completed the journey from India, through Lhassa, to China; and we have seen the Rajah defended (in 1775), as a feudatory of the Dalai Lama, against the aggression of Nepaul. We have seen how the hindrance of the old trade route through Nepaul, after the Goorkha conquest of that country in 1763, led Hastings to seek an alternative way through Bhootan. We have seen Sikhim indicated by Bogle as a sort of bye-lane between India and Thibet, of no great account owing to malaria and other causes; and we have seen its passes closed, in common with the whole Thibetan frontier, by the Chinese, in 1792. We have followed the development of British influence, from its inception, in 1814, to the acquisition of Darjeeling in 1835, the annexation of the Murung in 1849, and the emphatic assertion of Indian suzerainty in 1861. And we have traced the project of opening up Sikhim as a highway between India and Thibet, from the first conception of the idea, down to the Macaulay Mission and the incidents to which it has given rise. If the hostile attitude of the Lamas involve a contradiction of the hopes we had been led to entertain, Sikhimese history may, perhaps, help us to a solution of the puzzle. We have seen Dr. Campbell arrested by the official clique, in opposition to the popular wish; and we have seen the Lepchas warning him beforehand, and screening him after the attack at Rinchipoong, in defiance of the policy of their officials. The surmise might not be very wild that we have, here, an index to the situation in Thibet—

a hostile clique of Lama officials disposing of the State forces in opposition to the wish of a singularly submissive people. Nothing surprised Dr. Hooker more than the submission of the Sikhimese to the extortion and oppression of which the Dewan Namgay was guilty. His unpopularity was evident; he disposed of no repressive force; and nothing could, it seemed to the visitor, have been easier than to overthrow him. Yet the people submitted, and went on submitting, as they appear to submit to the oppression of his brethren, in Thibet.

These glimpses of the past enable us to appreciate also, more clearly, the rival claims of Thibetan and Indian suzerainty over which the negotiations at Gnatong made temporary shipwreck. If it is obvious, from the foregoing pages, that the Lamas were justified in regarding Sikhim as an ancient dependency of Lhassa, it is equally clear that the Cis-nivean region has passed under the influence of Calcutta. Bound by the treaty of Tumloong to join, with his whole force, any British troops engaged in the Himalayas, the Rajah was subsidized by Thibet to guard the very passes we have been concerned to open. If there is one province in respect to which he is a pensioned feudatory of India, there is another in respect to which he is a subsidized dependent of Lhassa. Owing his very possession of Cis-nivean Sikhim to British protection, he was bound by race, tradition, and every natural affinity to the Power which was arrayed against his real protectors.

We encountered, therefore, a Sikhimese question

in addition to a Thibetan question—a complicated question of Himalayan politics, in addition to one of complicated commercial rivalry—a storm in a teapot, perhaps—but a storm which it was rather more difficult to appease because it was concentrated in so small a focus.

CHAPTER XV.

PROGRESS OF NEGOTIATIONS.

So far, then, as the actual accomplishment of our purpose was concerned, the close of 1889 found matters very little advanced. We had driven the Thibetans out of British Sikhim, and cleared the passes into Chumbi; but the Lamas seemed as far as ever from coming to terms. The Chinese Government had become urgent in its instructions that a settlement should be arranged; but its envoy had only succeeded, so far, in superadding a question of suzerainty to the question of intercourse. Better sense and better counsels were, however, about to prevail. Mr. James Hart, of the Imperial Maritime Customs Service, was sent to assist in finding a solution, and—whether spontaneously or under instructions from Peking—Chang Keng was led to perceive that one half of Sikhim was really on the Indian slope. Negotiations were accordingly resumed, with a better prospect of success. The points at issue were, in fact, practically settled with this admission and the acceptance, in principle, of commercial intercourse. It remained, only, to consecrate them in a Convention; and the following terms were eventually reached:—

I.—The boundary of Sikhim and Thibet shall be the crest of the mountain range separating the waters flowing into the Sikhim Teesta and its affluents, from the waters flowing into the Thibetan Machu and northwards into other rivers of Thibet. The line commences at Mount Gipmochi, on the Bhootan frontier, and follows the above-mentioned water-parting to the point where it meets Nepal territory.

II.—It is admitted that the British Government, whose protectorate over the Sikhim State is hereby recognized, has direct and exclusive control over the internal administration and foreign relations of that State; and, except through and with the permission of the British Government, neither the ruler of the State nor any of its officers shall have official relations of any kind, formal or informal, with any other country.

III.—The Government of Great Britain and Ireland and the Government of China engage reciprocally to respect the boundary as defined in Article I., and to prevent acts of aggression from their respective sides of the frontier.

IV.—The question of providing increased facilities for trade across the Sikhim-Thibet frontier will hereafter be discussed, with a view to a mutually satisfactory arrangement, by the high contracting Powers.

V.—The question of pasturage on the Sikhim side of the frontier is reserved for further examination and future adjustment.

VI.—The high contracting Powers reserve for discussion and arrangement the method in which official communications between the British authorities in India and the authorities in Thibet shall be conducted.

VII.—Two joint commissioners shall, within six months from the ratification of this Convention, be appointed, one by the British Government in India, the other by the Chinese Resident in Thibet. The said commissioners shall meet and discuss the questions which, by the last three preceding articles, have been reserved.

VIII.—The present Convention shall be ratified, and the ratifications shall be exchanged in London, as soon as possible after the date of the signature thereof.

Having reached this conclusion, Chang Keng found no difficulty in continuing his journey to Calcutta; and it is satisfactory to learn that he appeared pleased and impressed with his visit. He had a fitting reception, and the signature of the Convention was accomplished with fitting ceremony. The incident was a memorable one, in many respects. It marked, probably, the most distinct recognition China had yet vouchsafed, of the change which had come over her relations with the outer world; and it marked the first act of direct intercourse between two great Asiatic Empires whose mutual interests must draw them into more and more intimate relations.

The Convention was ratified in August, 1890: but the terms of commercial intercourse have not even yet been settled. Mr. Hart has been pursuing the negotiations which he successfully inaugurated, but has found himself confronted by a problem of extreme difficulty. We have seen how great and how complicated are the interests concerned in the tea trade[1] between China and Thibet; and how gravely they must be affected by the sudden admission of a new competitor, whose produce could be placed on the market at a much less

[1] Not only is there the question of trade, but it has been stated lately, in the Shanghai press, that China distributes a great quantity of brick tea, in largess, to the Lama hierarchy which finds profit in selling it to the people; and that the Dalai Lama has made this the ground of a memorial to the Emperor *re* the proposed opening of Thibet to Indian tea.

comparative cost. It is not surprising, therefore, that prolonged discussion should have ensued; but it is understood that terms of compromise have been arranged, and that the announcement of a definite agreement may be shortly expected. The negotiations have been conducted with exemplary patience; but patience was called for, in dealing with a jealous and excited clique and a nervous people. There were mistakes, at first, on both sides. The constitution of the Macaulay Mission was a mistake: the *éclat* given to it was a mistake. The furious alarm of the Thibetans, and their advance into Sikhim were mistakes—mistakes both stupid and deplorable, but less incomprehensible than might have been the case if history were not at hand to suggest an explanation. Their prejudices and apprehensions will doubtless be considered, at the early stages of the intercourse which is now confidently anticipated. A British Consul at Chumbi, and the right to trade in Chumbi might satisfy, for the moment, the exigencies of the situation. The important object is to get the door ajar. Ulterior advance might be indicated for subsequent arrangement; but an important step would have been gained if an agreement were reached that Indians and Thibetans should meet, and trade, on Thibetan soil.